essentials

ACCESS 2000
intermediate

ROBERT FERRETT, EASTERN MICHIGAN UNIVERSITY
JOHN PRESTON, EASTERN MICHIGAN UNIVERSITY
SALLY PRESTON, WASHTENAW COMMUNITY COLLEGE

Prentice
Hall

A division of Pearson Education
Upper Saddle River, NJ 07458

Access 2000 Essentials Intermediate

Copyright © 2000 by Prentice Hall

International Standard Book Number: 1-58076-301-4

Library of Congress Catalog Card Number: 98-89902

Printed in the United States of America

First Printing: July 1999

03 02 01   4 3 2

Interpretation of the printing code: the rightmost double-digit number is the year of the book's printing: the rightmost single-digit number, the number of the book's printing. For example, a printing code of 00-1 shows that the first printing of the book occurred in 2000.

Trademark Acknowledgments

Access 2000 Essentials Intermediate is based on Microsoft Access 2000.

Publisher:
Robert Linsky

Executive Editor:
Sunthar Visuvalingam

Series Editors:
Marianne Fox and Larry Metzelaar

Annotated Instructor's Manual (AIM) Series Editor:
Linda Bird

Operations Manager:
Christine Moos

Director of Product Marketing:
Susan Kindel

Acquisitions Editor:
Sunthar Visuvalingam

Development Editor:
Jan Snyder

Technical Editor:
Asit J. Patel

Software Coordinator:
Angela Denny

Senior Editor:
Karen A. Walsh

Book Designer:
Louisa Klucznik

Design Usability Consultant:
Elizabeth Keyes

Project Editor:
Karen A. Walsh

Copy Editor:
Cynthia Fields

Proofreader:
Debbie Williams

Indexer:
Joy Dean Lee

Layout Technician:
Trina Wurst

Team Coordinator:
Melody Layne

Usability Testers:
Sarah Ann Margulies: B.A.
University of Michigan
Cathy Gillmore: Shell Chemical Company
Lakshmy Sivaratnam: M.Sc.
University of Missouri-Kansas City

About the Authors

Robert Ferrett is the Director of the Center for Instructional Computing at Eastern Michigan University. His center provides computer training and support to faculty at the university. He has authored or co-authored more than 30 books on Access, PowerPoint, Excel, Word, and WordPerfect, and was the editor of the *1994 ACM SIGUCCS Conference Proceedings*. He is a series editor for the *Learn 97* and *Learn 2000* books, and has been designing, developing, and delivering computer workshops for nearly two decades. He has a BA in Psychology, an MS in Geography, and an MS in Interdisciplinary Technology from Eastern Michigan University. He is ABD in the Ph.D. program in Instructional Technology at Wayne State University.

John Preston is an Associate Professor at Eastern Michigan University in the College of Technology, where he teaches microcomputer application courses at the undergraduate and graduate levels. He has been teaching, writing, and designing computer training courses since the advent of PCs, and has authored and co-authored more than two dozen books on Microsoft Word, Excel, Access, and PowerPoint. He is a series editor for the *Learn 97* and *Learn 2000* books. He has received grants from the Detroit Edison Institute and the Department of Energy to develop Web sites for energy education and alternative fuels. He has also developed one of the first Internet-based microcomputer applications courses at an accredited university. He has a BS from the University of Michigan in Physics, Mathematics, and Education, and an MS from Eastern Michigan University in Physics Education. He is ABD in the Ph.D. degree program in Instructional Technology at Wayne State University.

Sally Preston is President of Preston & Associates, a computer software-training firm. She utilizes her extensive business experience as a bank vice president in charge of branch operations, along with her skills in training people on new computer systems. She provides corporate training through Preston & Associates and through the Institute for Workforce Development at Washtenaw Community College, where she also teaches computer courses part-time. She has co-authored nearly 20 books on Access, Excel, PowerPoint, Word, and WordPerfect, including the *Learn 97* books, *Learn 2000* books, *Office 2000 Essentials*, and *Access 2000 Essentials* books. She has an MBA from Eastern Michigan University.

Acknowledgments

Although the authors are solely responsible for its content, this book and the *Essentials* series as a whole have been shaped by the combined experience, perspectives, and input of the entire authoring, editorial, and design team. We are grateful to the Series Editors, **Larry Metzelaar** and **Marianne Fox**, and to the College of Business Administration at Butler University for hosting the listserv on which the implications and value of every series element were thoroughly discussed and finalized even as this book was being written. They also hosted a November 1998 seminar for the *AIM* authors and coordinated much of the usability testing at the Butler campus. We acknowledge **Robert Linsky** (Publisher, Que Education and Training) for having provided the initial direction and for having allowed the Essentials 2000 team to shape this edition as we saw fit. You, the reader, are the greatest beneficiary of this ongoing online collaborative effort.

Chuck Stewart adapted the original Que E&T *Essentials* series for corporate training. In early 1998, however, he began revamping the *Office 2000 Essentials* pedagogy to better serve academic needs exclusively. He enlisted the services of Series Editors Metzelaar and Fox because of their extensive background in courseware development, many years of classroom teaching, and innovative pedagogy. Early discussion with the Series Editors revealed the need for the three new types of end-of-chapter exercises you find in the *Office*

2000 Essentials. Chuck continued to provide ideas and feedback on the listserv long after handing over the executive editorship to Sunthar. Together, they completely overhauled the *Essentials* series, paying particular attention to pedagogy, content, and design issues.

Sunthar Visuvalingam took over as Executive Editor for the *Essentials* series in October 1998. He stepped into a process already in full swing and moved quickly to ensure "a level of collaboration rarely seen in academic publishing." He performed admirably the daunting task of coordinating an army of widely dispersed authors, editors, designers, and usability testers. Among the keywords that characterize his crucial role in forging a well-knit "learning team" are decisive leadership, effective communication, shared vision, continuous pedagogical and procedural innovation, infectious enthusiasm, dogged project and quality management, active solicitation of feedback, collective problem-solving, transparent decision making, developmental mentoring, reliability, flexibility, and dedication. Having made his indelible mark on the *Essentials* series, he stayed on to shepherd the transition of the series to Alex.

Linda Bird (AIM Series Editor and author of both *PowerPoint Essentials* books) and **Robert Ferrett** (co-author of *Office Essentials*, all three *Access Essentials* books, and of the related *Learn* series) made significant contributions to enhancing the concept and details of the new series. A newcomer to the series but not to educational publishing, **Keith Mulbery** seized increasing ownership of *Essentials* and undertook the initiative of presenting the series at the April 1999 National Business Education Association Convention.

Alex von Rosenberg, Executive Editor, manages the Computer Applications publishing program at Prentice Hall (PH). The PH team has been instrumental in ensuring a smooth transition of the *Essentials* series. Alex has been ably assisted in this transition by **Susan Rifkin**, Managing Editor; **Leanne Nieglos**, Assistant Editor; **Jennifer Surich**, Editorial Assistant; **Nancy Evans**, Director of Strategic Marketing; **Kris King**, Senior Marketing Manager; and **Nancy Welcher**, Media Project Manager.

Operations Manager **Christine Moos** and Senior Editor **Karen Walsh** worked hard with Sunthar and Alex to allow authors maximum flexibility to produce a quality product, while trying to maintain a tight editorial and production schedule. They had the unenviable task of keeping the book processes rolling while managing the complex process of transitioning the series to Prentice Hall. Book Designer **Louisa Klucznik** and Consultant **Elizabeth Keyes** spared no efforts in making every detail of the new design attractive, usable, consistent and appropriate to the *Essentials* pedagogy. **Joyce Nielsen**, **Jan Snyder**, **Asit Patel**, **Nancy Sixsmith**, and **Susan Hobbs**—freelancers who had worked on earlier editions of the *Essentials* and the related *Learn* series in various editorial capacities—helped ensure continuity in procedures and conventions. **Tim Tate**, **Sherri Fugit**, **Melody Layne**, and **Cindy Fields** also asked sharp questions along the way and thereby helped us refine and crystallize the editorial conventions for the *Essentials*.

Debra Griggs, who has been teaching out of the *Access 97 Essentials* books at Bellevue Community College, offered many excellent comments and suggestions, and provided great technical expertise throughout the beta-testing stage. **Sarah Ann Margulies**, a retired lawyer and continuing learner, greatly enhanced this book by providing exceptional assistance during the usability testing phase.

Finally, the authors would like to thank **Asit Patel** for his great technical editing, and **Jan Snyder** for seeing this book through development during particularly trying times. **Karen Walsh**, assisted by **Cindy Fields**, did a remarkable job of editing this book for production. Also, thanks to **Marianne Fox** and **Larry Metzelaar** for taking on the series editorship and doing a great job, even though it must have been far more work than they could ever have imagined. Our particular thanks go to **Sunthar Visuvalingam**, for having a vision of what this series should be, and then seeing it through.

Contents at a Glance

Table of Contents

Project 3   Adding Useful Features to Your Forms   63

Introduction

Essentials courseware from Prentice Hall is anchored in the practical and professional needs of all types of students. This edition of the Office 2000 *Essentials* has been completely revamped as the result of painstaking usability research by the publisher, authors, editors, and students. Practically every detail—by way of pedagogy, content, presentation, and design—was the object of continuous online (and offline) discussion among the entire team.

The *Essentials* series has been conceived around a "learning by doing" approach that encourages you to grasp application-related concepts as you expand your skills through hands-on tutorials. As such, it consists of modular lessons that are built around a series of numbered, step-by-step procedures that are clear, concise, and easy to review. Explicatory material is interwoven before each lesson and between the steps. Additional features, tips, pitfalls, and other related information are provided at exactly the place where you would most expect them. They are easily recognizable elements that stand out from the main flow of the tutorial. We have even designed our icons to match the Microsoft Office theme. The end-of-chapter exercises have likewise been carefully graded from the routine Checking Concepts and Terms to tasks in the Discovery Zone that gently prod you into extending what you've learned into areas beyond the explicit scope of the lessons proper. Following, you'll find out more about the rationale behind each book element and how to use each to your maximum benefit.

How to Use This Book

Typically, each *Essentials* book is divided into seven or eight projects, concerning topics such as making data entry easier and more accurate, managing data using related tables, and using Access macros. A project covers one area (or a few closely related areas) of application functionality. Each project is then divided into seven to nine lessons that are related to that topic. For example, a project on special-purpose reports and advanced report features is divided into lessons explaining how to create labels for mailings, add calculated fields to reports, and create reports that group data. Each lesson presents a specific task or closely related set of tasks in a manageable chunk that is easy to assimilate and retain.

Each element in *Access 2000 Essentials Intermediate* is designed to maximize your learning experience. Following is a list of the *Essentials* project elements and a description of how each element can help you:

- **Project Objectives.** Starting with an objective gives you short-term, attainable goals. Using project objectives that closely match the titles of the step-by-step tutorials breaks down the possibly overwhelming prospect of learning several new features of Access into small, attainable, bite-sized tasks. Look over the objectives on the opening page of the project before you begin, and review them after completing the project to identify the main goals for each project.

- **Key Terms.** This book includes a limited number of useful vocabulary words and definitions, such as *dynaset*, *foreign key*, *subdatasheet*, and *switchboard*. Key terms introduced in each project are listed in alphabetical order immediately after the objectives on the opening page of the project. These key terms are shown in bold italic and are defined during their first use within the text. Definitions of key terms are also included in the Glossary.

- **Why Would I Do This?** You are studying Access so that you can accomplish useful tasks in the real world. This brief section tells you why these tasks or procedures are important. What can you do with the knowledge? How can these application features be applied to everyday tasks?

- **Visual Summary.** This opening section graphically illustrates the concepts and features that you will learn in the project. One or more figures, with ample callouts, show the final result of completing the project. This road map to your destination keeps you motivated as you work through the individual steps of each task.

- **Lessons.** Each lesson contains one or more tasks that correspond to an objective on the opening page of the project. A lesson consists of step-by-step tutorials, their associated data files, screen shots, and the special notes described as follows. Although each lesson often builds on the previous one, the lessons (and the exercises) have been made as modular as possible. For example, you can skip tasks that you have already mastered, and begin a later lesson using a data file provided specifically for its task(s).

- **Step-by-Step Tutorial.** The lessons consist of numbered, bold, step-by-step instructions that show you how to perform the procedures in a clear, concise, and direct manner. These hands-on tutorials, which are the "essentials" of each project, let you "learn by doing." Regular paragraphs between the steps clarify the results of each step. Also, screen shots are introduced after key steps for you to check against the results on your monitor. To review the lesson, you can easily scan the bold numbered steps. Quick (or impatient!) learners may likewise ignore the intervening paragraphs.

- **Need to Know.** These sidebars provide essential tips for performing the tasks and using the application more effectively. You can easily recognize them by their distinctive icon and bold headings. It is well worth the effort to review these crucial notes again after completing the project.

- **Nice to Know.** Nice to Know comments provide extra tips, shortcuts, alternative ways to complete a process, and special hints about using the software. You may safely ignore these for the moment to focus on the main task at hand, or you may pause to learn and appreciate these tidbits. Here, you find neat tricks and special insights to impress your friends and coworkers!

- **If You Have Problems…** These short troubleshooting notes help you anticipate or solve common problems quickly and effectively. Even if you do not encounter the problem at this time, make a mental note of it so that you know where to look when you find yourself (or others) in difficulty.

- **Summary.** This section provides a brief recap of the tasks learned in the project. The summary guides you to places where you can expand your knowledge, which may include references to specific Help topics or the Prentice Hall *Essentials* Web site (http://www.prenhall.com/essentials).

- **Checking Concepts and Terms.** This section offers optional True/False, Multiple Choice, Screen ID, and Discussion Questions that are designed to check your comprehension and assess retention. If you need to refresh your memory, the relevant lesson number is provided after each True/False and Multiple Choice question. For example, [L5] directs you to review Lesson 5 for the answer. Lesson numbers may be provided—where relevant—for other types of exercises as well.

- **Skill Drill Exercises.** This section enables you to check your comprehension, evaluate your progress, and practice what you've learned. The exercises in this section build on and reinforce what was learned in each project. Generally, the Skill Drill exercises include step-by-step instructions.

■ **Challenge Exercises.** This section provides exercises that expand on or relate to the skills practiced in the project. Each exercise provides a brief narrative introduction followed by instructions. Although the instructions are often written in a step-by-step format, the steps are not as detailed as those in the Skill Drill section. Providing less-specific steps helps you learn to think on your own. These exercises foster the "near transfer" of learning.

■ **Discovery Zone Exercises.** These exercises require advanced knowledge of project topics or the application of skills from multiple lessons. Additionally, these exercises may require you to research topics in Help or on the Web to complete them. This self-directed method of learning new skills emulates real-world experience. We provide the cues, and you do the exploring!

■ **Learning to Learn.** Throughout this book, you will find lessons, exercises, and other elements highlighted by this icon. For the most part, they involve using or exploring the built-in Help system or Web-based Help, which is also accessible from the application. However, their significance is much greater. Microsoft Office has become so rich in features that cater to so many diverse needs that it is no longer possible to anticipate and teach you everything that you might need to know. It is becoming increasingly important that, as you learn from this book, you also "learn to learn" on your own. These elements help you identify related—perhaps more specialized— tasks or questions, and show you how to discover the right procedures or answers by exploiting the many resources that are already within the application.

■ **Task Guide.** The Task Guide that follows the last project lists all the procedures and shortcuts you have learned in this book. It can be used in two complementary ways to enhance your learning experience. You can refer to it, while progressing through the book, to refresh your memory on procedures learned in a previous lesson. Or, you can keep it as a handy real-world reference while using the application for your daily work.

■ **Glossary.** Here, you find the definitions—collected in one place—of all the key terms defined throughout the book and listed on the opening page of each project. Use it to refresh your memory.

Typeface Conventions Used in This Book

We have used the following conventions throughout this book to make it easier for you to understand the material:

■ Key terms appear in ***italic and bold*** the first time that they are defined in a project.

■ Text that you type, as well as text that appears on your computer screen as warning, confirmation, or general information, appears in a special `monospace` typeface.

■ Hotkeys, the underlined keys onscreen that activate commands and options, are also underlined in this book. Hotkeys offer a quick way to bring up frequently used commands.

How to Use the CD-ROM

The CD-ROM that accompanies this book contains all the data files for you to use as you work through the step-by-step tutorials, Skill Drill, Challenge, and Discovery Zone exercises provided at the end of each project. The CD contains separate parallel folders for each project. The filenames correspond to the filenames called for in this book. The files are named in the following manner: The first three characters represent the software and the book level (such as AC2 for the *Access 2000 Essentials Intermediate*). The last four digits indicate the project number and the file number within the project. For example, the first file used in Project 1 is 0101. Therefore, the complete name for the first file in the Access Intermediate book is AC2-0101.

Files on a CD-ROM are Read Only; they cannot be modified in any way. To use the provided data files while working through this book, you must first transfer the files to a read-write medium, where you can modify them. Because classroom and lab rules governing the use of storage media vary from school to school, this book assumes the standard procedure of working with the file(s) on a 3.5-inch floppy disk.

A word of caution about using floppy disks: As you use a data file, it increases in size or automatically generates temporary work files. Ensure that your disk remains at least one-third empty to provide the needed extra space. Moreover, using a floppy for your work disk is slower than working from a hard drive. You will also need several floppy disks to hold all the files on the CD.

- **Copying to a 3.5-inch floppy disk.** For security or space reasons, many labs do not allow you to transfer files to the hard drive at all. The only way you can transfer Microsoft Access databases to a floppy disk is to manually copy the files. Unlike the other Office applications, Access does not have a Save As command for databases. This means that you cannot open and save each data file individually with a different name, as you may have done while working with Word, Excel, or PowerPoint.

  First, select the files on the CD that you want to copy and ensure that their combined size (shown on the status bar of the Explorer window) will fit on a 1.44MB floppy disk. Right-click on the selection with your mouse, choose Send To on the context menu that appears, and then choose 3 1/2 Floppy on the submenu. After copying, select the copied files on the floppy disk and right-click the selection with the mouse again. This time, choose Properties, choose the General tab on the Properties dialog box that appears, and then uncheck the read-only attribute at the bottom of this page. Because the original files on the CD-ROM were Read Only, the files were copied with this attribute turned on. You can rename files copied in this manner after you have turned off the Read Only attribute.

  Although you can use the same method to copy the entire CD contents to a large-capacity drive, it is much simpler to use the installation routine in the CD-ROM for this purpose. This automatically removes the Read Only attribute while transferring the files.

- **Installing to a hard drive or Zip drive.** The CD-ROM contains an installation routine that automatically copies all the contents to a local or networked hard drive, or to a removable large-capacity drive (for example, an Iomega Zip drive). If you are working in the classroom, your instructor has probably already installed the files to the hard drive and can tell you where the files are located. You will be asked to save or copy the file(s) you need to your personal work area on the hard drive, or to a floppy work disk.

Otherwise, run the installation routine yourself to transfer all the files to the hard drive (for example, if you are working at home) or to your personal Zip drive. You may then work directly and more efficiently from these high-capacity drives.

CD-ROM Installation Routine

If you were instructed to install the files on a lab computer or if you are installing them on your home computer, simply insert the CD-ROM into the CD-ROM drive. When the installation screen appears, follow these steps:

1. From the installation screen, click the Install button.

2. The Welcome dialog box displays. Click the Next button.

3. The Readme.txt appears. The Readme.txt gives you important information regarding the installation. Make sure that you use the scrollbar to view the entire Readme.txt file. When you finish reading the Readme.txt, click the Next button.

4. The Select Destination Directory displays. Unless you are told otherwise by your instructor, the default location is recommended. Click Next.

5. The Ready to Install screen appears. Click Next to begin the installation.

   A directory is created on your hard drive where the student files will be installed.

6. A dialog box appears, confirming that the installation is complete.

The installation of the student data files allows you to access the data files from the Start menu programs. To access the student data files from the Start menu, click Start, click Programs, and then click the *Essentials* title you installed from the list of programs. The student data files are in subfolders, arranged by project.

Uninstalling the Student Data Files

After you complete the course, you may decide that you do not need the student data files any more. If that is the case, you have the capability to uninstall them. The following steps walk you through the process:

1. Click on the Start menu, and then click Programs.

2. Click the *Essentials* title that you installed.

3. Click Uninstall.

4. Click one of the Uninstall methods listed:

   - Automatic—This method deletes all files in the directory and all shortcuts created.

   - Custom—This method allows you to select the files that you want to delete.

5. Click Next.

6. The Perform Uninstall dialog box appears. Click Finish. The Student data files and their folders are deleted.

The *Annotated Instructor's Manual*

The *Annotated Instructor's Manual* (AIM) is a printed copy of the student book—complete with marginal annotations and detailed guidelines, including a curriculum guide—that helps the instructor use this book and teach the software more effectively. The *AIM* also includes a Resource CD-ROM with additional support files for the instructor; suggested solution files that show how the students' files should look at the end of a tutorial; answers to test questions; PowerPoint presentations to augment your instruction; additional test questions and answers; and additional Skill Drill, Challenge, and Discovery Zone exercises. Instructors should contact Prentice Hall for their complimentary *AIM*. Prentice Hall can be reached via phone at 1-800-333-7945, or via the Internet at http://www.prenhall.com.

Project 1

Project 1

Making Data Entry Easier and More Accurate

Objectives

In this project, you learn how to

- ➤ Create Consistent Data Formats
- ➤ Create Conditional Formats for Positive, Negative, and Null Values
- ➤ Change the Data Input Structure Using Input Masks
- ➤ Restrict Entries to Those That Meet Validation Criteria
- ➤ Require Entry of Necessary Information
- ➤ Prevent Duplicate Entries Using Indexed Fields
- ➤ Create a Lookup Column to Allow Selection from a List

Key terms introduced in this project include

- Expression Builder
- format
- Indexed field
- Input mask
- null value
- placeholder
- primary key field
- validation rule
- validation text

Why Would I Do This?

I t is important that your data is stored in a consistent format. If some phone numbers are entered as (XXX) XXX-XXXX and some as 1-XXX-XXX-XXXX, it may be difficult to sort or extract the data. If one person designs and enters all the data, you may be able to get consistent input, but if that person is on vacation or out due to illness, your database could be filled with useless data by someone unfamiliar with your methods.

You may want your database to call attention to negative numbers or to suppress zeros in empty numeric fields. You learn how to use conditional formats to accomplish these goals.

To save time, you can create a list of possible entries. This allows you to choose an entry from a list rather than enter it from the keyboard.

It is also important to guard against common errors. You can check an entry against a set of rules to see if the entry is within allowable limits or matches a list of possible values. You may want to require that all records contain certain fields and to guard against duplicate entries.

In this project, you learn how to control the ***format*** of your data, check entries against a set of rules, and prevent duplicate entries. The database that you are modifying is designed to track the training employees have received on computer software packages.

Visual Summary

When you have completed this project, you will have created a document that looks like this:

Automatic data formatting has
been added to two fields

Figure 1.1
Automatic data formatting
and drop-down menus
make data entry easier
and more accurate.

A drop-down list
has been added

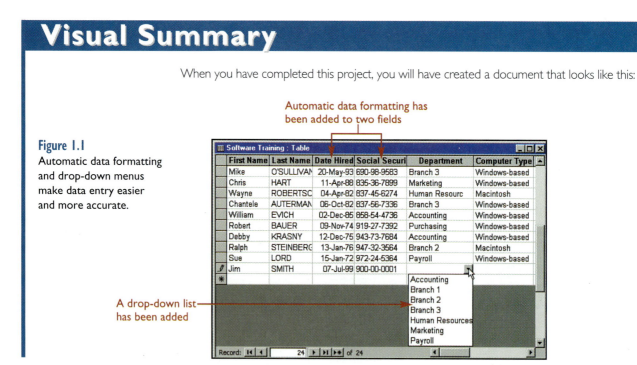

Lesson 1: Creating Consistent Data Formats

On many occasions you will want your data to be displayed in a specific format. For example, you might want to have text displayed in uppercase letters, or you might want dates to appear in a consistent format. Some of these formats can be activated by using a drop-down menu, whereas others require that you enter a symbol in a special format box.

In the following procedure, you learn how to change the appearance of two of the fields in the Software Training table. You change the format of the Last Name field to display all the names in uppercase letters, and modify the date format in the Date Hired field.

To Use a Display Format to Control the Appearance of the Data

1 **Launch Access. Click OK to open an existing file.**
The Open dialog box is displayed. Make sure you have a disk in drive A.

2 **Use the Look in box to locate the AC2-0101 file on your CD-ROM, right-click on it, and use the Send To option to send it to the floppy drive. Move to drive A, right-click on the filename, and select Properties from the shortcut menu. Select Archive and deselect Read-only from the Attributes section. Click OK to close the Properties dialog box.**

3 **Right-click on the filename, and select Properties from the shortcut menu. Select the Rename option, and then rename the file** PC Training. **Click OK, and then open the database.**
The database window should now be open to the Tables area (see Figure 1.2).

Figure 1.2
The database window displays the Tables area of the PC Training database.

> ❌ The file may appear as AC2-0101.mdb. This depends on whether the file extensions have been turned on in Windows. When renaming the file, make sure you add the .mdb extension if your original file shows it. Do not add it if the original file does not show it.

4 **Click the Tables object button, if necessary. Select the Software Training table, and then click the Open button to view the data.**
Notice that the data contained in the Last Name field is a mix of uppercase and lowercase letters, and the Date Hired field is displayed in the mm/dd/yy format.

5 **Click the View button on the toolbar to switch to Design view.**
The Table Design view is displayed (see Figure 1.3).

continues ▶

To Use a Display Format to Control the Appearance of the Data   (continued)

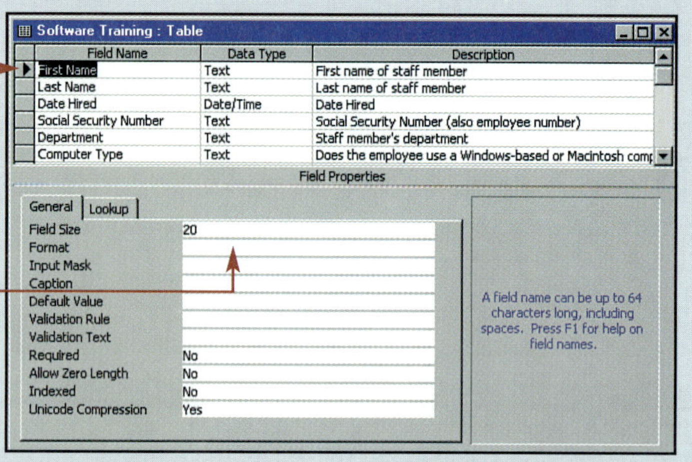

Figure 1.3

The Design view of the
Software Training table
includes detailed field
information.

Field selector

Format property box

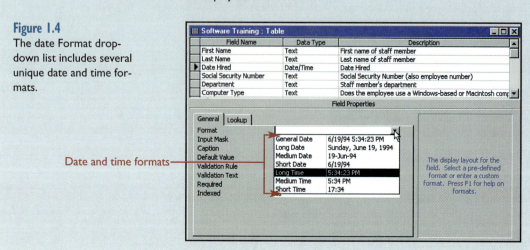

6 **Click anywhere in the Last Name field to select it.**
The Field Properties section in the bottom half of the window changes to display the properties of the Last Name field.

7 **Click in the Format property box in the Field Properties section.**

8 **Type the greater than symbol (>) as the Format property.**
The greater than symbol tells the program to display all text in the field as uppercase. The less than symbol (<) displays all the text in a field as lowercase. When no entry is made in the Format property box, text is displayed as entered.

9 **Click the View button on the toolbar to switch to Datasheet view.**
Whenever you make changes in field structures, the program asks if you want to save your changes. Click Yes whenever this message is displayed. Notice that all the last names in the Last Name field are now displayed in capital letters.

10 **Click the View button to return to Design view, and then click anywhere in the Date Hired field.**

11 **Select the Format property box, and then click the drop-down arrow.**
The date Format drop-down list is displayed (see Figure 1.4). Notice that a format can be selected for dates and times, or the General Date can be used to display both date and time.

Figure 1.4

The date Format drop-
down list includes several
unique date and time for-
mats.

Date and time formats

12 **Select the Medium Date format.**

Each format refers to the relative length of the date entries as they appear in the database.

 13 **Click the View button to return to Datasheet view.**

Once again, you have changed the structure of the table, so you will need to save your changes. The Date Hired field is now displayed in the dd-mmm-yy format (see Figure 1.5).

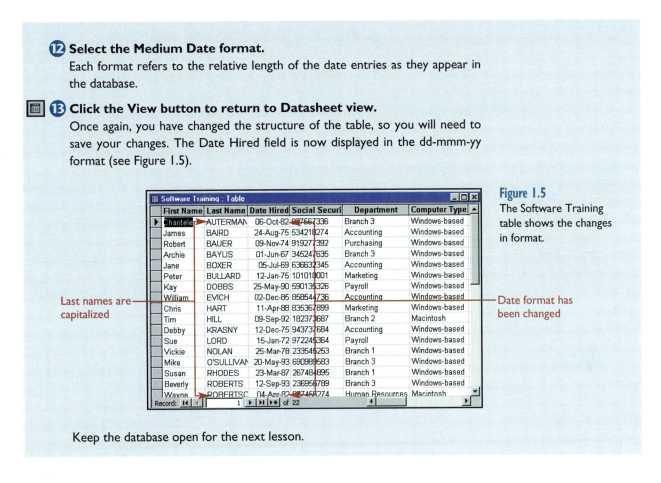

Last names are capitalized

Date format has been changed

Figure 1.5
The Software Training table shows the changes in format.

Keep the database open for the next lesson.

 How Formatted Data Is Saved

The Format property does not change the contents of the table, just how the data is presented. For example, the last names are still saved on your disk as you originally typed them.

Getting Help on Formatting Fields

Many more options are available for formatting fields. You can click in any of the Field Properties boxes, and then press F1 to get help on options for every data type.

Lesson 2: Creating Conditional Formats for Positive, Negative, and Null Values

More complex procedures are available to format fields than those shown in Lesson 1. These require a succession of components containing instructions separated by semi-colons. Each component represents a specific data format for a certain condition.

Conditional formats are particularly useful for dates and numbers. For example, you could set up a conditional format to display positive numbers with black text, negative numbers in red, and zeros or blanks when no data is entered in the field (a ***null value***). In this lesson, you set up the expense field to leave cells blank when you choose not to enter a number.

To Create a Conditional Format

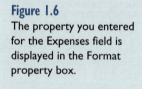 **1** **In the PC Training database, click the View button on the toolbar to switch to Design view of the Software Training table.**

2 **Scroll down the list of field names, and then click anywhere in the Expense field to select it.**

The Expense field is already formatted as Currency. Unfortunately, this displays fields with no entries as $0.00.

3 **Click in the Format box in the Field Properties area.**

4 **Select the Currency format and delete it.**

When formatting numeric fields (such as Number and Currency), the various components are separated by semicolons (;). The first component is always the format of a positive number, whereas the second is the format of a negative number. The third component tells the program how to display null values.

5 **Enter the following in the Format property box, exactly as shown:**
`$#,##0.00;$#,##0.00[Red];#`

The first component tells the program to display a dollar sign followed by the number for a positive number. The pound signs (#) to the right of the dollar sign tell the program to place a number there if one has been entered. If the number is less than a thousand, a zero will not be forced into that location, and the comma will be dropped. If a number under $1 is entered, a zero is displayed in the first position to the left of the decimal.

Sometimes you want to force a leading zero to identify decimal numbers that may be less than one. There is less possibility of overlooking the decimal point or confusing it with a period if it follows a zero (0.25) than if it does not (.25).

The second component uses the same format but displays negative numbers in red. This is indicated by typing the word Red surrounded by square brackets (not parentheses). The third component contains a pound sign (#), which tells the program to leave the field blank if no number is typed in.

The properties area should look like Figure 1.6.

Figure 1.6
The property you entered for the Expenses field is displayed in the Format property box.

New currency format —

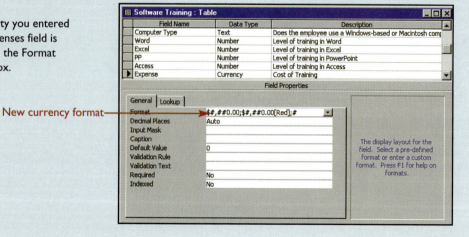

6 Click the View button on the toolbar to switch to Datasheet view.
Click Yes when prompted to save your changes to the table.

7 Scroll to the right and notice that the records that had no entries for the Expense field now display a blank instead of $0 (see Figure 1.7).
Keep the database open for the next lesson.

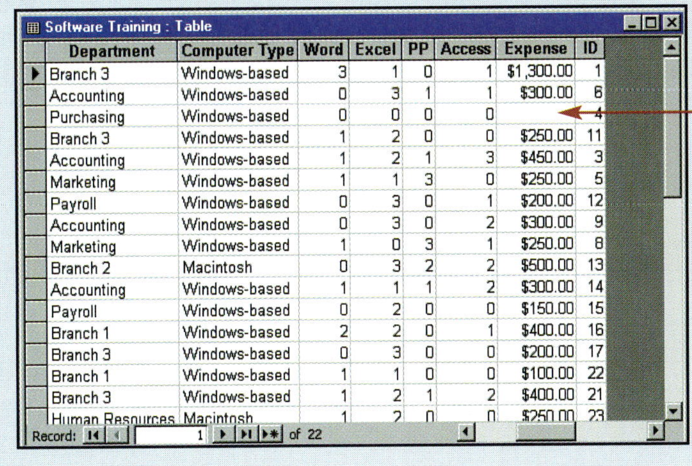

Department	Computer Type	Word	Excel	PP	Access	Expense	ID
Branch 3	Windows-based	3	1	0	1	$1,300.00	1
Accounting	Windows-based	0	3	1	1	$300.00	6
Purchasing	Windows-based	0	0	0	0		4
Branch 3	Windows-based	1	2	0	0	$250.00	11
Accounting	Windows-based	1	2	1	3	$450.00	3
Marketing	Windows-based	1	1	3	0	$250.00	5
Payroll	Windows-based	0	3	0	1	$200.00	12
Accounting	Windows-based	0	3	0	2	$300.00	9
Marketing	Windows-based	1	0	3	1	$250.00	8
Branch 2	Macintosh	0	3	2	2	$500.00	13
Accounting	Windows-based	1	1	1	2	$300.00	14
Payroll	Windows-based	0	2	0	0	$150.00	15
Branch 1	Windows-based	2	2	0	1	$400.00	16
Branch 3	Windows-based	0	3	0	0	$200.00	17
Branch 1	Windows-based	1	1	0	0	$100.00	22
Branch 3	Windows-based	1	2	1	2	$400.00	21
Human Resources	Macintosh	1	2	0	0	$250.00	23

Record: 1 of 22

Figure 1.7
The Software Training table shows a blank rather than a zero.

A blank replaces a zero

Getting Help with Conditional Formats
The first few times that you use conditional formats, you will probably need to use help. The quickest way to get the right kind of help is to go to Design view, select the field you want to format, place the insertion point in the Format properties box, and press F1. This will take you directly to format help.

Lesson 3: Changing the Data Input Structure Using Input Masks

Input masks are data formats that make data entry more meaningful. They can be used to make certain types of data, such as telephone numbers and Social Security numbers, easy to enter. Input masks can be entered in the Input Mask properties box. They can also be added using the Input Mask Wizard.

In this lesson, you add an input mask to the Social Security Number field to divide the number into the familiar XXX-XX-XXXX format. Input masks can also control the format of the data as it is stored in the table.

To Create an Input Mask

 1 In the PC Training database, click the View button on the toolbar to switch to Design view of the Software Training table.

continues ▶

To Create an Input Mask   (continued)

2 Click anywhere in the Social Security Number field to select it.

The Social Security numbers in this database have been entered as text. Because all Social Security numbers contain three blocks of numbers of 3, 2, and 4 digits, it would make data entry easier if the field was also set up in this format.

3 Click the Input Mask box in the Field Properties area.

A Build button (the one with three dots) is displayed on the right-hand side of the Input Mask box (see Figure 1.8).

Figure 1.8
Use the Input Mask property box Build button to start the Input Mask Wizard.

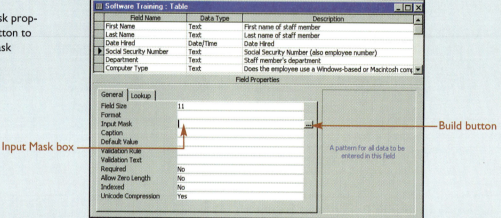

4 Click the Build button.

Before the wizard opens, a dialog box is displayed telling you that you must first save the table. Click Yes to save the table. The first dialog box of the Input Mask Wizard is displayed, showing several of the preset masks (see Figure 1.9). The Input Mask Wizard is used to control the formatting for Text and Date fields only. You can also set an Input Mask manually for Number or Currency fields.

Figure 1.9
The first Input Mask Wizard dialog box asks how you want your data to look.

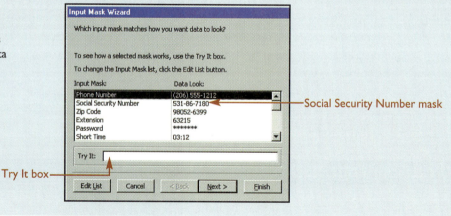

X   You might get a message that Microsoft Access cannot start this wizard. This means that the Input Mask Wizard has not been installed on your machine. If this is the case, click Yes to install it. A dialog box will ask for the first Microsoft Office installation CD. Place the CD in your CD drive and click OK. Select Add or Remove Features from the installation window. Expand the Microsoft Access for Windows button and click the drop-down arrow for Typical Wizards. Choose whether you want to run the wizard from the hard disk or the CD, and whether you want to install just the feature you need (in this case the Input Mask Wizard) or all the typical wizards. Click Update Now to complete the installation.

It is not absolutely necessary to use the Input Mask Wizard. If you know the expression you want to use, you can type it directly into the Input Mask property box. Look at the examples of the input masks in the following section and enter the expression directly into the Input Mask property box.

5 **Select the Social Security Number option, and then click in the Try It area to see the format that appears in the field.**

6 **Click the Next button.**
The second Input Mask Wizard dialog box is displayed (see Figure 1.10). The basic format is shown, and you are asked if you are satisfied with the format and the *placeholders* used to reserve spaces for the data. In this example, you accept the default settings.

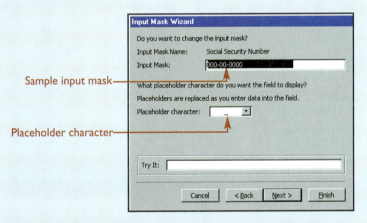

Sample input mask

Placeholder character

Figure 1.10
The second Input Mask Wizard dialog box enables you to modify the selected input mask.

7 **Click the Next button.**
The third Input Mask Wizard dialog box is displayed (see Figure 1.11). This dialog box asks whether the program should save the characters, in this case dashes, used to separate the three parts of the Social Security number. The dashes will be displayed in forms and reports that use this field but will not be part of the actual data stored in each field. If you export the data to another program, the dashes will not be there. The default choice is not to save the extra characters.

continues ▶

To Create an Input Mask   (continued)

Figure 1.11
The third Input Mask
Wizard dialog box asks
you how you want to
store the data.

Save without the symbols option ─┐

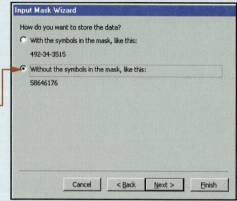

8 **Click the <u>N</u>ext button to accept the default.**
The fourth Input Mask Wizard dialog box is displayed. This dialog box tells
you that you have completed the Wizard.

9 **Click the <u>F</u>inish button to complete the Input Mask Wizard.**
The Input Mask property box contains the following:

000-00-0000;;_

The Input Mask contains three components that are separated by semicolons.
The first component shows the input format. The next component has noth-
ing in it, which indicates that there is no special format for an empty field. The
third component has an underscore to indicate that the placeholder for the
field is an underscore.

10 **Click the View button on the toolbar to switch to Datasheet view.**
Click <u>Y</u>es when prompted to save your changes to the table. Notice that the
Social Security numbers are now in the familiar format (see Figure 1.12).

Figure 1.12
An Input Mask for the
Social Security Number
field has been added.

Social Security Number ─
with input mask

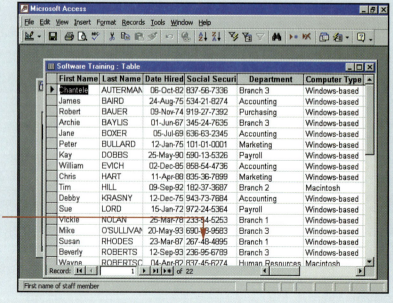

⑪ Click on the New Record button and add another record to see how the data is entered into the field. Use your own name and make up the rest of the information.

Do not use a Social Security number that is a duplicate of a number in the table. You learn how to automatically guard against this type of error in Lesson 6, "Preventing Duplicate Entries Using Indexed Fields."

Keep the database open for the next lesson.

Input Mask Limitations

Adding an Input Mask puts certain limitations on data entry. If you have place-holders for nine characters, you need to enter all nine. If you enter eight or fewer characters, you get an error message, and you are not able to move out of the field until you correct the problem. If you do not have all the characters to enter, don't put any of them in, but press (Esc) to leave the field blank for now.

Lesson 4: Restricting Entries to Those That Meet Validation Criteria

The data entered in some fields in a database needs to be restricted in some way. For example, a field set up for coded data might only use 0s and 1s, whereas a text field might be used to enter only two possible values. Several fields in the PC Training table fit this category. The Computer Type field has only two possible answers: Windows-based or Macintosh. The four software fields, Word, Excel, PP, and Access, use only four numbers (0, 1, 2, and 3).

Access gives you the option of restricting the information that will be accepted into a field. This is done by constructing a **validation rule**, which is an expression that the program compares entered data against to see if it is acceptable. If the data is not acceptable, **validation text** can be displayed to explain the reason the data is not acceptable.

Validation rules are used for two purposes: to make sure the user does not enter incorrect data, and to help avoid typographical errors. In this lesson you use the **Expression Builder** to build a validation rule for the four software fields. You also create validation text to be used as an error message for incorrect data entry.

To Create Validation Rules and Validation Text Using the Expression Builder

 ❶ In the PC Training database, click the View button on the toolbar to switch to Design view of the Software Training table.

❷ Click anywhere in the Word field to select it, and then click the Validation Rule box in the Field Properties area.

You may have to scroll down to see the Word field. Notice that a Build button (containing three dots) is displayed to the right of the Validation Rule property box.

continues ▶

To Create Validation Rules and Validation Text Using the Expression Builder (continued)

3 Click the Build button on the right side of the Validation Rule box.

The Expression Builder dialog box is displayed (see Figure 1.13). You now build a Function, which is the default.

Figure 1.13
Use the Expression Builder dialog box to build a function in a Validation Rule.

Functions is the default option —

Or button —

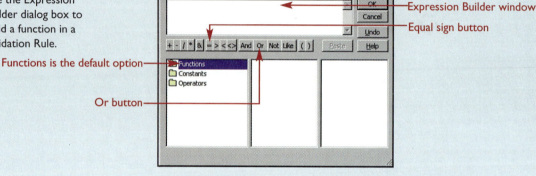

Expression Builder window

Equal sign button

4 Click the button with the = (equal sign) to begin building the expression.

The equal sign is displayed in the upper-left corner of the Expression Builder window.

5 Type the number 0 (zero).

6 Click the Or button.

7 Follow this procedure until your expression reads:

= 0 Or 1 Or 2 Or 3

The Expression Builder window should look like Figure 1.14.

Figure 1.14
The Expression Builder window now contains a validation rule.

Validation rule —

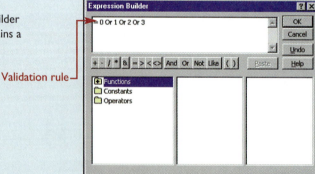

8 Click OK, and then place the cursor in the Validation Text box of the Field Properties area.

9 Type the following in the Validation Text property box: That is not a valid option. Please enter the number 0, 1, 2, or 3.

You should now have entries in both the Validation Rule box and the Validation Text box (see Figure 1.15).

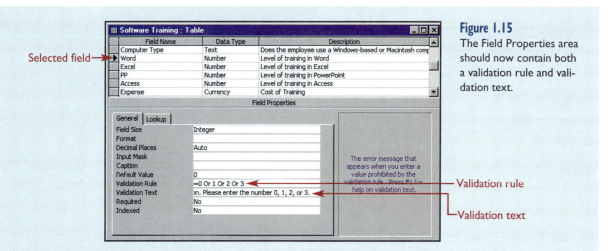

Figure 1.15
The Field Properties area should now contain both a validation rule and validation text.

10 Repeat steps 2 through 9 for the other three software fields (Excel, PP, and Access).

To save time and effort, you can use the Copy and Paste commands with Field Properties. Highlight the Validation Rule text in the Word property box and click the Copy button. Then select the Excel field, click the Validation Rule property box, and click the Paste button. Do this to the other two fields (PP and Access), and then go back and repeat the procedure with the Validation Text property boxes.

11 Click the View button on the toolbar to switch to Datasheet view.

Click Yes when prompted to save your changes to the table.

As usual, when you change the structure of the table, you will be prompted to save your changes. This time, however, an additional dialog box is displayed (see Figure 1.16). This dialog box warns you that Data integrity rules have been changed; existing data may not be valid for the new rules. Whenever a validation rule is added or modified, this warning is displayed. It is important that you are familiar with the content of your data so you can assess whether, in fact, the data in the table violates the new rule that has just been added. In this case, the data will cause no problem.

Figure 1.16
The Data Integrity warning dialog box notifies you that data integrity rules have been changed.

12 Click Yes. The program tests your fields to find any conflicting data.

If data integrity is violated, you receive an additional warning box telling you that data has been detected that violates the rules, but the program does not specifically identify the data. You then need to create a query to search for the data that was outside of the rules and change that data, if appropriate.

13 Attempt to enter the number 5 in one of the software fields and press ↵Enter to move to the next field.

Notice how the message you typed in the Validation Text property box is displayed in the error message window (see Figure 1.17).

continues ▶

To Create Validation Rules and Validation Text Using the Expression Builder (continued)

Figure 1.17
The Validation Rule text is displayed when an incorrect number is entered.

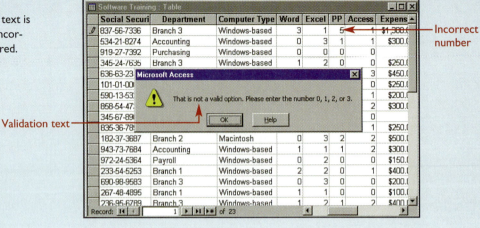

Incorrect number

Validation text

14 Click OK in the error message box, and then press Esc to return the field to its original number.

Keep the database open for the next lesson.

Testing Structural Changes on a Backup File

It is a good idea to test your changes on a backup file before you make major changes to your table structure. If you change the structure of a table on the only file you have and choose yes when it checks for data integrity, it is always possible that some data could be lost. By testing the structure change on a backup file, you can thoroughly test the change without having to worry that you are going to incorrectly change the "real" data.

Lesson 5: Requiring Entry of Necessary Information

At times you will want to force the user to fill in a field. Access enables you to require a data entry in a field. Required responses can be added to all field types except the AutoNumber fields, which are used when sequential numbering is required.

In this lesson, you require that data be entered into the Last Name field.

To Require Entry of Necessary Information

 1 In the PC Training database, click the View button on the toolbar to switch to Design view, and then click the Last Name field to select it.
You may have to scroll up to find the Last Name field.

2 Click the Required box in the Field Properties area.

3 Click the drop-down arrow to reveal the choices.
The screen should look like Figure 1.18.

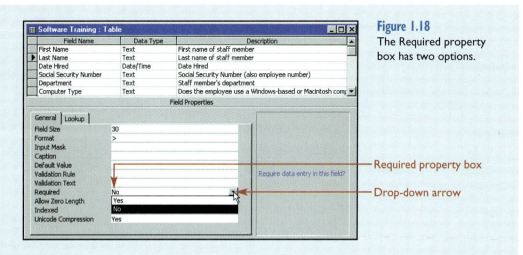

Figure 1.18
The Required property box has two options.

Required property box

Drop-down arrow

4 Select Yes to make an entry into this field required.

5 Click the View button on the toolbar to switch to Datasheet view.
Click Yes when prompted to save your changes to the table. You are warned about data integrity rule changes as you were when you changed the Validation Rule in Lesson 4, "Restricting Entries to Those That Meet Validation Criteria." Click Yes to move to the datasheet.

> **X** If you entered any records without a last name, you will see another warning box that states Existing data violates the new setting for the 'Required' property for the field 'Last Name'. Choose Yes to continue testing with the new setting.

6 Scroll down to the bottom of the table and enter a new record, but leave the Last Name field blank.
The program enables you to continue entering data to the end of the record; however, when you press ⏎Enter after the last field, another dialog box is displayed (see Figure 1.19), warning you that the Last Name field cannot contain a Null value.

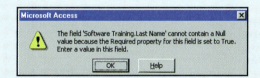

Figure 1.19
The Null value warning dialog box is displayed if you try to skip the Last Name field.

7 Click OK in the warning box.

8 Press Esc to back out of the entry.
Keep the database open for the next lesson.

Lesson 6: Preventing Duplicate Entries Using Indexed Fields

In Access it is possible to build an index for a field. This acts like an index in a book; it speeds up searching and sorting for that field. Indexes can be created for all but Memo, Hyperlink, and OLE fields. **Indexed fields** can also be set up to prevent duplicate entries in a field. If a field has been designated as the **primary key field**, it is automatically indexed, with no duplicate entries allowed. Other fields can also be indexed and set to disallow duplicate entries.

In this lesson, you index the Social Security Number field and prevent duplicate entries, because all Social Security numbers should be unique.

To Prevent Duplicate Entries Using Indexed Fields

 1 **In the PC Training database, click the View button on the toolbar to switch views to Design view of the Software Training table.**

2 **Click anywhere in the Social Security Number field to select it, and then click the Indexed property box.**
A drop-down arrow is displayed at the right side of the property box.

3 **Click the drop-down arrow and select Yes (No Duplicates) from the drop-down list.**
The Social Security Number properties area should look like Figure 1.20.

Figure 1.20
The Social Security Number Field Properties area now shows "Yes (No Duplicates)" in the Indexed property box.

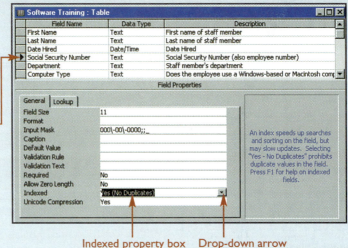

Selected field ─

Indexed property box   Drop-down arrow

4 **Click the View button on the toolbar to switch to Datasheet view.**
Click Yes when prompted to save your changes to the table.

5 **Scroll down to the bottom of the table.**

6 **Add a new record, but this time enter a Social Security number from a previous record.**
When you try to complete the record, an error message is displayed (see Figure 1.21). Notice that the error message tells you that you have entered a duplicate value in an index, primary key, or relationship, but does not tell you in which field the error occurred. This can be a big problem in a database with many indexed fields.

> ### Checking For the Primary Key or Indexed Fields
> If you get an error message and can't remember which field is the primary key, switch to Design view and look for the key icon to the left of the list of fields. You can also check to see which fields are indexed by selecting each field and checking the Indexed box in the Field Properties area.

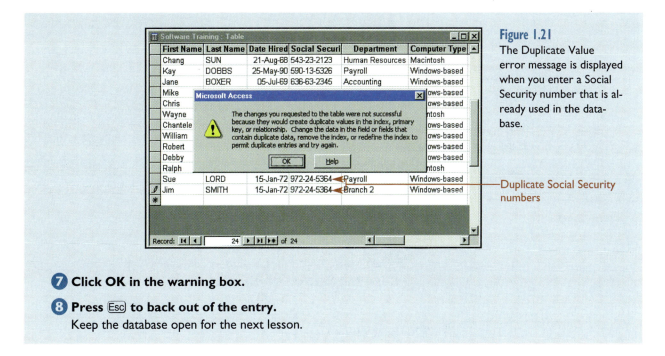

Figure 1.21
The Duplicate Value error message is displayed when you enter a Social Security number that is already used in the database.

Duplicate Social Security numbers

7 **Click OK in the warning box.**

8 **Press Esc to back out of the entry.**
Keep the database open for the next lesson.

Searching For Duplicate Entries

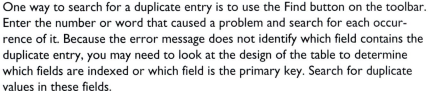
One way to search for a duplicate entry is to use the Find button on the toolbar. Enter the number or word that caused a problem and search for each occurrence of it. Because the error message does not identify which field contains the duplicate entry, you may need to look at the design of the table to determine which fields are indexed or which field is the primary key. Search for duplicate values in these fields.

Lesson 7: Creating a Lookup Column to Allow Selection from a List

There are times when you will have a field that has several common entries. This is particularly true of fields designed for such things as city or state names, job titles, and military ranks.

Access contains a Lookup Wizard in the Data Type column in the Table Design view. This wizard enables you to either enter the common items or have the program make up a list from a field in another table. Having pre-typed choices available makes data entry far easier, and also prevents the user from making typographical errors. When entering data, if the value you need is not on the list, you can type it in the field.

In this lesson, you add a Lookup list for the Department field. The Lookup Wizard walks you through the steps of creating the data list, and you end up with a drop-down list containing all the department names in the database.

To Create a Lookup Column Using the Lookup Wizard

1 In the **PC Training database, click the View button on the toolbar to switch views to Design view of the Software Training table.**

2 Click on the **Data Type box of the Department field.**
A drop-down arrow is displayed on the right side of the box.

3 Click the **arrow in the Department Data Type box.**
A drop-down menu is displayed (see Figure 1.22). The various data types are shown in this box. At the bottom of the box is the Lookup Wizard choice.

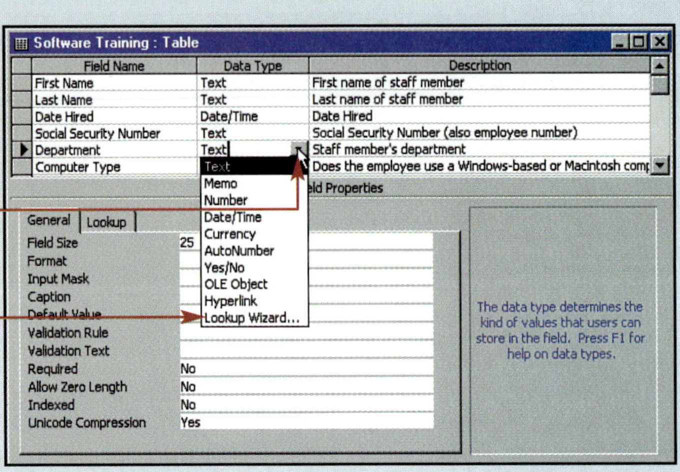

Figure 1.22
The Lookup Wizard option is displayed at the bottom of the drop-down list.

Drop-down arrow ⟶

Lookup Wizard option ⟶

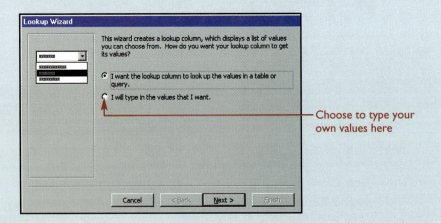

4 Select **Lookup Wizard from the drop-down list.**
The first Lookup Wizard dialog box is displayed (see Figure 1.23).

Figure 1.23
The first Lookup Wizard dialog box asks how you want your lookup column to get its values.

Choose to type your own values here ⟶

5 Choose the **second option to type the values you want, and then click Next.**
The second Lookup Wizard dialog box is displayed.

6 **Accept the default number of columns, and then type the departments listed below in the box labeled Col1:**

Do not press ⏎Enter after each entry. This takes you to the next dialog box. Use ↓ or Tab↹ to move down. If you accidentally move to the next dialog box before you finish entering the department names, click <u>B</u>ack to return to the data entry area.

```
Accounting
Branch 1
Branch 2
Branch 3
Human Resources
Marketing
Payroll
```

As you enter the seven department names (see Figure 1.24), the first one may scroll off the screen. If you need to move up to edit an entry that has scrolled off the screen, use ↑.

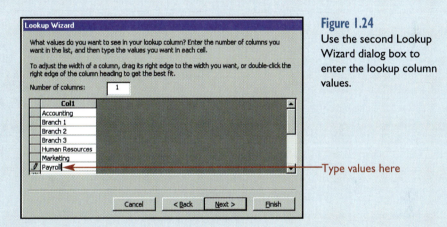

Figure 1.24
Use the second Lookup Wizard dialog box to enter the lookup column values.

Type values here

7 **Click <u>N</u>ext to move to the third Lookup Wizard dialog box.**

This dialog box asks what you want to name your lookup column (see Figure 1.25).

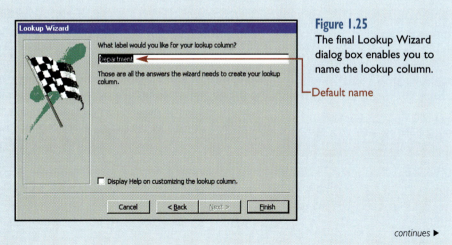

Figure 1.25
The final Lookup Wizard dialog box enables you to name the lookup column.

Default name

continues ▶

To Create a Lookup Column Using the Lookup Wizard   (continued)

8 Accept the default, Department, as the lookup column name, and then click <u>F</u>inish.

 9 Click the View button on the toolbar to switch to Datasheet view.
Click <u>Y</u>es when prompted to save your changes to the table.

10 Scroll down to the bottom of the table and enter a new record.
When you get to the Department field, notice that a drop-down arrow is displayed.

11 Click the arrow to display the drop-down box you just created, and then select one of the departments.
You have now created a timesaving feature for your table (see Figure 1.26).

Figure 1.26
The Lookup Wizard created a drop-down box for the Department field.

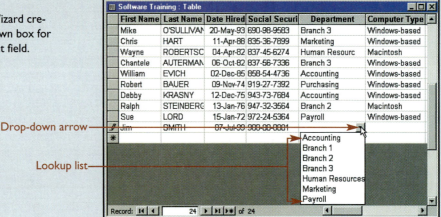

12 Press Esc to back out of the entry. Close your table and Exit Access.
If you have completed your session on the computer, select Sh<u>u</u>t Down from the Start menu. Otherwise, continue with the exercises for this project.

Effects of Format Changes in a Table
The changes made to the text and number formatting in table design carry over to new forms and reports that are based on this table. Some of the changes, such as required fields, validation rules, and default values, also show up in existing forms. It is always best to have the table structure complete before creating other objects to ensure that all the formatting characteristics flow from the table to the objects based on that table. If you make changes to the table structure after other objects have been created, you can add those same formatting characteristics directly to the design of the form, reports, or queries.

Features That Improve Data Accuracy

All the topics in this project were performed and tested in the table view. By changing the text and number formatting in table design, the formatting carries over to new forms and reports. All the following features help improve accuracy in forms, tables, and reports:

- Consistent data formats
- Conditional formats
- Input masks
- Validation criteria
- Required fields
- Prevention of duplication

Summary

In this project, you were introduced to some of the techniques used to refine and control data entry. You learned how to make field entries appear as all upper- or lowercase letters, and how to make data look different depending on data characteristics. You also set up input masks to assist with entry of consistently formatted data. You learned how to set conditions for accepting data entry, how to require the entry of data in a field, and how to avoid duplicate entries by indexing a field. Finally, you created a lookup list to make data entry quicker and more accurate.

You can learn more about taking control of data entry in Access by looking a little more closely at some of the other options available in input masks, conditional and data formatting, and validation criteria in Microsoft Help. The best way to do this is to go to the help index and explore the topic you are interested in. Create a new database and try out these features.

Checking Concepts and Terms

True/False

For each of the following statements, check *T* or *F* to indicate whether the statement is true or false.

__T __F **1.** When you change the display format of a field in an existing table, the data already stored on your disk is changed also. [L1]

__T __F **2.** If you want to show negative numbers in red text, you would create a conditional format. [L2]

__T __F **3.** You must use the Input Mask Wizard to enter an input mask. [L3]

__T __F **4.** Text you enter into the Validation Text property box will appear in an error message dialog box if the Validation Rule is violated. [L4]

__T __F **5.** Data entry can be required in every type of field except AutoNumber. [L5]

__T __F **6.** If you want a text field displayed in all capitals, enter the > (greater than) symbol in the format properties box for that field. [L1]

__T __F **7.** When you add an input mask to a field after data has been entered, it does not change the way the existing data is displayed; you must re-enter the data to have the new format take effect. [L3]

__T __F **8.** If the Input Mask Wizard does not work when you click the Build button, it means that it has not yet been installed on your hard drive. [L3]

__T __F **9.** When indexing a field, the Yes (No duplicates) option can only be used for the primary key field. [L6]

__T __F **10.** A null value is the same as a zero. [L2]

Multiple Choice

Circle the letter of the correct answer for each of the following questions.

1. In a conditional format, components are separated by _____. [L2]
a. commas
b. semicolons
c. colons
d. quotation marks

2. The Input Mask Wizard creates formats for _____. [L3]
a. all types of fields
b. all types of fields except OLE
c. text fields only
d. text and date fields only

3. A program that helps the user create formulas for Validation Rules is called a(n)_____. [L4]
a. Expression Builder
b. Validation Text
c. Rule Wizard
d. Restriction Builder

4. If you enter duplicate information in a field where duplicates are not allowed, how do you back out of that entry? [L6]
a. Press Del.
b. You can't delete the record.
c. Press Esc.
d. Press ↵Enter and go on.

5. One way to speed up searching and sorting on a field is to _____. [L6]
a. prevent duplicate entries in the field
b. make it a required field
c. index it
d. make the data format consistent

6. Validation Text is used to_____. [L4]
a. explain to the person entering data the reason why the data entered is not acceptable
b. verify that only valid data is entered
c. validate text fields only
d. intimidate the user for making a mistake

7. Formats for the Date/Time data type can be set for _____. [LI]
a. dates
b. times
c. date and time
d. all the above

8. Which of the following best describes a null value? [L2]
a. zero in a number field
b. spaces in a text field
c. $0 in a currency field
d. no entry at all

9. A required property can be set for every type of field except _____. [L5]
a. Memo
b. OLE
c. AutoNumber
d. Yes/No

10. A lookup list would be most useful for a field that contained _____. [L7]
a. Social Security numbers
b. department names
c. last names
d. account numbers

Screen ID

Label each element of the Access screens shown in Figure 1.27 and Figure 1.28.

Figure 1.27

A. Build button

B. Allows more than one condition

C. Special format for negative number

D. Begins an expression

E. Conditional format

F. Duplicate entries can be eliminated here

G. Selected field

H. Dialog box text

I. Data must meet this condition

J. Validation condition being built

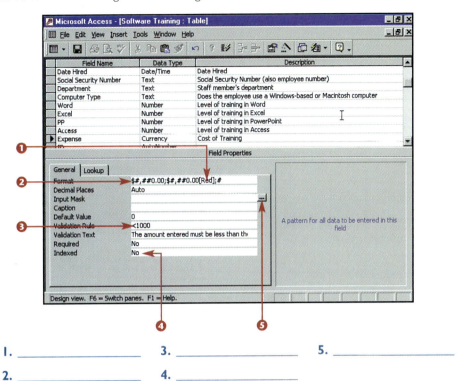

1. _____ 3. _____ 5. _____

2. _____ 4. _____

Figure 1.28

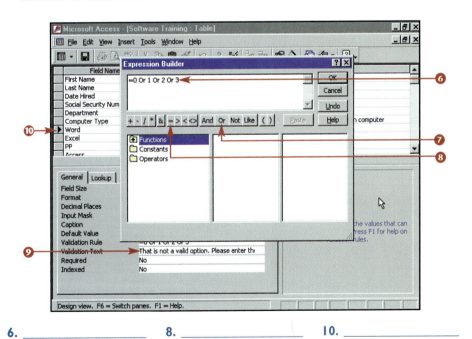

6. _____ 8. _____ 10. _____

7. _____ 9. _____

Discussion Questions

1. You learned how to use display formats and input masks in this project. In what situations would you use an input mask rather than a display format, and vice versa? When might you want to use both in the same field?

2. In the Software Training table of the PC Training database you worked with in this project, you used a conditional format on the Expense field. Are there any other fields that could use a conditional format?

3. If you wanted to index on the Last Name field, what would you have to do differently from what you did with the index you used in the Social Security Number field? Why?

4. In the Software Training table, which fields should be required? What problems could arise from making too many of the fields required fields?

5. Which other field(s) should use lookup columns? Would lookup columns be helpful for the Word, Excel, PP, and Access fields? Why or why not?

Skill Drill

Skill Drill exercises reinforce project skills. Each skill reinforced is the same, or nearly the same, as a skill presented in the project. Each exercise includes a brief narrative introduction, followed by detailed instructions in a step-by-step format.

The database you will use in the Skill Drill exercises contains information about a company's computers. It consists of two tables—one with information about the characteristics of the computers and one with information about the vendors who sold you the computers.

1. Creating a Consistent Data Format

The first thing you want to do is set the computer processor type to all capital letters.

To change the format of text in a field, complete the following steps:

1. Find the AC2-0102 file on your CD-ROM, right-click on it, and send it to the floppy drive. Move to drive A, remove the read-only status, and rename the file **Computer Inventory**.

2. Open the Computer Inventory database, and then open the PC Hardware table in Design view.

3. Place the insertion point anywhere in the Processor field.

4. Click in the Format box in the Field Properties area.

5. Type a greater than (>) symbol.

6. Click the View button to move to Datasheet view. Save your changes when prompted.

7. Widen the Processor column so that you can read the data.

8. Close the table. Because you changed the structure of the table (column width), you will be prompted to save your changes.

2. Adding an Input Mask to a Text Field

The Phone Number field in the Vendors table has a text data type. You will want to add an input mask to this field. This will prompt the user to enter an area code for the number.

To add an input mask for a telephone number, complete the following steps:

1. With the Computer Inventory database open, select the Vendors table.

2. Open the Vendors table in Design view.

3. Click anywhere in the Phone Number field.

4. Click in the Input Mask box in the Field Properties area.

5. Click the Build button to start the Input Mask Wizard.

6. Select the Phone Number option and click Next.

7. Accept the default input mask, placeholder, and method of saving, and click Next when necessary.

8. Click Finish to complete the input mask.

9. Click the View button to switch to Datasheet view. Save your changes.

10. Make sure your phone numbers are in the proper format, and then close the table.

3. Adding Validation Rules

All your computers have RAM of one of six sizes—4, 8, 16, 32, 64, or 128 MB. You think it is highly likely that any new machines you add in the near future will fit into one of these categories. Therefore, you want to restrict the data input to one of these numbers. (Note: You can edit or remove validation rules at any time.)

To add validation rules to the RAM field, complete the following steps:

1. With the Computer Inventory database open, select the PC Hardware table.
2. Open the PC Hardware table in Design view.
3. Click anywhere in the RAM field.
4. Click in the Validation Rule box in the Field Properties area.
5. Click the Build button to open the Expression Builder.
6. Click the equal button, or type the = symbol in the Expression Builder work area.
7. Type **4**, and then click the Or button.
8. Repeat this procedure to enter **8**, **16**, **32**, **64**, and **128**. When you are finished, click OK.
9. Click the View button to switch to Datasheet view. Save your changes when prompted, and have the program check for data integrity errors.
10. Add a new field and try to enter a number other than one of those you typed into the Expression Builder. Click OK to acknowledge the error.
11. Back out of the new field and record by pressing Esc twice.

4. Preventing Duplicate Entries Using the Index Property

Many of the entries in the Inventory Code Number field are similar. To make sure the user doesn't type the code number from another computer, you will want to index on the field and prevent duplicates from being entered. (Note: If you were sure that no numbers would ever be duplicated in this field, you could make it a primary key field, which would automatically prevent duplicate entries.)

To prevent duplicate entries using the Index property, complete the following steps:

1. With the Computer Inventory database open, select the PC Hardware table, if necessary.
2. Open the PC Hardware table in Design view.
3. Click anywhere in the Inventory Code Number field.
4. Click in the Indexed box in the Field Properties area.
5. Click the drop-down arrow and select Yes (No Duplicates).
6. Click the View button to switch to Datasheet view, and save your changes when prompted.
7. Enter a new record and enter **B324231** in the Inventory Control Code field. When you press Enter after the last field, notice that the error message does not tell you which field contains the error.
8. Click OK, and then back out of the new record by pressing Esc.

5. Adding a Lookup Column

One of the fields in the PC Hardware table is the name of the vendor that sold you the computers. You have deals with three vendors—Acme Computer, General Comp, and Wilson Electric. Because all your computers will come from one of these three companies, you can add a drop-down list to the field by using the Lookup Wizard.

To add a lookup column to a field, complete the following steps:

1. With the Computer Inventory database open, select the PC Hardware table, if necessary.
2. Open the PC Hardware table in Design view.
3. Click in the Data Type column of the Vendor field.
4. Click the drop-down arrow in the Data Type box and select Lookup Wizard from the data type menu.
5. Choose to type the values yourself.

6. Accept the default of one column, and then type **Acme Computer**, **General Comp**, and **Wilson Electric** and click <u>N</u>ext. Use (Tab⇆) or (↓) to move from one field to the next. If you accidentally press (↵Enter), click the <u>B</u>ack button in the dialog box.

7. Accept Vendor as the name of the label.

8. Click the View button to switch to Datasheet view. Save your changes when prompted.

9. Move to the Vendor field and click anywhere in the column. Click the down arrow to see if your lookup column is working.

6. Requiring a Field Entry

Computers are first sent through your company's Receiving department, which places an Inventory Code Number on each computer. Once this is done, the item is placed in the database. An entry into the Inventory Code Number field is required, so you need to make sure that a number is entered for every record.

To require the entry of an inventory code, complete the following steps:

1. With the Computer Inventory database open, select the PC Hardware table, if necessary.

2. Open the PC Hardware table in Design view.

3. Click anywhere in the Inventory Code Number field.

4. Click in the Required box in the Field Properties area.

5. Click the drop-down arrow and select Yes.

6. Click the View button to switch to Datasheet view, save your changes when prompted, and let the program check for data integrity problems.

7. Enter a new record and skip the entry for the Inventory Code Number field. Read the error message you receive, and then click OK.

8. Back out of the new field by pressing (Esc).

9. Close the table, and then close the database.

Challenge 💡

These exercises expand on or are somewhat related to skills practiced in the project. Each exercise provides a brief narrative introduction followed by instructions in a numbered step format that are not as detailed as those in the Skill Drill section.

The database you will be using for the Challenge section is for a small online chess club that started out as a chess-by-mail club. Yearly dues help pay for space on a file server where games can be played and saved. Like most clubs, some members have paid in advance, and some are behind in their dues. The database currently contains only one table—a membership list that you are responsible for. You decide that if you must take care of the list, you will set it up the way you want it!

I. Placing Default Text in Empty Fields Using Custom Formats

You have two address fields for each of the members. Some of the members don't have second address lines, and you'd like to place the word 'None' in the field if it is left empty.

To place default text in empty fields using a custom format, complete the following steps:

1. Copy the file AC2-0103 from your CD-ROM, place it on your floppy drive, and rename it **Chess Club**. Change it to an Ar<u>c</u>hive file, and deselect the <u>R</u>ead-only attribute.

2. Open the database and the Membership Information table. Notice that two of the records have no entry in the Address2 field.

3. Switch to Design view, select the Address2 field, and click in the Format properties box.

4. Type @;"None" in the Format properties box.

5. Press F1 to find out what each of the two sections of the custom format do.

6. Switch to Datasheet view and look at the Address2 fields that were formerly blank to make sure your custom format is working.

2. Creating a Two-Column Lookup Column

You want to save the State field in the standard two-character format, but you sometimes have trouble remembering what code is used for what state. You decide to add a lookup column that contains both the two-character state code and the full state name. Right now, you have members from Colorado, Georgia, Indiana, and Michigan. You are also pretty sure a person from Missouri will be joining soon.

To create a two-column lookup column, complete the following steps:

1. Select the Design view of the Member Information table and select the State field.

2. Change the Data Type to Lookup Wizard.

3. Indicate that you want to type the values, but change the number of columns to 2.

4. Enter the following information in the columns:

Col1	Col2
CO	Colorado
GA	Georgia
IN	Indiana
MI	Michigan
MO	Missouri

5. Double-click on the line between the Col1 and Col2 column headings to reduce the width of the Col1 column.

6. Continue through the rest of the wizard. Choose to store the value from Col1 in your table and accept the default name.

7. Switch to Datasheet view and add another member. The membership information should read: **9998765, Ms., Hawken, Charity, S., 1885 Burtchville Rd.,** [leave Address2 blank], **Jeddo, MO, 63460, (573) 555-1234, 25, 9/9/99, 47.** Use the lookup column for the State field. Notice that the two-character code and the state name both appear, but only the code is entered into the table.

3. Using Validation Rules to Set a Minimum Value for a Field

By club rules, the minimum membership age is 18 years. You want to make sure that you don't accidentally type an incorrect age, so you want to create a validation rule to have the program tell you if you type a number less than 18.

To set a minimum value for a field, complete the following steps:

1. With the Chess Club database open, open the Member Information table in Design view.

2. Use the available help to make sure that the number entered is 18 or greater. There are two ways to do this—either way will do.

3. Type **The age must be at least 18** as validation text.

4. Switch to Datasheet view and change the age in the first record (Mr. Jones) from 24 to **15**. Try changing it to **17** (this is the critical one in determining whether your validation rule is correct).

5. Change the age back to **24**.

4. Using Conditional Formats to Emphasize Negative Numbers

You want to display the negative numbers in the Dues field in red. In Lesson 2, "Creating Conditional Formats for Positive, Negative, and Null Values," you set up a conditional format that included red for negative numbers, but there were no negative numbers in the field. In the Dues field, use the available help to figure out how to display the negative numbers in red and with no decimal places. Also, have the negative numbers surrounded by parentheses.

5. Indexing Multiple Fields

You can create indexes for more than one field in a table. You can also create an index that is based on multiple fields. Because you are anticipating a lot more members in the future, you want to create an index on the Last Name and First Name fields so that the program will sort on these fields faster.

To index on more than one field at a time, complete the following steps:

1. With the Chess Club database open, open the Member Information table in Design view.

2. Click the Indexes button on the toolbar. The Indexes dialog box shows two current indexes.

3. Type **Name** in the first available Index Name box.

4. Select the Last Name field from the drop-down list in the Field Name column.

5. Move down one row and select the First Name field from the drop-down list in the Field Name column. Leave the Index Name box blank in this row.

6. Switch to Datasheet view. The multiple-field index will make little difference with only a few fields, but will be very important when you work with tables with many records.

Discovery Zone

Discovery Zone exercises help you gain advanced knowledge of project topics and application of skills. These exercises focus on enhancing your problem-solving skills. Numbered steps are not provided, but you are given hints, reminders, screen shots, or references to help you reach your goal for each exercise.

The database you will be using in this Discovery Zone is a slightly modified version of the Chess Club database you used in the Challenge section.

I. Creating Your Own Input Mask

The Member ID# is set up with the last two digits of the year the member joined followed by a randomly generated five-digit number. You would like to create an input mask that would separate the first two digits from the last five digits with a dash.

Copy the file AC2-0104 from your CD-ROM, place it on your floppy drive, and rename it **Chess Club 2**. Change it to an Ar<u>c</u>hive file and deselect the <u>R</u>ead-only attribute.

Goal: Create a custom input mask that results in a Member ID # with the following format: **ID 92-23434** (this is the Member ID # for the first record in the table). The input mask should

- Start each Member ID # with the following characters: **ID**.
- Use a dash to separate the first two digits (the year) from the last five digits.
- Make all seven digits required entries.
- Use the underscore as a placeholder.
- Not store the literal characters (for example, the dash) in the table.

Hint #1: All the information you need is in the Input Mask help section.

Hint #2: You will need three sections for this input mask.

2. Creating Your Own Custom Date Format

Date fields give you great flexibility in customizing formats. You want to show as much information as possible for the Date Joined field in your Member Information table.

Goal: Create a custom display format that results in the Date Joined field with the following format: **Monday, January 9, 1995** (this is the Date Joined for the first record in the table). This format will be displayed even though you only type in **1/9/95**. The format should

- Include commas after the weekday and the date, as shown above.
- Display just the number of digits needed for the date (January 9 should not read January 09).
- Display the full year.
- Include a single space after each of the commas.

Hint #1: The table of custom formats in the Format Property-Date/Time Data Type help will give you all the necessary information to create this date format.

Hint #2: It may not seem logical, but the same symbol is used for two of the four parts of this input mask.

Project 2

Managing Data Using Smaller, Related Tables

Objectives

In this project, you learn how to

➤ **Design Related Tables to Hold Repetitive Data**

➤ **Define the Relationship Between the Tables**

➤ **Create Queries That Draw Data from Both Tables**

➤ **Automatically Fill In Data from One of the Joined Tables**

➤ **Update Tables by Entering or Deleting Data in the Query**

➤ **Find Duplicate Records in an Existing Table**

Key terms introduced in this project include

- cascade
- combo box
- dynaset
- expand indicator
- Find Duplicate Query Wizard
- Find Unmatched Query Wizard
- foreign key
- one-to-many
- subdatasheet

Why Would I Do This?

To manage your data effectively, you need to be able to reduce the size of databases and limit repetitive data entry. Instead of using large tables with many fields that contain identical entries, you need to know how to create separate tables and join them when necessary.

Once you have separated your data into smaller, single-purpose tables, you can recombine the data as needed by creating queries that draw data from the tables.

If a form is based on a query that is, in turn, based on more than one table, it is possible to have the program automatically fill in some of the needed information. It is also possible to enter new data into the tables by entering it into the query.

In some cases, you may want to be sure that all the records in one table have a corresponding record in another table. For example, if you have a table of vendor names and a table of purchases, you might want to make sure that you have a vendor name for each purchase. You might also want to know if you have a vendor from whom you have made no purchases. In this case, the data about the vendor might be unnecessary and could be deleted.

Visual Summary

When you have completed this project, you will have created a document that looks like this:

Figure 2.1
Selecting one field from a drop-down list results in the automatic update of several related fields.

A query drop-down box automatically fills in other data

Select this field   These fields are automatically updated

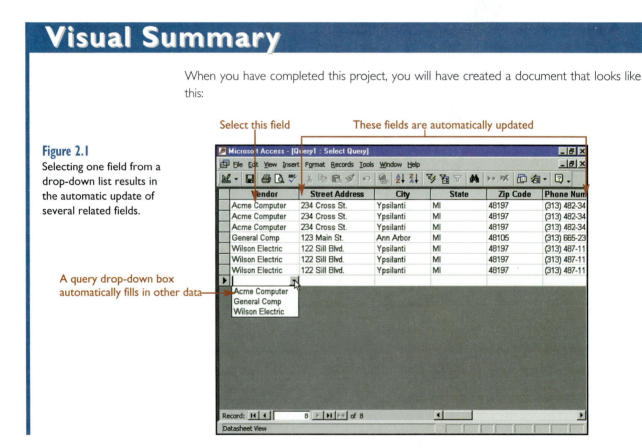

Lesson 1: Designing Related Tables to Hold Repetitive Data

In this lesson, you see how two tables are designed to store related data and how to use them to minimize duplicate data entry. The database used in the first five lessons of this project is a modified version of the Computer Inventory database you worked on in the Skill Drill section of Project 1, "Making Data Entry Easier and More Accurate."

To Examine the Structure of Related Tables

1 **Find the AC2-0201 file on your CD-ROM, right-click on it, and send it to the floppy drive. Move to drive A, right-click on the filename, and select Properties from the shortcut menu. Select Ar_c_hive and deselect _R_ead-only from the Attributes section.**

2 **Right-click on the filename and select Rena_m_e from the shortcut menu. Rename the file** Computer Inventory 2. **Click OK, and then open the database.**

The database window should now be open to the Tables area (see Figure 2.2).

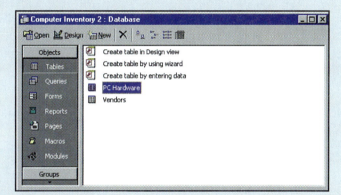

Figure 2.2
The Computer Inventory 2 database includes the PC Hardware and Vendors tables.

3 **Click the Vendors table to select it, then click _O_pen.**

You could also double-click the Vendors table to open it. This table contains data that is necessary to contact the vendor by mail or by phone. Notice that each vendor's name only appears one time.

4 **Click the View button to switch to Design view.**

The Name of Vendor field is the primary key field in this table (see Figure 2.3).

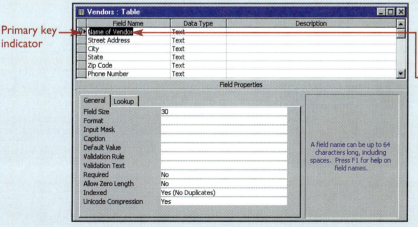

Primary key indicator

Figure 2.3
The Vendors table displays a primary key field in Design view.

Primary key field

5 **Close the Vendors table so that you can look at the PC Hardware table.**

6 **Click the PC Hardware table to select it, and then click _O_pen.**

The PC Hardware table is displayed in Datasheet view.

continues ▶

To Examine the Structure of Related Tables . (continued)

7 **Scroll the table to the right to display the Vendor field.**

8 **Click anywhere in the Vendor field, and then click the arrow on the right side of the Field box.**
Notice that the Lookup Wizard has been used to attach a lookup box to the Name of Vendor field (see Figure 2.4). This lookup box (also referred to as a ***combo box***) uses the contents of the Name of Vendor field in the Vendors table to form its list. This makes it easy to enter the Vendor's name so that there will be an exact match. Notice that the same vendor's name can appear more than once in this table.

Figure 2.4
The Name of Vendor field of the PC Hardware table contains a lookup box.

Lookup box showing contents of the Name of Vendor field —

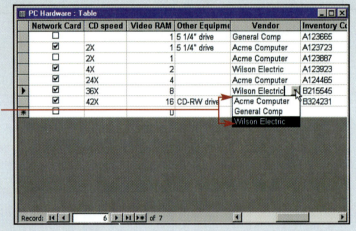

9 **Close the table.**
Keep the database open for the next lesson.

Lesson 2: Defining the Relationship Between the Tables

Whenever the same information is repeated in numerous records, it is more efficient to create two tables and join them with a single field. In this example, the name of the vendor is used to link the two tables. When the user enters the name of the vendor in a record in one table, all the data for that vendor is available from the other table without entering it again.

Linking a pair of similar fields, one from each of the two tables, joins those tables. The two fields do not have to have the same name, but they must be the same data type. If they are Number fields, they must also have the same Field Size property setting.

The most common type of database relationship is called a ***one-to-many*** relationship. In the following lesson, you learn how to join the Vendors table to the PC Hardware table using a one-to-many link between the Name of Vendor field in the Vendors table and the Vendor field in the PC Hardware table. In the Vendors table, there is only one record for General Comp, while in the PC Hardware table there are three (many) records for General Comp.

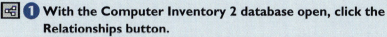

To Join Two Tables with a One-to-Many Relationship

 ❶ **With the Computer Inventory 2 database open, click the Relationships button.**

The Relationships dialog box is displayed in the background, with a Show Table dialog box in the foreground (see Figure 2.5). The Relationships dialog box enables you to create and edit relationships between tables.

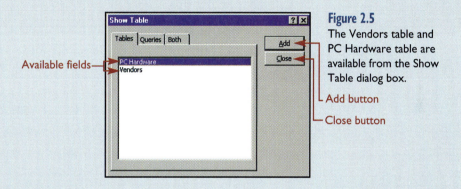

Figure 2.5
The Vendors table and PC Hardware table are available from the Show Table dialog box.

— Add button

— Close button

> ❌ If the Show Table dialog box is not shown, click the Show Table button on the toolbar.

❷ **Click the Add button to add the PC Hardware table to the Relationships dialog box.**

The PC Hardware list box is displayed in the Relationships dialog box.

❸ **Select the Vendors table and click the Add button to add the Vendors table to the Relationships dialog box. Click the Close button to close the Show Table dialog box.**

List boxes for both tables are displayed in the Relationships dialog box.

❹ **Scroll down to the bottom of the list of fields in the PC Hardware list.**

Notice that the Name of Vendor field in the Vendors table is indicated in boldface type. This is because it is the key field in the Vendors table. The corresponding field in the PC Hardware table, Vendor, is not in boldface type because it is not the key field in the PC Hardware table. When the tables are linked, the non-key field is identified as the ***foreign key***. It is important that you know which field from which table is identified in this manner (see Figure 2.6).

continues ▶

To Join Two Tables with a One-to-Many Relationship (continued)

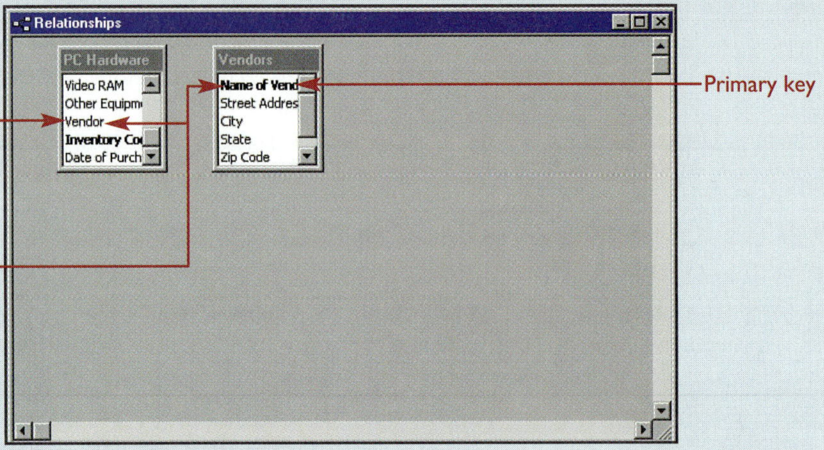

Figure 2.6
The Name of Vendor field in the Vendors table corresponds to the Vendor field in the PC Hardware table.

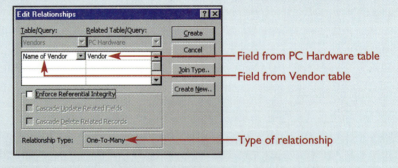

5 **Click the Name of Vendor field name in the Vendors list to select it.**

6 **Click and drag this field name to the corresponding field, Vendor, in the PC Hardware field list, and then release the mouse.**

This creates a relationship between the two tables. Once this relationship is created, you are able to create queries that draw from both tables.

The Edit Relationships dialog box is displayed, showing that the fields from both tables are ready to be linked (see Figure 2.7).

Figure 2.7
The Edit Relationships dialog box shows that the two tables are ready to be linked.

7 **Click the Join Type button to view the options.**

The Join Properties dialog box is displayed (see Figure 2.8).

Figure 2.8
The Join Properties dialog box enables you to specify the type of join you want to use.

These join properties influence the query you create in a later lesson. For this example, you list all the PC Hardware records and any of the Vendor records that match. In other words, if you have a Vendor listed in the Vendors table, but have not purchased PCs from them, their name and address will not appear in the resulting query.

8 Select the third option and click OK to return to the Edit Relationships dialog box.

This option will include all records from the PC Hardware table and only those that match from the Vendors table.

9 Select the Enforce Referential Integrity text box.

Checking this box prevents the user from entering a record in the PC Hardware table that does not have a corresponding entry in the Vendors table (see Figure 2.9). Likewise, you cannot delete a record in the Vendors table as long as it is related to records in the PC Hardware table. Enforcing reference integrity prevents having orphan (unmatched) records in the many table.

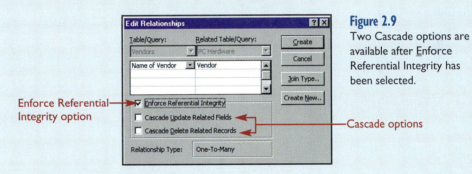

Figure 2.9
Two Cascade options are available after Enforce Referential Integrity has been selected.

When this box is checked you also have two other options that enable you to *cascade* changes: to change a field in one table and to automatically update related fields. Do not select either of them for this lesson.

 Using Cascade Updates and Deletes

If you select Cascade Update Related Fields in the second Relationships dialog box, changes in the Vendor table are automatically transferred to the PC Hardware table. For example, if the General Comp company changes its name to Allied Computers, all occurrences of its name would be changed in the PC Hardware table as well. Similarly, if you select Cascade Delete Related Records, deleting a vendor name from the Vendors table would delete all related records from the PC Hardware table.

These two features should be used sparingly and only after careful consideration.

10 Click Create to establish the relationship.

The Relationships box appears with a new line displaying the one-to-many relationship (see Figure 2.10). The "one" field is labeled 1, whereas the "many" field is indicated by an infinity symbol (∞).

continues ▶

To Join Two Tables with a One-to-Many Relationship   (continued)

"Many" field indicator   "One" field indicator

Figure 2.10
A one-to-many relation-ship has been created.

Relationships line

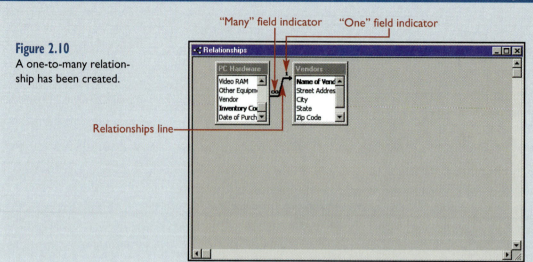

11 **Close the Relationships box, highlight the Vendors table, and click the Open button. Save the changes when prompted.**

Notice that there are now pluses to the left of each Vendor record. The plus is called an *expand indicator*, which means that there is information related to that record in another table, in this case the PC Hardware table. If you click the expand indicator, all the related information from the PC Hardware table will be displayed in a *subdatasheet*.

12 **Click the expand indicator on the left side of the Acme Computer record.**

The subdatasheet is displayed, showing the information about all computers purchased from that company (see Figure 2.11). The expand indicator for the Acme Computer record has been changed to a minus, showing that the sub-datasheet is open for that record.

Figure 2.11
A subdatasheet shows re-lated information from another table.

Click here to close a subdatasheet

Click here to open a subdatasheet

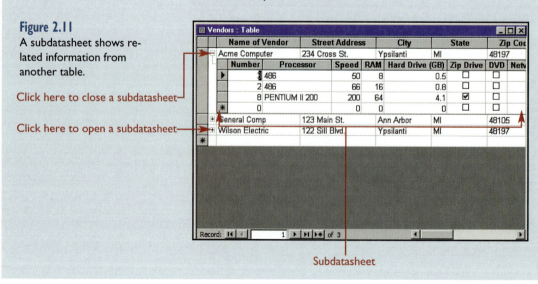

Subdatasheet

Navigating the Subdatasheets
When the subdatasheet is displayed, you can use the navigation buttons at the bottom of the table window to move between records and (Tab⁺) to move between fields in the subdatasheet.

⓭ Click the minus sign on the left of the Acme Computer field to close the subdatasheet, and then click the Close button to close the table window.
Save your layout changes when prompted. Keep the database open for the next lesson.

Lesson 3: Creating Queries That Draw Data from Both Tables

Queries can be used to look at subsets of data from a single table or to combine fields from more than one table. Because the queries draw from existing tables, they do not take up large amounts of space on your disk. This lets you create as many special-purpose queries as you desire. Queries can also be used as the basis for forms. If a form requires data from more than one table, it should be based on a query.

In this lesson, you learn how to create a query that includes data from the Vendors table and from the PC Hardware table.

To Create a Query Based on Two Tables

① With the Computer Inventory 2 database open, click the Queries object button and click the New button.
The New Query dialog box is displayed (see Figure 2.12).

In this exercise, you design your own query. The other options that appear in the dialog box are query wizards that are used for specific purposes. You can click each option and read the explanation on the left side of the dialog box to get a brief description of what each wizard will do.

Figure 2.12
Use the New Query dialog box to start a query.

② Click Design View to select it, if necessary, and then click OK.
The Select Query window opens with the Show Table dialog box in front of it (see Figure 2.13).

continues ▶

To Create a Query Based on Two Tables   (continued)

Figure 2.13
The Show Table dialog box opens in front of the Select Query window.

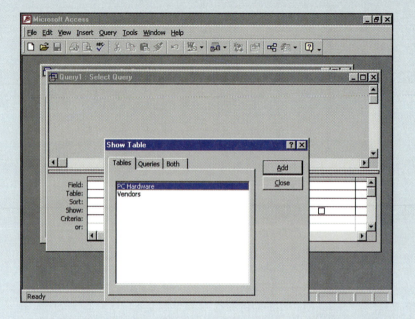

3 **Click the Add button to add the PC Hardware table to the Select Query window in the background, click Vendors to select the table, and then click the Add button to add the Vendors table to the Select Query window.**

4 **Click the Close button to close the Show Table dialog box.**
The Select Query window becomes active, showing that the Vendors table and the PC Hardware table have been selected for use in this query. The relationship between the tables is also shown, although the Vendor field is hidden for the PC Hardware table.

5 **Click the Maximize button in the upper-right corner of the Select Query window to maximize the window.**

6 **Point your mouse pointer at the thick line dividing the Select Query window into two parts. When the mouse pointer turns into a double-headed black arrow, click and drag the line down to expand the upper portion of the window (see Figure 2.14).**

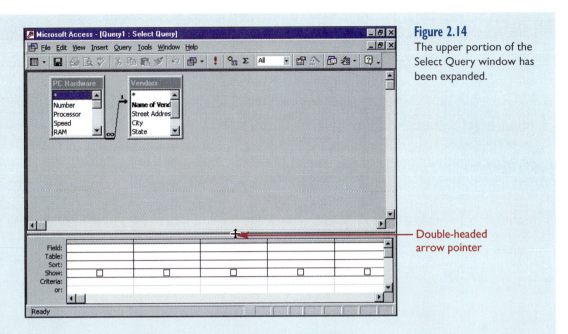

Figure 2.14
The upper portion of the Select Query window has been expanded.

Double-headed arrow pointer

7 **Point to the lower edge of the PC Hardware list box. When the mouse pointer turns into a double-headed black arrow, drag the lower edge of the box until you can see most of the field names. Do the same for the Vendor list box.**

You can move the fields by clicking in the field list title bar and dragging. You can also drag the right border of each box to the right to adjust the size and position of the boxes so that you can see the full width of the field names (see Figure 2.15).

Notice that the Name of Vendor field is the primary key field in the Vendors table, but Vendor is not the primary key field in the PC Hardware table.

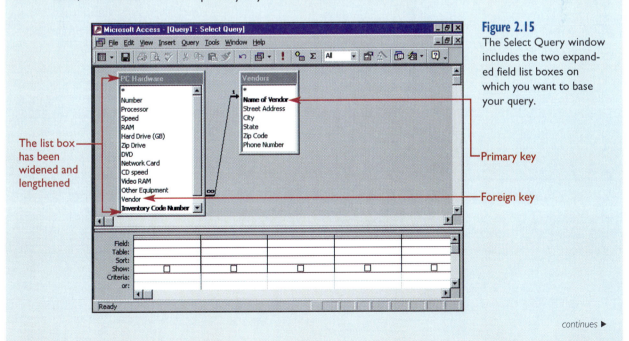

Figure 2.15
The Select Query window includes the two expanded field list boxes on which you want to base your query.

The list box has been widened and lengthened

Primary key

Foreign key

continues ▶

To Create a Query Based on Two Tables   (continued)

8 **Drag the Vendor field from the PC Hardware list to the first Field box in the query design area.**

Notice that the Table box in the query design indicates that this field comes from the PC Hardware table (see Figure 2.16).

Figure 2.16
The foreign key field, Vendor, is selected from the PC Hardware table.

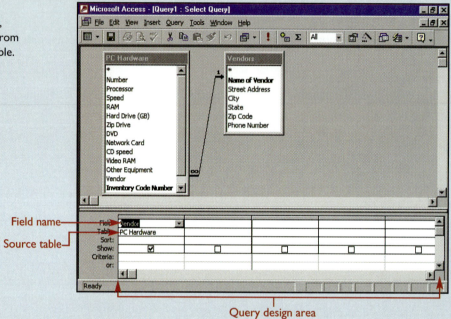

Field name
Source table

Query design area

The foreign key is used in this case to enable automatic updates. This feature is explained later in this project.

In the next several steps, additional fields are moved to the query design. These fields are being selected so that a maintenance contact list can be created with pertinent information needed to call for repair or maintenance.

9 **Drag the Phone Number field from the Vendors table to the second Field box of the query design.**

10 **Drag the Processor field and then the Inventory Code Number field from the PC Hardware list to the next two fields of the query design.**

11 **Use the horizontal scrollbar to reveal the next available column, if necessary, and then drag the Date of Purchase field from the PC Hardware table to the next available Field Box.**

You may have to scroll down in the PC Hardware list box to find the Date of Purchase field. The final query design should look like Figure 2.17.

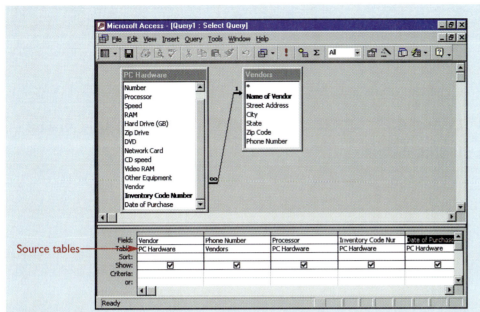

Figure 2.17
The completed query design includes five fields.

Source tables

⑫ Click the View button to switch to Datasheet view.

The query displays the *dynaset* of data from both tables (see Figure 2.18). A dynaset is a temporary table of data that is assembled from other tables, but is not permanently stored as a separate table.

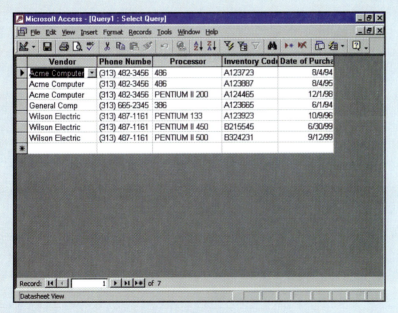

Figure 2.18
The query dynaset appears when you switch to Datasheet view.

⑬ Close the query, and then click Yes to save the changes.

⑭ When prompted for a Query Name, type Vendor Name and Phone Number for each PC, **and then click OK.**

Keep the database open for the next lesson.

Using Multiple Tables in a Query
You can use any number of tables as the basis for a query. The tables do not need to be related to be used in the query.

Lesson 4: Automatically Filling In Data from One of the Joined Tables

When you create a query that is based on joined tables, you need to be careful how you deal with the two fields that are used to join the tables. In the Vendors table, the Name of Vendor field is the primary key. The corresponding Vendor field in the PC Hardware table that is used to join the tables is the foreign key.

When you design a query that draws data from two or more tables, you can require it to fill in some of the fields automatically by using the foreign key of the linked fields rather than the primary key. In the following example, the Vendor field from the PC Hardware table will be used. This is the foreign key. Information relative to that vendor will be added to the query from the Vendors table. When new data is entered using this query, the fields that have been added from the Vendors table will be automatically filled in once the Vendor field (foreign key) has been entered. This saves time in entering repetitive data and helps ensure that the correct information is entered.

To Automatically Fill In Fields from Joined Tables

1 In the Computer Inventory 2 database, click the Queries object button, if necessary.

2 Click <u>N</u>ew to design a new query, select Design View, and then click OK.

3 Add both tables to the query design and close the Show Table dialog box.

4 Scroll down and drag the Vendor field from the PC Hardware list of fields to the first Field box in the query design area.
Notice that this field is at the "many" end of the join line, distinguished by the infinity symbol. It is the foreign key.

 Shortcuts for Adding Fields to the Query Design Window
Several timesaving shortcuts are available when you add fields in the query design window. You can double-click a field name to add it to the query design in the next available field box. You can also click the down arrow in a field box and select the field from the drop-down list. To select several fields at once, click the first name in the list and ⟨✦Shift⟩+click a name farther down the list to select those two fields plus all the field names between them. You can then drag the entire list over to the next available field box. Finally, you can click one field to select it, and then select one or more non-adjacent fields by holding down ⟨Ctrl⟩ and clicking the other fields you want to select.

5 **Add the Street Address, City, State, Zip Code, and Phone Number fields from the Vendors list to the next five Field boxes in the query design area.**

Your query design window should look like Figure 2.19.

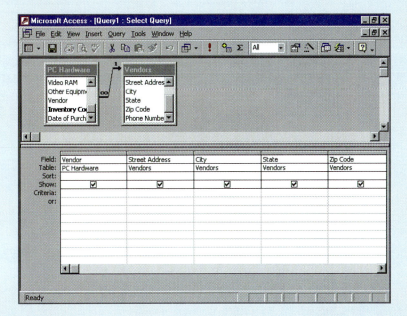

Figure 2.19
The query design window is shown after the vendor information has been added.

6 **Add the remaining fields from the PC Hardware list by selecting every field except the Vendor field, and then click and drag the group of fields to the next open field in the query.**

(i) **Selecting Multiple Fields**

You can click on the first field, scroll to the end of the field list, hold down ⬆Shift, and click on the last field name. Then hold down Ctrl and click the Vendor field to deselect it.

Access will spread out the fields, one to each of the next available query columns. Be sure you do not include the Vendor field a second time.

 7 **Click the View button to view the dynaset, and then go to the bottom of the list and click in the empty Vendor field.**

Notice that the Lookup list included in the table design also works in the query.

8 **Click the list button to reveal the list of vendors (see Figure 2.20).**

continues ▶

To Automatically Fill In Fields from Joined Tables   (continued)

Figure 2.20
The list of vendors from the Vendors table appears in the query.

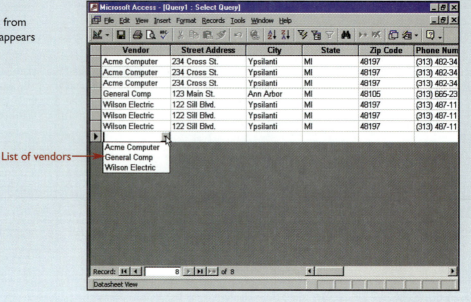

List of vendors

9 **Click Acme Computer to select it.**

Access automatically retrieves the data from the other fields in the Vendors table that have been included in the query (see Figure 2.21). At this point, you could scroll to the right and fill in information about a new computer purchase.

Figure 2.21
Data from the vendors table is automatically filled in.

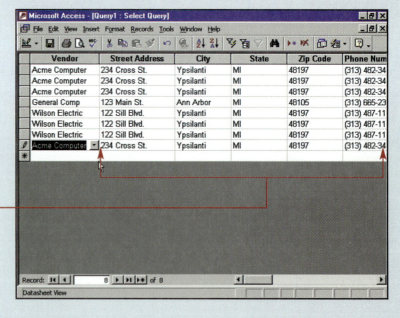

Data has been automatically filled in

10 **Do not enter a new record at this time. Press** Esc **to abort the input process.**

11 **Close the query, and click** **Y**es **to save the changes. When prompted for a Query** **N**ame, **type** Vendor and Hardware, **and then click OK.**

Keep the database open for the next lesson.

Lesson 5: Updating Tables by Entering or Deleting Data in the Query

Queries can be used to enter data into the tables on which they are based. This must be done with care. In some cases you will get error messages that are difficult to understand. In this lesson, you will learn some guidelines for successful data entry and how to interpret some of the error messages that you may receive.

To Enter New PC Hardware Data Using the Vendor and Hardware Query

1 **In the Computer Inventory 2 database, select the Vendor and Hardware query and click the Open button.**

2 **Go to the bottom of the list and click in the empty Vendor field.**

3 **Click the drop-down button and then select Acme Computer from the drop-down list.**

The remaining fields that are linked to the Vendor table are filled in automatically.

4 **Press Tab⇆ until you get to the Number field.**

Enter the following data in the remaining fields in this record. (Use the mouse to click the checkbox to indicate the presence of a zip drive, DVD, or network card.) You can also press the Spacebar to place the check mark in the box or Tab⇆ to skip over a box and leave it empty.

```
4

Pentium II

450

64

8.6

✓ for the Zip Drive

No ✓ for the DVD

✓ for the Network Card

24X

8

CD-RW Drive

B763423

9/25/99
```

5 **Close the query, click on the Tables object button, and click Open to look at the PC Hardware table in Datasheet view.**

Notice that the new PC has been entered in the table (see Figure 2.22).

continues ▶

To Enter New PC Hardware Data Using the Vendor and Hardware Query (continued)

Figure 2.22

The PC Hardware table includes the new record for the new PC.

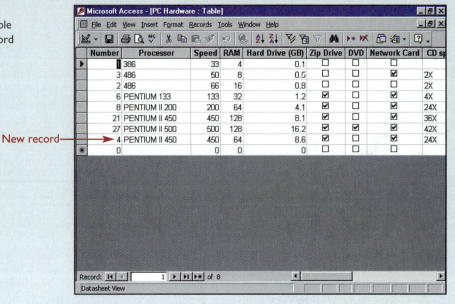

New record →

6 **Close the PC Hardware table, click the Queries object button, and open the Vendor and Hardware query in Datasheet view.**

7 **Click the record selector button to select the record for the computers that you just entered.**

You will have to scroll to the right to find the record you just added, because it is not the bottom record anymore (see Figure 2.23). It has been sorted on the foreign key field.

Figure 2.23

Because of automatic sorting, the record you just entered is no longer at the end of the table.

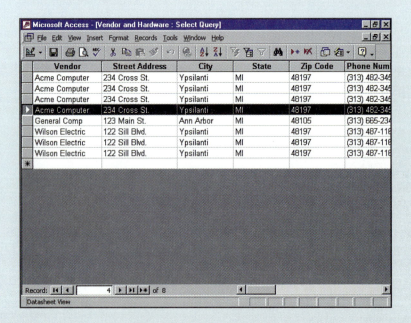

8 **Press Del to delete the record, and then click Yes to confirm that you want to delete the record.**

9 **Close the query.**

10 **Click the Tables object button and open the PC Hardware table in Datasheet view.**
Confirm that the record has been deleted from the table.

11 **Close the table and close the database.**

 Changing the Contents of the Foreign Key Field
You should not try to change the contents of the Vendor field from this query. The Vendor field in this query is the foreign key from the PC Hardware table, not the primary key field from the Vendors table. When you defined the join between these two tables, you specified that referential integrity should be enforced. This meant that there could not be a value in the Vendor field in the PC Hardware table that did not already exist in the Vendors table. Use the list box to select an existing vendor.

 Dealing with Multiple Primary Keys in a Query
This query also contains the primary key field from the PC Hardware table, Inventory Code Number. When you use this query to add new records to the PC Hardware table, you must enter a new inventory code number that is not the same as any other code number in the table. If you leave this field empty or enter a duplicate number, you get an error message.

Lesson 6: Finding Duplicate Records in an Existing Table

In some cases, you inherit a table of data from another source where the data entry was not carefully controlled. This table may contain duplicate entries that are difficult to find. Locating duplicates can also be useful when you append two data tables together and are uncertain if there is duplication of some records. Finally, it is useful to look for duplicates when you want to establish a field as the primary key field but are uncertain if there are duplicates in that field.

Fortunately, Access provides a special query that can be used to locate duplicate records. The **Find Duplicates Query Wizard** creates a query that lists the duplicate values in a single table or query.

Another type of error may occur when two related tables have records in one table without corresponding records in the second table. This occurs when referential integrity has not been enforced. The **Find Unmatched Query Wizard** can be used to locate these types of errors. Both of these special purpose queries work in a similar manner. In this lesson, you use the Find Duplicate Query Wizard to locate duplicate entries in a database of economic data. The database used in this lesson was compiled by the government and contains information about the number of service businesses in each ZIP code area in Michigan. Some duplicate records have been added for this exercise. The database does not have a primary key, but the natural choice is the ZIP code. When you try to set a primary key, you get an error message that says there is a duplicate value in the primary key, indexed field, or relationship.

You could scroll through the records looking for the duplicate, but there are more than 900 records and you do not know how many duplicates there are! This is an instance where you need the Find Duplicates Query Wizard.

To Find Duplicate Entries

1 **Find the AC2-0202 file on your CD-ROM, right-click on it, and send it to the floppy drive. Move to drive A and rename the file** `Service Businesses in Michigan-1987`.

2 **Right-click on the filename and select Properties from the shortcut menu. Select Archive and deselect Read-only from the Attributes section. Click OK and open the database.**

3 **Click the Queries object button, and then click New.**
The New Query dialog box is displayed (see Figure 2.24).

Figure 2.24
The New Query dialog box enables you to select the wizard you want to use.

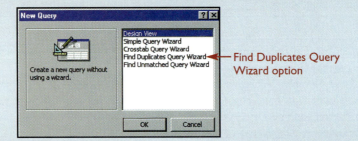
Find Duplicates Query Wizard option

4 **Select the Find Duplicates Query Wizard, and then click OK.**
The first Find Duplicates Query Wizard dialog box is displayed (see Figure 2.25).

Figure 2.25
The first Find Duplicates Query Wizard dialog box asks which table or query you want to search for duplicates.

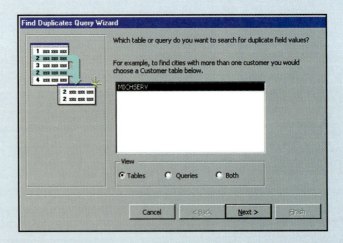

X The Find Duplicate Queries Wizard may not have been installed on your machine. If this is the case, the program will prompt you to add it. Follow the screen instructions to install this feature.

5 **Click the Next button to accept the default selection of the MICHSERV table.**
The second Find Duplicates Query Wizard dialog box is displayed (see Figure 2.26).

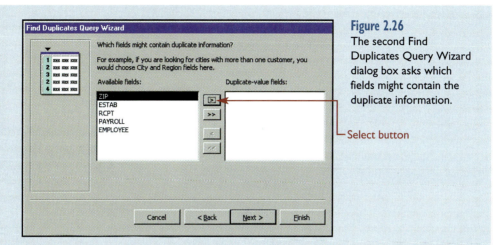

Figure 2.26
The second Find Duplicates Query Wizard dialog box asks which fields might contain the duplicate information.

Select button

6 **Click the ZIP field to select it.**

7 **Click the Select button to move the ZIP field into the Duplicate-value fields box, and then click Next to move to the next dialog box.**
The third Find Duplicates Query Wizard dialog box is displayed (see Figure 2.27).

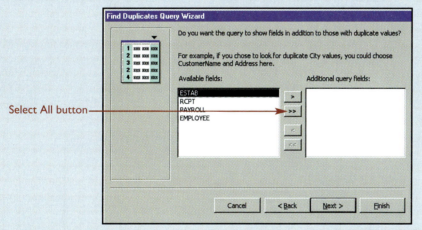

Select All button

Figure 2.27
Use the third Find Duplicates Query Wizard dialog box to specify other fields you want to use in the Find.

8 **Click the Select All button, which selects and moves all the remaining fields into the Additional query fields box.**
These additional fields help you determine how to deal with the duplicate records when you find them.

9 **Click the Finish button.**
This accepts the default name for the query and displays the final results of your query (see Figure 2.28). It shows each instance of a duplicate entry in the ZIP field, and also shows the contents of each of the other four fields.

continues ▶

To Find Duplicate Entries   (continued)

Figure 2.28
The Find duplicates for MICHSERV: Select Query found two sets of duplicate ZIP code entries.

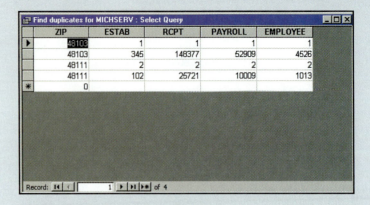

	ZIP	ESTAB	RCPT	PAYROLL	EMPLOYEE
▶	48103	1	1	1	1
	48103	345	148377	52909	4526
	48111	2	2	2	2
	48111	102	25721	10009	1013
✳	0				

Record: ◀◀ ◀   1   ▶ ▶◀ ▶✳ of 4

When you display the duplicate entries, you need to decide what to do with them. In this example, the two entries for each of the ZIP codes might need to be added together. Let's assume that you do a little research and find that the smaller duplicate entries are errors.

10 **Click the record selector to the left of the first record for ZIP code 48103 (the one that shows 1 in the ESTAB field) and press (Del).** Choose Yes when prompted.

11 **Delete the next erroneous record (the one that shows 2 in the ESTAB field) for ZIP code 48111.**

12 **Close the query.**
Access creates a query called Find duplicates for MICHSERV (see Figure 2.29).

Figure 2.29
Access created the query and automatically named it Find duplicates for MICHSERV.

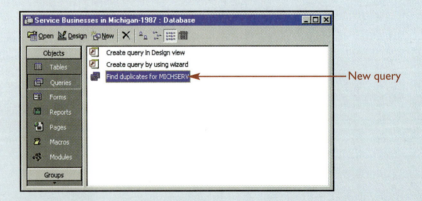

New query

The MICHSERV table can now use the ZIP field as a primary key. (Do not perform that operation at this time.)

13 **Close the database and close Access, unless you want to continue working on the following exercises.**
If you have completed your session on the computer, exit Access and shut down Windows before you turn off the computer. Otherwise, continue with the exercises.

Filenames of Older Databases

This table was created by the federal government using a database program called dBASE III. Programs that use older operating systems that predate Windows 95 (not including Macintosh computers) were restricted to filenames of eight characters or less. Notice how much more descriptive your filename of Service Businesses in Michigan-1987 is compared to MICHSERV.

Summary

In this project you were introduced to some fairly sophisticated methods of managing data. You learned how to join two tables using a one-to-many relationship, and to create queries that draw data from more than one table. You filled in data from several fields in a table by entering just the foreign key field, and you updated the information in tables by entering or deleting data in a query. Finally, you learned how to find and eliminate duplicate records in a table.

You can learn more about managing data by looking through the help on the topics mentioned above. You might especially want to look at the different types of relationships and when each might be useful. You might also want to explore the pros and cons of using cascading updates and deletes.

Checking Concepts and Terms

True/False

For each of the following statements, check *T* or *F* to indicate whether the statement is true or false.

__T __F **1.** It is best to put as many fields as possible in the same table to keep the organization of the database as simple as possible. [L1]

__T __F **2.** If there is one record for Sally Jones in a table of employee records and her name occurs several times in a table of sales commissions, those two tables could be linked in a one-to-many relationship. [L2]

__T __F **3.** When you create a query that automatically fills in fields from table A, you drag the primary key from table A into the query design. [L4]

__T __F **4.** The contents of tables cannot be changed by entering new data into queries. [L5]

__T __F **5.** A special wizard exists to help you find unmatched records between two tables. [L6]

__T __F **6.** To create a query based on two tables, both tables must have a field with the same name and data type. [L2]

__T __F **7.** If you choose a wizard and it doesn't work, you may have to install it from the Microsoft Office CD. [L6]

__T __F **8.** When you create a Find Duplicate query, you need to include enough fields to enable you to decide what to do with the duplicate records. [L6]

__T __F **9.** The Find Duplicates query could be useful if you wanted to use the selected field as a primary key field. [L6]

__T __F **10.** To base a form on more than one table, you can first create a query that is based on those tables and then base your form on the query. [L3]

Multiple Choice

Circle the letter of the correct answer for each of the following questions.

1. One-to-many means _____. [L2]
   a. one field can have many different entries
   b. one record can relate to many records in a different table
   c. one table can have many records
   d. one database can have many tables

2. In a one-to-many relationship, _____. [L2]
   a. the field in the many table is the foreign key
   b. the field in the one table is the foreign key
   c. the field in the many table is the primary key
   d. neither field is indexed

3. To create a query that automatically fills in data from one of the joined tables, _____. [L4]
   a. use the primary key and the other fields from the same table
   b. use the foreign key from the second table and the other fields from the table that has the primary key
   c. select a one-to-one join
   d. select Automatic Fill from the Tools menu

4. The best way to find records that have the same entry in a given field is to _____. [L6]
   a. use the Find Unmatched Query Wizard
   b. use the Find Duplicates Query Wizard
   c. scroll down the list and visually inspect the contents of the fields
   d. sort the table using the Sort button on the toolbar. If there are duplicates, a message appears asking if you want to delete them.

5. If you have created a query that uses a foreign key and fills in fields automatically, _____. [L4]
   a. you should not try to enter a completely new value in the foreign key field
   b. you can change any field in either table
   c. you can only change values in the table that contains the primary key of the two joined fields
   d. you can look at the contents of the table, but you can't make changes

6. When you choose to enforce referential integrity in a relationship, it means _____. [L2]
   a. you cannot enter a record in the many table that does not have a corresponding entry in the one table
   b. you cannot delete a record in the one table that has an entry in the many table
   c. your data is protected from having orphan records
   d. all of the above

7. To create a query on your own, use the query _____. [L3]
   a. Design Wizard
   b. Datasheet vew
   c. Design view
   d. template

8. To change the size of the field list box, point to the edge of the box and drag the edge of the box when the mouse pointer turns into a(n) _____. [L3]
   a. pointing finger
   b. open hand
   c. double-headed black arrow
   d. single-headed vertical arrow

9. To include a field in a query, _____. [L4]
   a. click on the field and drag it to an open field box
   b. double-click on the field name
   c. click on the down arrow in the field box and select the field
   d. all of the above

10. To create a join between tables, click the relationship button, select the tables, and then _____. [L2]
    a. drag the primary key field from one table to the matching field in the second table and click the Create button in the second relationship window
    b. click the Join button to join the two tables, and then specify the fields that are to be joined
    c. make sure the field names and data types are the same
    d. click the Join button, match the fields, select enforce referential integrity, and save your changes

Screen ID

Label each element of the Access screen shown in Figure 2.30.

Figure 2.30

A. Relationship line

B. Primary key field

C. Foreign key

D. View button

E. Table source

F. Field list

G. One symbol

H. Selected field

I. Close button

J. Many symbol

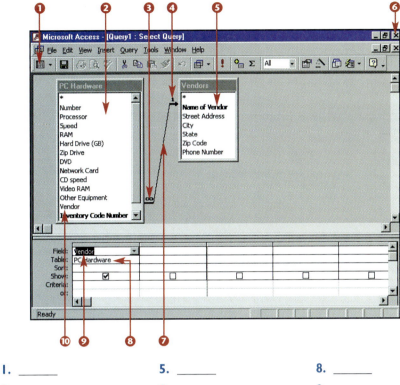

1. _____	5. _____	8. _____
2. _____	6. _____	9. _____
3. _____	7. _____	10. _____
4. _____		

Discussion Questions

1. When you first design your tables, you need to minimize the entry of repetitive information. If you were designing a database to keep detailed information about your CD collection (including information on artists, the company that put out the CDs, the songs on each CD, and whatever other information you might desire) what fields might you use? How many tables would you need to create to keep repetitive data entry to a minimum?

2. What are the advantages of creating queries that draw information from more than one table? From your basic knowledge of Access reports, are there advantages to basing reports on queries rather than on tables?

3. In this project you worked on relationships that were defined as one-to-many. Can you think of a situation where you might use a one-to-one relationship? How about a many-to-many relationship?

4. In Lesson 6, "Finding Duplicate Records in an Existing Table," you created a Find Duplicates query using the Query Wizard. When would you need to save the query once it has done its work? What situations would make saving the query irrelevant?

5. The Find Duplicates Query Wizard finds duplicate entries in a field. Its companion is the Find Unmatched Query Wizard, which identifies fields in one table that do not have corresponding fields in a second table. Why might that be useful?

Skill Drill

Skill Drill exercises reinforce project skills. Each skill reinforced is the same, or nearly the same, as a skill presented in the project. Each exercise includes a brief narrative introduction, followed by detailed instructions in a step-by-step format.

The database you will use in the Skill Drill exercises contains information about your book collection and the people to whom you have loaned books.

1. Enforcing Referential Integrity in Your Library Database

In this exercise, you have a database that has a table of information about the books in your library and another table that tracks the books others have borrowed from you. Every book that has been borrowed should be listed in the table of books in the library.

When this database was created, referential integrity between the two tables was not enforced, so it is possible that a book was loaned out before it was recorded in the master list of books.

To enforce the referential integrity of an existing relationship, complete the following steps:

1. Find the AC2-0203 file on your CD-ROM, right-click on it, and send it to the floppy drive. Move to drive A, right-click on the filename, and change the Attribute from Read-only to Archive. Right-click on the filename again, select Rename, rename the file **Home Library** and open it.

2. Click the Relationships button on the toolbar.

3. Double-click the line that joins the tables to display the Edit Relationships dialog box. Notice that the

Enforce Referential Integrity check box was not selected when this relationship was established. There may be unmatched records in the Borrowed table.

4. Select the Enforce Referential Integrity check box and click OK. An Error message appears. There are unmatched records in the Borrowed table.

5. Click OK to acknowledge the message.

6. Close the Relationships window. You work with this problem in the next section.

2. Finding an Unmatched Record

In Lesson 6, you learned how to use a query design wizard to find duplicate records. In this case, you can use a similar wizard to find unmatched records.

To find an unmatched record, complete the following steps:

1. Open the Home Library database, if necessary.

2. Click the Queries object button and click New to start a new query.

3. Use the Find Unmatched Query Wizard to find the borrowed book that is not listed in the Books table.

4. Select Borrow as the table containing the records you want in the query results.

5. Select Books as the table containing the related records.

6. Accept Book Title as the related field in both tables.

7. Click the Select All button to see all the fields in the query, and then accept the default name.

8. When you have identified the book, enter a new record in the Books table for this book. The author

is **Robert Heinlein**, and the name of the book, as you found out in the previous step, is **Notebooks of Lazarus Long**. It is a **Science Fiction** book that was originally published in **1973**. (The type of book is not limited to those in the attached lookup list. You may enter a new type, such as Science Fiction.)

9. Close the Books table, and then go back to the previous exercise and follow those steps to enforce referential integrity. This procedure should work now that there are no unmatched records. The relationship line should now show a one-to-many relationship. (Make sure that the title is an exact match in both tables. It is the joined field.)

10. Leave the database open for use in the next exercise.

3. Viewing Related Information Using a Subdatasheet

The Books table and the Borrow table are related in a one-to-many relationship using the Book Title field. You can now go into the Books table and see whether any of the books have been loaned to friends.

To view related information using a subdatasheet, complete the following steps:

1. Open the Home Library database, if necessary.

2. Click the <u>O</u>pen button to open the Books table.

3. Click on the expand indicator to the left of the Robert Heinlein book you just added to the field. The subdatasheet displays the name and phone number of the borrower and the date the book was borrowed.

4. Click the expand indicator to close the subdatasheet.

5. Click the expand indicator to the left of the next record (the book by William Coughlin). The subdatasheet is empty, indicating that the book is not on loan.

6. Click the minus sign to close the subdatasheet.

7. Close the table, but leave the database open for use in the next exercise.

4. Creating a Query Based on Two Tables

In the Home Library database you can create a query to automatically fill in data from one table while you are entering data into another table.

To create a query based on two tables, complete the following steps:

1. Open the Home Library database, if necessary.

2. Click the Queries object button.

3. Click <u>N</u>ew to start a new query and choose Design View.

4. Add both tables to the query design and close the Show Table dialog box. Notice the relationship between the two tables is displayed as one-to-many.

5. Select the Book Title field from the Borrow table (not the Books table) as the first field in the query design.

6. Select the Author Last Name and Type of Book fields from the Books table.

7. Select the rest of the fields from the Borrow table.

8. Switch to Datasheet view. Click the New Record button on the navigation bar and enter the name of one of the books shown. When you press ⏎Enter, the information in the next two fields appears automatically.

9. Make up a name, phone number, and date and enter them in the following fields.

10. Close the query and name it `Books on Loan`.

11. Click the Tables object button, and then open the Borrow table. The new record should be in the table.

12. Close the table and the database.

5. Enforcing Referential Integrity for the Sound Byte Music Company

A database for a small music retail business keeps a table of music orders and a table of suppliers. Each order table has an entry for the supplier that should match an entry in the supplier table. In this exercise, you will discover some of the problems involved in enforcing referential integrity. You will discover that some of these problems could have been avoided by careful initial planning!

To check for unmatched records in the Orders and Suppliers tables, complete the following steps:

1. Find the AC2-0204 file on your CD-ROM, right-click on it, and send it to the floppy drive. Move to drive A, right-click on the filename, and change the Attribute from <u>R</u>ead-only to Ar<u>c</u>hive. Right-click on the filename again, select Rena<u>m</u>e, rename the file `Sound Byte Music`, and open the database.

2. Click the Relationships button to determine which fields are linked between the Orders and Suppliers tables.

3. Double-click the link between the two tables. The Edit Relationships dialog box opens. Notice that the Relationship type is listed as Indeterminate. In order to enforce referential integrity, you will need to create a one-to-many relationship between these fields. One way to do this is to make the Record Company field in the Suppliers table a key field (if you are sure there will be no duplicate entries).

4. Click Cancel to close the Edit Relationships dialog box, and then close the Relationships window.

5. Open the Suppliers table in Design view, make sure the Record Company field is selected, and then click the Primary Key button. (You can also select Edit, Primary Key from the menu.)

6. Close the table Design view window and save your changes when prompted.

7. Click the Relationships button, and then double-click the relationships line. The Edit Relationships dialog box opens again and indicates that the type of relationship is now a one-to-many.

8. Click the Enforce Referential Integrity check box, and then click OK. An error message appears that informs you that there are unmatched records. Click OK, and then close the Relationships window.

9. Click the Queries object button, and then click New to create a new query.

10. Use the Find Unmatched Query Wizard to look for unmatched records in the Orders table that do not have a matching record in the Suppliers table.

11. Compare the name of the supplier in the unmatched order to the Record company name in the Suppliers table to determine why there is no match. Notice that a mismatch was caused by entering the name of the company incorrectly. The names must match exactly (which is one reason to use a lookup list for this type of field). Open the Orders table and correct that mistake.

12. Click the Relationships button and double-click the relationships line to open the Edit Relationships dialog box.

13. Select Enforce Referential Integrity, and then click OK. The relationship should display a one at the Supplier Name end of the line and an infinity symbol at the Record Company end. This indicates a successful one-to-many relationship with enforced referential integrity.

14. Close the Relationships window, but leave the database open for use in the next exercise.

6. Creating a Query Based on Two Tables in the Sound Byte Music Company

The Orders and Suppliers tables in your Sound Byte Music database contain related information. You want to set up a query that draws information from both tables.

To create a query based on two tables, complete the following steps:

1. Open the Sound Byte Music database, if necessary.

2. Click the Queries object button.

3. Click New to start a new query and choose Design View.

4. Add the Orders and Suppliers tables to the query design and close the Show Table dialog box. Notice the relationship between the two tables is displayed as one-to-many.

5. Select the Supplier Name field (foreign key) from the Suppliers table as the first field in the query design.

6. Select the Contact Name and Phone fields from the Suppliers table.

7. Select the rest of the fields from the Orders table. Make sure you don't insert the Suppliers Name field twice.

8. Switch to Datasheet view. Click the New Record button on the navigation bar and enter the name of one of the suppliers shown. When you press ↵Enter, the information in the next two fields appears automatically.

9. Make up values for the remaining fields.

10. Close the query and name it **Orders and Supplier Contact**.

11. Open the Orders table. The new record should be in the table.

12. Close the table and the database.

Challenge

Challenge exercises expand on or are somewhat related to skills presented in the lessons. Each exercise provides a brief narrative introduction followed by instructions in a numbered step format that are not as detailed as those in the Skill Drill section.

1. Adding a Table, Relating to the Table, and Creating a Query Based on Both Tables

The chess club databases you used in Project 1 had a single table design. If you want to track several donations or several months of dues payments, the database needs a second table. Copy the AC2-0205 file to your floppy disk, change the Read Only status to archive, rename the file **New Chess Club**, and open the database.

1. Open the Member Information table in Design view. The Member ID # field is the primary key field. Remember what the data type is for this field. Close the table.

2. Create a new **Member Dues** table to track how much was paid and when. Include a **Member ID #** field, a **Dues** field, and a **Date Paid** field. Make sure the Member ID # field in this table is the same data type as in the other table.

3. Create a one-to-many relationship between the two tables using the Member ID # field in each.

4. Create a query that uses the Member ID # field from the Member Dues table (foreign key), the first and last name fields from the Member Information table, and the other fields from the Member Dues table. Save this query as **Names and Dues**. Keep the database open for the next exercise.

2. Changing a Data Type Using the Lookup Wizard

So far, you haven't entered any information in the Member Dues table, and if you look at the Names and Donations query or the Member Dues query, you will have no way to know what Member ID #s you have to work with. In this exercise, you will change the data type of the Member ID # field in the Member Dues table to Lookup Wizard.

1. Open the Member Dues table in Design view. Select Lookup Wizard from the Data Type drop-down list for the Member ID # field.

2. Choose to look up the information from another table, and then select the Member Information table.

3. Choose the Member ID # field from the field list and accept the defaults for the last two wizard dialog boxes.

4. Try out the lookup box in Datasheet view of the Member Dues table. Close the table and open the Names and Dues query.

5. Select 9223434 from the Member ID # drop-down list. Notice that the last and first names are filled in. Type **25** in the Dues field and today's date in the Date Paid field.

6. Close the query and close the database.

3. Establishing Referential Integrity Among Tables

The database used in this exercise contains information about research on the television viewing habits of 20 households. The study focused on six news and education cable channels. This database has four tables and three relationships. The relationships were created without enforcing referential integrity so that there could be orphan records. Copy the AC2-0206 file to your floppy disk, change the read-only status to archive, rename the file **Customer Research**, and open the database.

1. Open the Customer Research database. View the relationships. Notice that each of the relationships is between the key field of one table and a non-key field of another table. All three of these relationships should be one-to-many.

2. Double-click on each of the relationship lines and attempt to enforce referential integrity. This is easy to do in two of the three.

3. When you identify which relationship has a problem with unmatched records, close the Relationships window and run an unmatched records query to find the problem. (Warning: It makes a difference which table you pick first when looking for unmatched records. If your first try doesn't find the problem, run the query again but reverse the order of the two tables.)

4. Do not try to fix the problem until you've identified exactly what the problem is. (Hint: Look closely at the data in each of the unmatched records queries you ran, and then look at the list of participants. The problem is a typographical error that will become apparent as you look at the queries and tables.)

5. You can attempt to fix the problem in either of the related tables, but one of them is an AutoNumber field that can't be changed. Fix the problem, and then go back and attempt to enforce referential integrity again. Notice how much easier this would have been if referential integrity had been enforced from the beginning.

4. Enforcing Referential Integrity and Creating One-to-Many Relationships Among Tables

The database used in this exercise contains information about the locations, suppliers, repair, and types of vending machines. The tables in this database were created without concern for data integrity. In this exercise, you establish key fields where appropriate and create one-to-many relationships with referential integrity. Copy the AC2-0207 file to your floppy disk, change the read-only status to archive, rename the file **Vending Machines**, and open the database.

1. Open the Vending Machines database and open the Relationships window. Notice that only one of these tables, Locations, has a primary key. The name of the supplier should be a unique field in the Suppliers table and the Machine Type field should be the key field in the Machines table.

2. Right-click the Name field in the Suppliers table and select Table Design from the shortcut menu. (This is faster than closing the Relationship and opening the table.) Make the Name field the primary key field, close the Design view, and save your changes.

3. Use the same procedure to make the Machine Type field the primary key in the Machines table.

4. Double-click the relationship line between the Locations and the Machines table. Try to enforce referential integrity. It will not work. Close the Edit Relationships box and delete the relationship line.

5. Create a new relationship line between the two Machine Type fields, and then enforce referential integrity.

6. Remove and replace the other relationships lines and enforce referential integrity. Do these one at a time so you don't forget which fields were related!

7. Create a query that uses fields from the Locations and Machines tables. Name the query `Machines and Sites`.

8. Look at your new query, and then close the query and the database.

5. Revising Tables and Relationships in a Database

In this exercise, you remove three redundant fields from one of the tables, enforce referential integrity, and create a query based on three tables.

1. Locate the AC2-0208 database, copy it to your disk drive, turn off read-only status, and rename it `Video Store`. Open the Video Store database and click the Relationships button to view the relationships between the tables. Maximize the window and expand the field lists so you can see all the fields.

2. Double-click one of the relationship lines to open the Relationships window. Click the check box to enforce referential integrity. Repeat this process for the other relationship. Close the Relationship window.

3. Study the fields in each of the three tables. The Video Tapes table has three fields that actually describe the rental activity; therefore, they are redundant. Open the Video Tapes table and delete the Currently Rented, Current Renter, and Number of Rentals fields.

4. Create a query that uses fields from all three tables. It should at least include the customer's first and last name and phone number, the title of the video rented, and the date rented, date returned, and late fee. Do not include any of the fields that are used to provide links between the tables.

5. Switch to the Datasheet view to test your query. Save the query as `Three Tables`.

Discovery Zone

Discovery Zone exercises help you gain advanced knowledge of project topics and application of skills. These exercises focus on enhancing your problem-solving skills. Numbered steps are not provided, but you are given hints, reminders, screen shots, or references to help you reach your goal for each exercise.

The database you will be using in this Discovery Zone deals with short stories from the turn-of-the century (19th to 20th, not 20th to 21st). These are short stories from books of stories by different authors, not books of stories by a single author. There are three tables in the database—one with information about the authors, one with information about the short stories, and one with information about the books.

1. Improving an Existing Database

Copy the file AC2-0209 from your CD-ROM, place it on your floppy drive, and rename it `Short Story Collection`. Change it to an Archive file and deselect the Read-only attribute.

The three tables in the Short Story Collection database have not had the primary key fields identified, and they are not related; therefore, orphan records and inconsistent data entry may have occurred and will likely continue to occur unless something is done.

Goal: Identify primary key fields, create relationships, and enforce referential integrity, where possible. (Note: Because of the nature of the fields, some relationships can never have referential integrity enforced.) In this database you should

- Use the Book Title field as the key field in the Book information table.
- Use the Author field as the key field in the Author information table.
- Create a relationship between the Book Title field in the Book information table and the Source field in the Short stories table. You should attempt to enforce referential integrity between the tables.
- Create a relationship between the Author field in the Author information table and the Author field in the Short stories table. You should attempt to enforce referential integrity between the tables.

Hint #1: You will need to use a query to check for duplicates before you can identify one of the primary key fields.

Hint #2: You will discover one relationship that can never have referential integrity enforced. See if you can figure out which one won't work, and why, before you try to set it up.

2. Adding Information Using Subdatasheets

Subdatasheets are particularly useful when you want to add information to related tables with small numbers of fields. The one-to-many relationship will become much clearer by the time you have finished this exercise, which uses the Short Story Collection database you created in the previous exercise.

Goal: Update records in one table from inside another table using the subdatasheet.

Use the help menu to learn about using subdatasheets. While you are looking through the available help, notice the relationship required between the two fields for this procedure to work. In the Book information table

- Find the book of Great English Short Stories edited by Christopher Isherwood.
- Using the subdatasheet, add the following stories:

  ```
  Lawrence, D. H.   "Blind Man, The" 1922  27  England, My England
  Kipling, Rudyard "Mary Postgate"  1915  22  Diversity of Creatures, A
  ```
- Check to make sure the two stories you added in the Book information table have been added to the Short stories table.

Project 3

Project 3

Adding Useful Features to Your Forms

Objectives

In this project, you learn how to

➤ **Add Formats in the Form Design View**

➤ **Select Entries from a List**

➤ **Look Up Valid Entries from a Table or Query**

➤ **Use Information from a Query to Fill In Fields Automatically**

➤ **Enter the Current Date in a Field Automatically**

➤ **Add the Current Date and Time to a Form Automatically**

➤ **Change the Tab Order**

➤ **Create Subforms**

➤ **Print the Form for Filing Purposes**

Key terms introduced in this project include

■ list box   ■ tab order

■ subform

Why Would I Do This?

Consistent data input is one of the primary reasons for using a form. This is particularly true when several people are entering information into the same tables. In Project 1, you looked at ways of creating consistent data input structures, and you learned how to change the look of the data when it is displayed in the datasheet. You can also customize the fields in a similar manner in a form.

You also know how to use a default value to avoid unnecessary typing if a field often contains the same data. A default value solves this problem if there is one piece of information that is used in a field the majority of the time. But what if there are five or six items, such as city names, that all occur frequently? The Lookup Wizard helped you build a list that appeared in a drop-down list in Table view. Forms have a similar feature that offers additional options.

Another way to avoid extra typing is to set up a form based on more than one table. You can set up the form to look up information from a table and automatically fill in several fields when you enter the information for only one field.

Frequently, you will be required to enter the current date (and even time) in a record. There are ways of automating that procedure so that the user does not have to enter anything.

When you enter data, the cursor jumps from one text box to the next when you press [Tab⁴]. This is called the *tab order*. If you move the fields around in the form, the tab order may no longer make sense. You learn how to change this sequence to match the layout of the form.

Another useful form is the main form/subform. This design places a form within a form and is very useful for displaying a one-to-many relationship between tables. In the main part of the form you see the one side of the relationship, and in the *subform* you see the many related records from the second table. This type of design could be used to display the entire inventory that was purchased from each vendor, or all the employees who work in each department in a company.

In this project, you learn how to improve data entry speed and accuracy by adding lists and combo boxes. You also add dates that are needed in two different situations. You create a main form/subform and use it to enter new records. Finally, you learn how to print the Form view of a single record. You will use modified versions of two of the databases you used in the first two projects throughout this project.

Visual Summary

When you have completed this project, you will have created a document that looks like this:

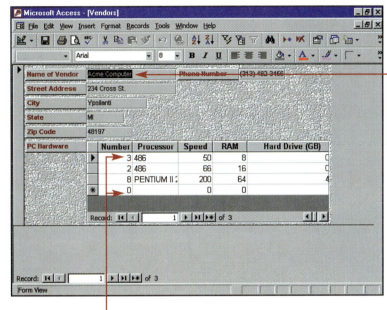

Figure 3.1
A subform displays the related records in the "many" table to the selected record in the main form.

Primary key field in main form

Subform records related to the selected record in the main form

Lesson 1: Adding Formats in the Form Design View

The database used in this exercise is similar to the one you worked on in Project 1, "Making Data Entry Easier and More Accurate." An extra table and a query have been added for the lessons in this project, and a basic form has been created. A new text field, called City, has also been added.

To Open the Data Entry Form

1 **Find the AC2-0301 file on your CD-ROM, right-click on it, and send it to the floppy drive. Move to drive A, right-click on the filename, and select P**_r_**operties from the shortcut menu. Select Ar**_c_**hive and deselect R**_ead_**-only from the Attributes section.**
This is an expanded version of the Software Training Database you used in Project 1.

2 **Right-click on the filename and select Rena**_m_**e from the shortcut menu. Rename the file** Software Training**. Click OK, and then open the database.**

3 **Click the Forms object button, if necessary.**
Only one form should appear—the PC Training Data Entry Form—and it should be highlighted (see Figure 3.2).

continues ▶

To Open the Data Entry Form (continued)

Figure 3.2
One form is listed in the Forms area of the Software Training database.

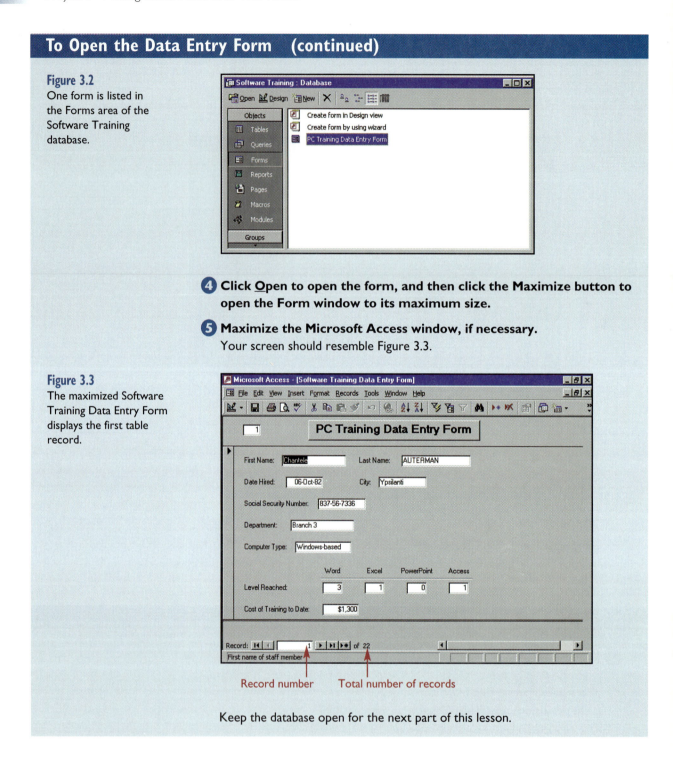

4 **Click Open to open the form, and then click the Maximize button to open the Form window to its maximum size.**

5 **Maximize the Microsoft Access window, if necessary.**
Your screen should resemble Figure 3.3.

Figure 3.3
The maximized Software Training Data Entry Form displays the first table record.

Record number   Total number of records

Keep the database open for the next part of this lesson.

When you create a form, any input masks, data format expressions, validation rules, and required field properties are brought to the form from the underlying table or tables. You can add properties to any field, although you cannot add or change the Required property option in the property boxes.

In the following procedure, you use two formatting techniques to change the look of your data. You make the Department name all capital letters, much the same as you did with the Last Name field in Project 1. You then use a standard formatting button to right-align the Social Security Number field.

To Use Buttons and Properties to Control the Appearance of the Data

1 With the PC Training Data Entry form open, click the View button to switch to Design view.

> The field list box or the toolbox may cover the fields on the screen. If the field list box is open, click the Close button in the list box to close it. If the toolbox is in the way, click in the toolbox title bar and drag it to the right side of the screen.

2 Click the Department text box to select it.

Handles appear around the text box, and a single large handle should appear in the upper-left corner of the label box. Make sure you have selected the Department text box and not the label box, which is the field name on the left of the text box.

3 Click the Properties button on the Form Design toolbar.

The property sheet is divided into five sections. Take a moment to look at each of them by clicking on the five tabs.

Another way to activate the property sheet is to right-click on the field text box and choose Properties from the shortcut menu.

4 Click the Format tab.

Once the Format tab is chosen, the property sheet for the Department field appears as in Figure 3.4.

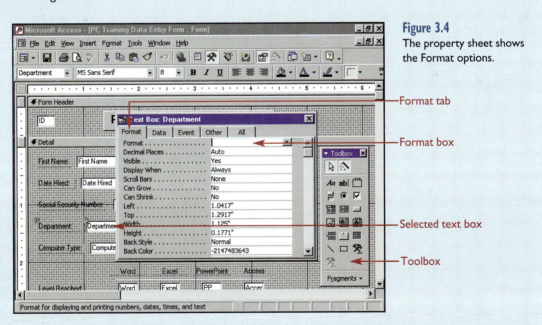

Figure 3.4
The property sheet shows the Format options.

— Format tab
— Format box
— Selected text box
— Toolbox

5 Type the greater than symbol (>) in the Format box.

This is the same procedure you used in the Table view in Project 1.

6 Click the Text Box Close button to close this property sheet.

continues ▶

To Use Buttons and Properties to Control the Appearance of the Data (continued)

7 Click the View button to return to Form view.

The Department name should now be capitalized, along with the Last Name field, which you formatted in Project 1.

You can also control the alignment of the text within the box.

8 Click the View button to move back to Design view.

9 Click the Social Security Number text box to select it.

10 Click the Align Right button on the Formatting toolbar.

You have now aligned the Social Security number to the right, the way users expect numbers to be displayed. The reason that this number was aligned left was that it was originally set up as a text field to take advantage of input masking.

You can use any of the Formatting buttons on either the text box or its label. This means that you can display the data using boldface or italic, and you can even change the color of the text.

11 Click the View button to return to Form view.

Notice that the Social Security Number field is right-aligned (see Figure 3.5).

Figure 3.5
The PC Training Data Entry Form shows the changes made to the form.

The Social Security Number field is right-aligned

The Department field is now capitalized

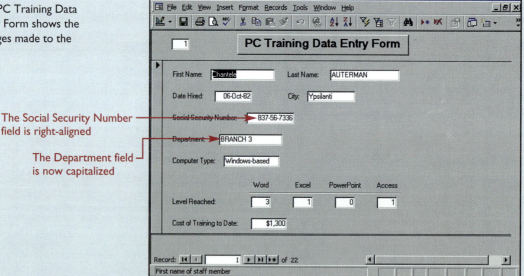

12 Click the Close Window button to close the form. Save your changes when prompted.

13 Click the Tables object button, and then open the Software Training table.

Notice that the Department field is not uppercase, and the Social Security Number is still left-aligned (see Figure 3.6).

Field formatting in forms has not
changed formatting in tables

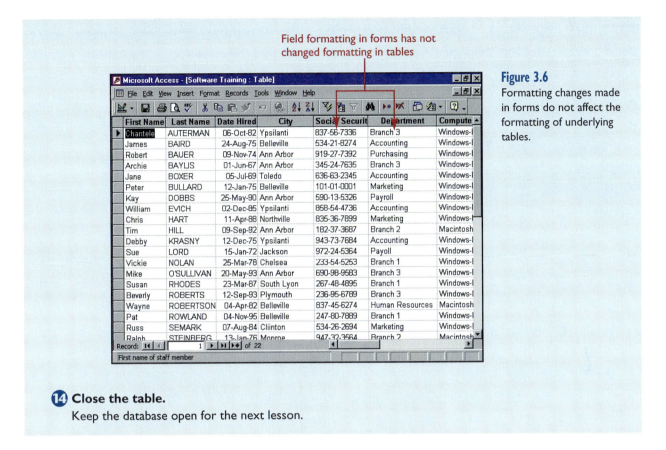

Figure 3.6
Formatting changes made
in forms do not affect the
formatting of underlying
tables.

 Close the table.

Keep the database open for the next lesson.

Formatting Changes in Forms Don't Affect Table Fields

It is very important to remember that formatting changes you make go one way
but not the other. The changes you make in a field's properties in the Form view
do not affect the formatting of the data in the underlying table. If you want to
create formats that appear universally throughout the database, make those
changes in the table Design view.

Lesson 2: Selecting Entries from a List

Sometimes, when the number of possible values that will go in a field is small, you can put
the entire list of values on the screen. This way the user can simply click the correct value
for that record. The **list box** is easy to set up and easy to use. The user does not have
the option of adding a value that is not on the list, which helps to ensure that correct data
is entered.

The Software Training table contains a field called Computer Type. There are only two
values for this field: Windows-based and Macintosh. In this lesson, you create a short list
for this field.

To Create a List Box

1 **Click the Forms object button, select the PC Training Data Entry Form, and click the Design button. Maximize the form, if necessary.**
The form opens in Design view.

2 **Right-click on the Computer Type text box, and then move the pointer to Change To in the shortcut menu.**
Make sure you click on the Computer Type text box and not the label box. The Change To submenu appears to the right of the shortcut menu (see Figure 3.7).

Figure 3.7
Use the shortcut Change To menu to change the field type to a list box.

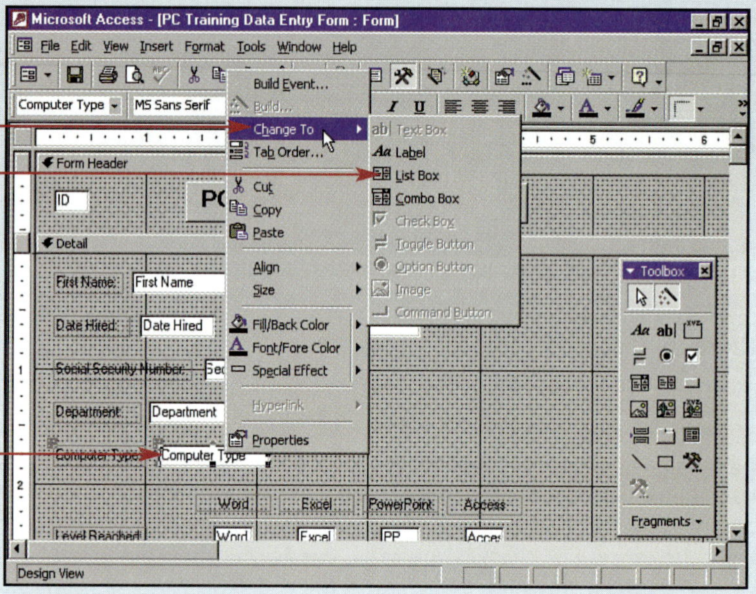

Change To option in the shortcut menu

List Box option

Selected field text box

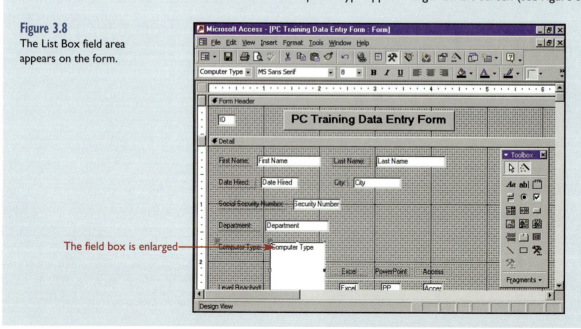

3 **Click the List Box option.**
The text box for Computer Type appears larger on the screen (see Figure 3.8).

Figure 3.8
The List Box field area appears on the form.

The field box is enlarged

4 **Click the right mouse button on the new text box, and then select Properties from the shortcut menu.**

The List Box property sheet appears on the screen.

5 **Click the Data tab.**

6 **Click the Row Source Type option, and then click the drop-down arrow.**

The Row Source Type drop-down menu is displayed (see Figure 3.9).

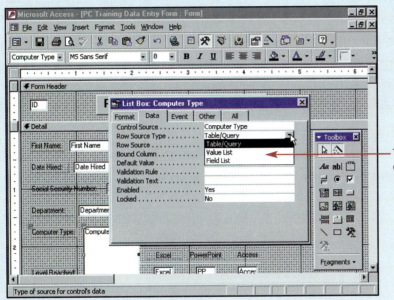

Figure 3.9
The Row Source Type drop-down menu gives you three options.

The Row Source Type drop-down menu

7 **Click Value List from the Row Source Type drop-down menu.**

This tells the program to look for the data for the list in the Row Source box, just below the Row Source Type box. You type the values into the Row Source box. All values must be separated by semicolons.

The table/query option could be used with a list box, but for very short lists, this method is easier.

8 **In the Row Source box, type the following:**

`Windows-based;Macintosh`

The Data tab in the List Box property sheet should look like Figure 3.10.

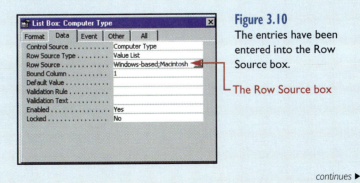

Figure 3.10
The entries have been entered into the Row Source box.

The Row Source box

continues ▶

To Create a List Box (continued)

9 Close the List Box property sheet.

 Editing the Entries in a List Box
At times you will make a spelling error or want to add another word to the list box. You can edit the list box in the Design view by clicking on the text box field with the right mouse button and choosing <u>P</u>roperties.

10 Use one of the handles on the bottom of the Computer Type text box to decrease the height of the box to the height of about two lines of text.
You may have to use the vertical scrollbar to move down to the bottom of the text box (see Figure 3.11).

Figure 3.11
You can resize the Computer Type text box.

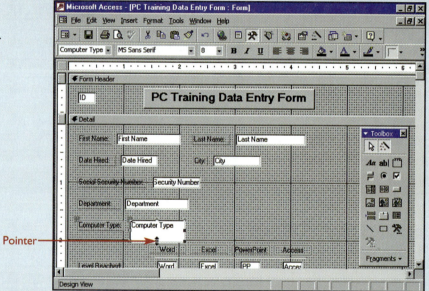

Pointer ———→

11 Click the View button to move to the Form view.

12 Scroll through your records using the Next Record button.
Notice that when you come to a record that contains "Macintosh" for the Computer Type field, the word is highlighted in the list. Try adding a record to see how this would work if you were entering data.

Keep the database open for the next lesson.

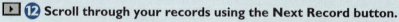

 A Quick Way to Enter List Selections
You can type the first letter of a selection in a list. The first word in the list beginning with that letter will be highlighted. When there is only one word beginning with that letter, as there is in this case, you can use this method to select the entry for the field. This is one of the advantages of a list box. A list box remains visible on your screen at all times and is generally best used when the list is short. For further information on how to set up a list box, use F1 or the Office Assistant for help.

Lesson 3: Looking Up Valid Entries from a Table or Query

When the number of possible values that will go in a field is small, you can put the entire list of values in a list box, as you did in Lesson 2. If there are many possible entries, you will want to use a combo box that can look up values in an existing field or query. With a combo box you also have the option to prevent or allow the user to enter items that are not in the list. You created a combo box in Lesson 1 by using the Lookup Wizard data type, but you have more control over it if you create the combo box manually.

In this lesson, you create a combo box for the City field, and then have the program look up the city names in the City and County Names Query. The query was created so that the records are sorted on the City field. By doing this, the list in the combo box is alphabetized.

To Look Up Valid Entries from a Table or Query Using a Combo Box

1 In the **PC Training Data Entry Form, click the View button on the toolbar to switch to Design view.**

2 **Position the pointer on the City text box, and then click the right mouse button.**
The shortcut menu is displayed.

3 **From the <u>C</u>hange To option in the shortcut menu, choose <u>C</u>ombo Box.**
The text box should now have a drop-down arrow on the right edge.

4 **Right-click on the City text box, choose <u>P</u>roperties, and click the Data tab, if necessary.**
The Data properties for the City field are displayed. The default for the Row Source Type should be Table/Query. If it is not, activate the drop-down box for the Row Source Type and change it.

5 **Click the Row Source option, and then click the drop-down arrow.**
The Row Source drop-down list displays all the tables and queries associated with this database (see Figure 3.12). Notice that there are two buttons available on the right side of the Row Source list—a Build button and a drop-down arrow. Make sure you choose the drop-down arrow.

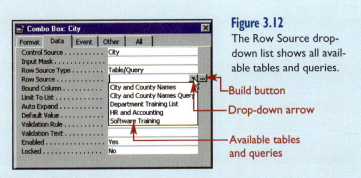

Figure 3.12
The Row Source drop-down list shows all available tables and queries.

Build button
Drop-down arrow
Available tables and queries

6 **Choose City and County Names Query from the list.**

continues ▶

To Look Up Valid Entries from a Table or Query Using a Combo Box (continued)

 Other Data Options in the Properties Box

You have several other options available in the properties box. You can add input masks for text and date fields, set default values, and validate data. You also have the ability to restrict the user to only those items on the list by changing the Limit to List box from No to Yes.

7 **Close the Combo Box property sheet, and then click the View button on the toolbar to switch to Form view.**

Notice that the City field now has a drop-down list attached to it.

8 **Click the drop-down box of the City field.**

A list is displayed (see Figure 3.13). Notice that there is a vertical scrollbar on the list, indicating that there are more items than are shown on the screen. Scroll down to look at the rest of the items.

Figure 3.13

The combo box for the City field displays a list of cities.

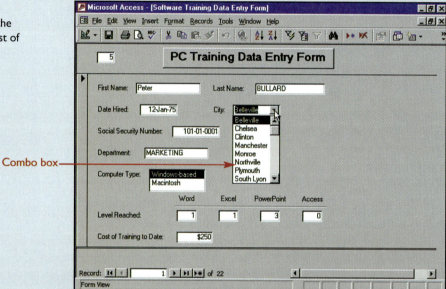

Combo box

9 **Add a new record to try out your new combo box, but press Esc to back out of the data entry when you get to the last field.**

10 **Close the form, save your changes when prompted, and then close the Software Training database.**

 A Quick Way to Enter Combo Box Selections

In a list box, you can type the first letter of a selection in a list. The first word in the list beginning with that letter is highlighted. Using a combo box, however, you can then type the second letter of the word, and you can get the value you are looking for by typing enough letters to make your desired value unique.

Lesson 4: Using Information from a Query to Fill In Fields Automatically

In Project 2, "Managing Data Using Smaller, Related Tables," you worked on a database containing two tables: PC Hardware and Vendors. To save a lot of work entering all the vendor information each time you entered a new record into the query, you used the foreign key field to automatically update the other fields in the Vendors table.

Because most data is entered in Form view, it is helpful to automatically fill in repetitive data in the same manner you did using queries. In this lesson, you create a form based on the query you built in Project 2.

To Create a Form That Fills In Data Automatically

1 **Find the AC2-0302 file on your CD-ROM, right-click on it, and send it to the floppy drive. Move to drive A, right-click on the filename, and select Properties from the shortcut menu. Select Archive and deselect Read-only from the Attributes section.**

2 **Right-click on the filename and select Rename from the shortcut menu. Rename the file** Computer Inventory 3. **Click OK, open the database, and click the Forms object button.**
The New Form dialog box is displayed.

3 **Click New, select Form Wizard, and then choose Vendor and Hardware as the query or table to be used as a source for the form.**
The New Form dialog box should look like Figure 3.14.

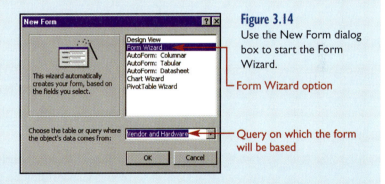

Figure 3.14
Use the New Form dialog box to start the Form Wizard.

Form Wizard option

Query on which the form will be based

4 **Click OK.**
The first Form Wizard dialog box is displayed. It may take several seconds for the Form Wizard dialog box to appear as the program builds the Wizard. You may also experience similar delays between other wizard screens.

5 **Click the Select All button to move all the fields from the Available Fields window to the Selected Fields window.**
The fields should all move to the right window (see Figure 3.15).

continues ▶

To Create a Form That Fills in Data Automatically   (continued)

Figure 3.15
In the first Form Wizard dialog box, select the fields you want to include on your form.

Select All button →

All the fields have been selected

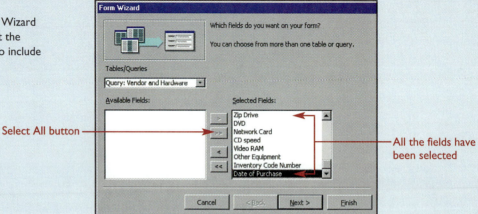

6 **Click Next.**
The second Form Wizard dialog box is displayed (see Figure 3.16). This dialog box gives you the option of four layouts for your form. Click each of them. A preview of the formats appears in a window on the left side of the dialog box.

Figure 3.16
Choose a form layout in the second Form Wizard dialog box.

Form layout preview area

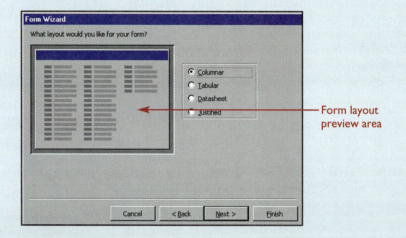

7 **Choose Columnar format, and then click Next.**
The third Form Wizard dialog box is displayed (see Figure 3.17). This dialog box gives you the various style options. Click a few of them to see what styles are available.

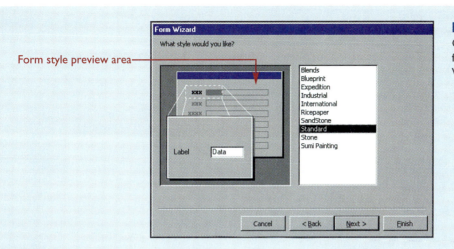

Figure 3.17
Choose a style for your form in the third Form Wizard dialog box.

Form style preview area

8 **Choose Blends, and then click Next.**

The fourth (and final) Form Wizard dialog box is displayed (see Figure 3.18). A default name of Vendor and Hardware has been entered in the title box. At this point you have the choice of moving to Form view, or going to Design view to modify the form design. Accept the default name and the default option to open Form view.

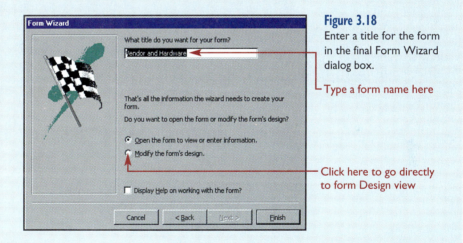

Figure 3.18
Enter a title for the form in the final Form Wizard dialog box.

Type a form name here

Click here to go directly to form Design view

9 **Click Finish.**

The Vendor and Hardware form is created (see Figure 3.19).

continues ▶

To Create a Form That Fills in Data Automatically   (continued)

Figure 3.19
The form has been auto-
matically created by the
Form Wizard.

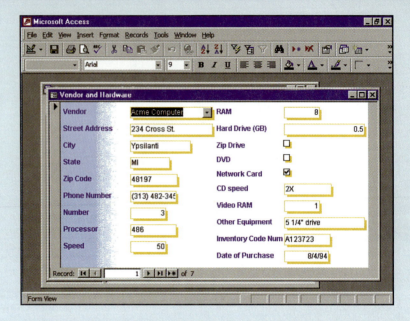

10 Click the **New Record** button and select **General Comp** from the drop-down list in the **Vendor** field.

Notice that the other fields from the Vendors table are entered automatically. The default values for the RAM and Hard Drive Size fields are also entered.

11 Press Esc to back out of the data entry, and then close the database.

Lesson 5: Entering the Current Date in a Field Automatically

There are many occasions where a database calls for the current date. This is particularly true in the business world, where orders are dated as they are received and when they are sent out.

In the PC Training Data Entry Form of the Software Training database, where Date Hired is the only date field, let's assume that the vast majority of the personnel files are started on the day the employee is officially hired. On those occasions when the data is not entered on the date of hiring, the user has the option of typing a new date.

In this lesson, you change the default for the Date Hired field to the current date.

To Enter the Current Date in a Field Automatically

1 Open the **Software Training** database and click the **Forms** object button, if necessary.

This is the database you used in Lessons 1-3 of this project.

2 Select the **PC Training Data Entry Form**, click the **Design** button, and maximize the window, if necessary.

3 **Right-click on the Date Hired text box and choose Properties from the shortcut menu.**

4 **Click the Data tab, if necessary, and then click in the Default Value property box.**

A Build button is displayed on the right side of the box (see Figure 3.20).

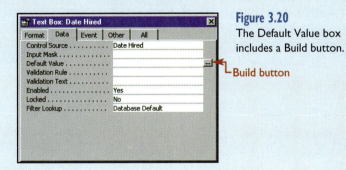

Figure 3.20
The Default Value box includes a Build button.

└─ Build button

5 **Click the Build button.**

An Expression Builder dialog box is displayed.

6 **Select Common Expressions from the left column.**

A list of common expressions appears in the middle column (see Figure 3.21).

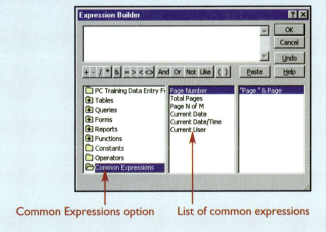

Figure 3.21
The Expression Builder is shown with Common Expressions selected.

Common Expressions option   List of common expressions

7 **Double-click the Current Date option.**

Notice that the expression Date() appears in the third column and in the Expression Builder window (see Figure 3.22).

continues ▶

To Enter the Current Date in a Field Automatically   (continued)

Figure 3.22
The Expression Builder is
shown with the Date()
expression selected.

Code for current date

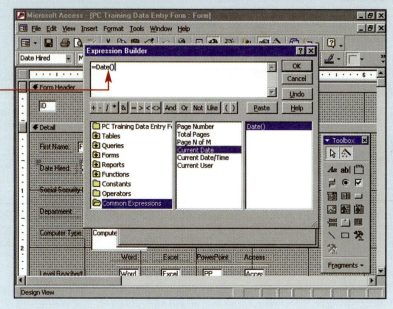

Other Uses for the Expression Builder Code
When you become more familiar with Access, you can save yourself time by typing
the code directly into the properties box without going to the Expression Builder.
You can type the code in the Expression Builder window directly into the Default
Value property box.

8 Click OK, and then close the property sheet.

9 Click the View button on the toolbar to switch to Form view.

10 Click the New Record button and enter a new record.
Notice that the current date is automatically posted in the Date Hired field.

Keep the database open for the next lesson.

Lesson 6: Adding the Current Date and Time to a Form Automatically

There are times when you want to print out an individual form. It is possible to type a
date or time on the form using the Label tool, but Access gives you a way to add this information automatically. This information, sometimes called a date stamp or a time stamp,
is usually placed in the form's Header or Footer area.

In this lesson, you add a date to the Header area of the PC Training Data Entry Form, and
then use the same procedure to add the time.

To Add the Current Date and Time to a Form Automatically

1 In the PC Training Data Entry Form, click the View button to
switch to Design view.

2 **From the Insert menu, select Date and Time.**

The Date and Time dialog box is displayed (see Figure 3.23). You see your current date and time in the dialog box.

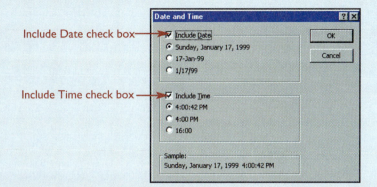

Include Date check box ──→

Include Time check box ──→

Figure 3.23
Use the Date and Time dialog box to add a date or time to a form.

3 **Click the check box next to Include Time to deselect this option.**

The Include Time area should now be grayed out.

4 **Click the top option button, if necessary, in the Include Date area.**

5 **Click OK.**

The date expression is automatically placed in the upper-left corner of the Form Design work area.

6 **Drag the date to the upper-right corner of the work area.**

Your date expression should be in the Form Header area.

7 **Drag the middle handle on the left side of the date box to reduce the length of the date control box to about 1 1/4".**

The Form work area should now resemble Figure 3.24.

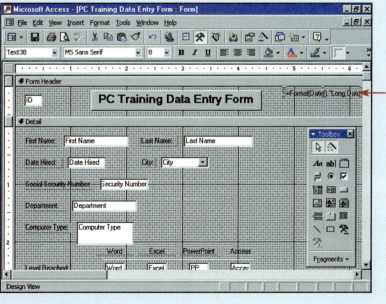

Figure 3.24
The Form window is shown with a date added to the Form Header.

←── The Date text box

continues ▶

To Add the Current Date and Time to a Form Automatically   (continued)

🔲 **8** **With the date expression still selected, use the Align Right button to align the date to the right.**

9 **Follow steps 2-8 to add a right-aligned time stamp just below the date stamp.**

You may have to move the toolbox to place the time control properly. Use the middle format (2:17 PM). Make sure you deselect Include Date.

🔲 **10** **Click the View button on the toolbar to switch to Form view.**

Notice that the date and time are to the right of the title (see Figure 3.25). If necessary, move back to Design view and adjust the location of the date and time.

Figure 3.25
The form displays the final location of the date and time.

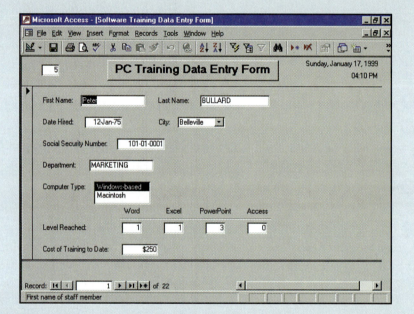

🔲 **11** **Click the Save button on the toolbar to save your work.**

Keep the database open for the next lesson.

Lesson 7: Changing the Tab Order

When you enter data into the text boxes in a form, the cursor jumps from one text box to the next in a certain sequence. This sequence is called the tab order. In the case of an AutoForm, the tab order is initially determined by the order of fields in the underlying table or query. If you use the Form Wizard to create a form, the original order in which the fields are selected determines the tab order. When you move fields around in Design view, the tab order needs to be adjusted so that the cursor moves from field to field in the order in which fields are arranged. Fortunately, it is easy to change the tab order to read left-to-right, or in columns, depending on how the information flows in your form.

In this lesson, you learn how to change the tab order.

To Change the Tab Order

1 **In Form view of the PC Training Data Entry Form, click on the First Name text box.**

2 **Press** `Tab⇆` **repeatedly and watch how the cursor jumps from one text box to another.**

Notice that the cursor skips the City text box and does not return to it until after going to the Cost of Training to Date box.

3 **Click the View button to switch to Design view.**

4 **From the Y̲iew menu, select Ta̲b Order. Click the D̲etail option button, if necessary.**

The Tab Order dialog box is displayed, with the form fields displayed in the Custom Order list box (see Figure 3.26).

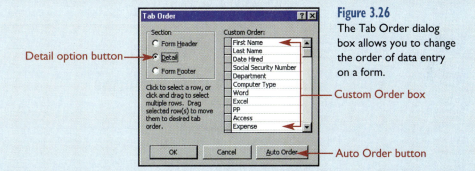

Detail option button

Custom Order box

Auto Order button

Figure 3.26
The Tab Order dialog box allows you to change the order of data entry on a form.

5 **Scroll to the bottom of the list of field names to show the City field.**

The order of the field names in this dialog box represents the order in which they are selected when you tab through the form.

6 **Click the A̲uto Order button.**

This changes the tab order automatically so that the text boxes are selected from left to right and top to bottom, the way you would normally read a page of text.

Notice that the City field has been moved up in the list to follow Date Hired (see Figure 3.27).

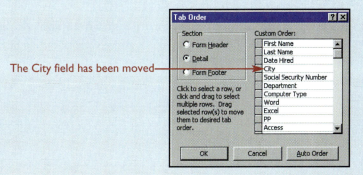

The City field has been moved

Figure 3.27
The tab order is shown after it has been automatically rearranged.

continues ▶

To Change the Tab Order (continued)

⑦ **Click OK to save the change and close the Tab Order dialog box.**

 ⑧ **Click the View button to switch to Form view.**

⑨ **Press** Tab⇄ **repeatedly and observe how the cursor now jumps from the Date Hired text box to the City text box.**

⑩ **Save the changes to the form, close the form, and close the database.**

⚠ **Manually Rearranging the Tab Order**
You can rearrange the fields to appear in any order you desire. With the Detail option button selected on the Tab Order dialog box, select a field by clicking on the select box to the left of the field name. Click on the same area, hold the mouse button down, and drag the field up or down to a new location.

Lesson 8: Creating Subforms

At times you might want a form that shows the one-to-many relationship between two tables. The main form/subform design is useful for displaying the one side of a relationship in the main part of a form and the related records in a subform. The subform is usually displayed in a datasheet layout. Although these are technically two forms, they can be created together using the Form Wizard.

With this design, you can display such things as all the employees who work in each department, the furniture and equipment that is assigned to each department, or the clients assigned to each sales representative.

In this lesson, you create a main form/subform that shows all the computers that were purchased from each vendor in the Computer Inventory 3 database you worked on earlier in this project. To create a form/subform design, a relationship must be established between the two tables. This was done in Project 2.

To Create a Subform

① **Open the Computer Inventory 3 database and click the Forms object button, if necessary. Click the New button to create a new form.**
The New Form dialog box is displayed.

② **Select the Vendors table from the drop-down list, select the Form Wizard, and then click OK.**
The first Form Wizard dialog box is displayed (see Figure 3.28).

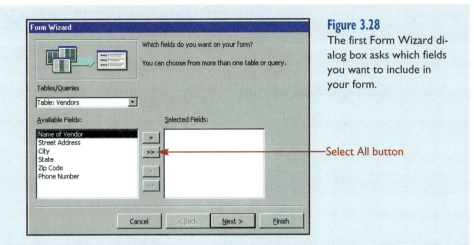

Figure 3.28
The first Form Wizard dialog box asks which fields you want to include in your form.

3 **Click the Select All button to move all the fields to the Selected Fields box.**

All the fields from the Vendor table are included in the main part of the form.

4 **Click the down arrow at the end of the Tables/Queries drop-down list box and select Table: PC Hardware.**

Once you click on the new table name, the fields for that table are displayed in the Available Fields box (see Figure 3.29).

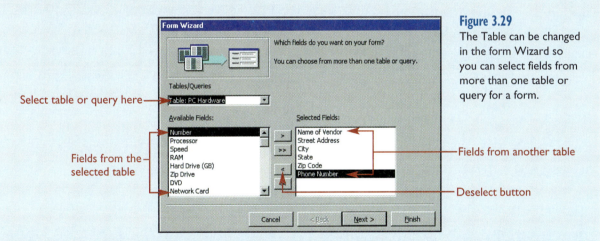

Figure 3.29
The Table can be changed in the form Wizard so you can select fields from more than one table or query for a form.

5 **Move all the fields to the Selected Fields box except the Vendor field.**

The selected fields from the PC Hardware table area are added to the fields already included in the subform (see Figure 3.30).

A Quick Way to Enter List Selections
You can use the Select All button to move all the fields to the Selected Fields box, and then highlight the Name of Vendor field from the PC Hardware table and use the Deselect button to move this field back to the Available Fields box. When there are two fields with the same field name, they are displayed in the Selected Fields box preceded by the name of the table. In this case, the Name of Vendor field from the PC Hardware table is listed as: PC Hardware.Name of Vendor.

continues ▶

To Create a Subform (continued)

Figure 3.30
The fields for the subform are selected from a second table.

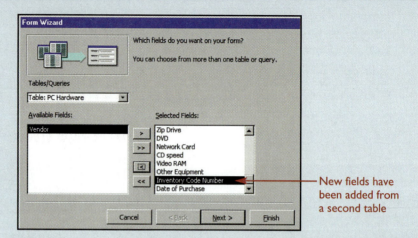

New fields have been added from a second table

6 **Click Next. The second dialog box asks how you want to view your data.**
Because you included the primary key field from the "one" (Vendors) table, the Vendors fields are displayed at the top of the preview area. Notice the option button for Form with subform(s) is also selected by default (see Figure 3.31). Accept the default settings.

Figure 3.31
The main form shows the vendor information and the subform shows the related records.

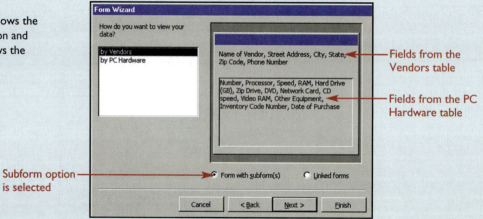

Fields from the Vendors table

Fields from the PC Hardware table

Subform option is selected

7 **Click Next.**
The next wizard dialog box asks which layout you want for the subform. Accept the default setting of Datasheet.

8 **Click Next to accept the default setting of Datasheet. Choose the Stone style and then click Next.**
The final wizard dialog box is displayed.

9 **Default titles are suggested for the two parts of this form. Accept the suggested titles by clicking the Finish button, and then maximize the form window.**
The form is created and displayed on your screen (see Figure 3.32). Notice that the form has two sets of navigation buttons. The navigation buttons at the bottom of the form scroll through the vendors. As the vendor changes, the related records in the datasheet (subform area) change. The navigation buttons in the subform scroll through the PC records that are displayed for each vendor.

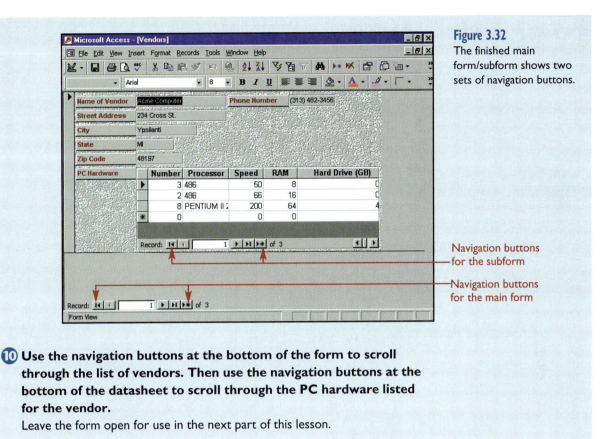

Figure 3.32
The finished main form/subform shows two sets of navigation buttons.

Navigation buttons for the subform

Navigation buttons for the main form

🔟 **Use the navigation buttons at the bottom of the form to scroll through the list of vendors. Then use the navigation buttons at the bottom of the datasheet to scroll through the PC hardware listed for the vendor.**
Leave the form open for use in the next part of this lesson.

 An Alternative Way to Edit New Records
A main form/subform can also be used to edit or add new records to your two tables. You want to make sure that if you use this type of form for adding records, all the fields for each of the tables are included. Otherwise, you will end up with records with missing information. For this to work properly, the primary key from the "one" side of the relationship must be included.

Next, you add a record to the main form and to the subform.

To Add Records Using a Main Form/Subform

⬛1 **With the Vendors form open, click on the New Record button in the main form navigation buttons (in the status bar) to move to an empty record.**

2 **Enter the following vendor information:**
Computer Tyme, 1233 Second Street, Macon, MI 48134, (517) 555-2233
You have added a new vendor to the list of available vendors. Now add a record of hardware purchased from Computer Tyme.

continues ▶

To Add Records Using a Main Form/Subform (continued)

3 Press [Tab↹] to move to the first field for the hardware information
and enter the following information.

```
1, Pentium II, 500, 128, 19.2, Yes, Yes, Yes, 48X, 32, CD-RW,
C112233, 1/10/00
```

A record for the PC Hardware table has been added (see Figure 3.33).

Figure 3.33
New records can be
added using the main
form and the subform.

A new record has been
added to the main form

A new record has been
added to the subform

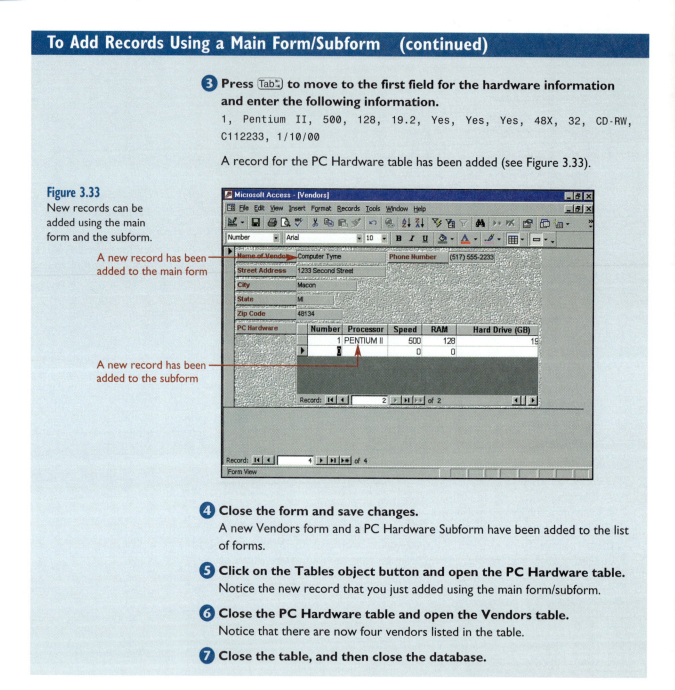

4 **Close the form and save changes.**
A new Vendors form and a PC Hardware Subform have been added to the list
of forms.

5 **Click on the Tables object button and open the PC Hardware table.**
Notice the new record that you just added using the main form/subform.

6 **Close the PC Hardware table and open the Vendors table.**
Notice that there are now four vendors listed in the table.

7 **Close the table, and then close the database.**

Lesson 9: Printing the Form for Filing Purposes

You might want to print the form for an individual record for filing purposes, as a rough
draft to check on a particular piece of data, or as a check on the layout when the form is
longer than the screen. Although most of the printing in Access is done in reports, some
is also done in forms.

In this lesson, you print the information for one of the records in the Software Training database. You then change the background color to try to make the printout more readable.

To Print the Form

1 Open the Software Training database, and then open the PC Training Data Entry Form. Maximize the window, if necessary.

2 From the File menu, choose Page Setup.

The Page Setup dialog box is displayed, with the Margins tab selected (see Figure 3.34).

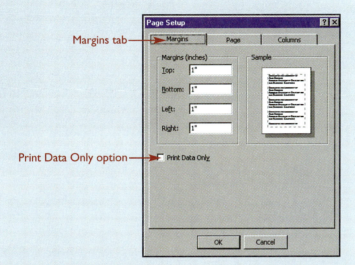

Margins tab

Print Data Only option

Figure 3.34
The Page Setup dialog box appears with the Margins tab selected.

3 Change the left and right margins to .75".

To do this, highlight the old margin settings and type the new margins over them.

4 If the Print Data Only checkbox is checked, deselect it, and then choose OK.

The Print Data Only selection might be used if you are printing a lot of records and have a slow printer, or if you only want to archive the data.

5 Click the Print Preview button.

The preview screen shows that the printout is continuous; two complete records are shown, along with most of a third (see Figure 3.35). You can use the pointer, which has changed into a magnifying glass, to zoom in or out on the preview page.

continues ▶

To Print the Form (continued)

Figure 3.35
The Print Preview screen shows nearly three complete records.

Close button

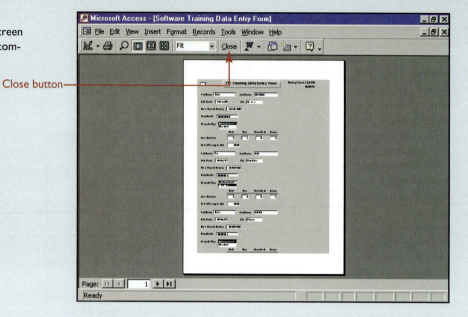

6 **Click the Close button on the toolbar to close the Print Preview window.**
Before you send this form to the printer, there are a few more steps you need to perform.

7 **Click the View button on the toolbar to switch to Design view.**

8 **Click the right mouse button on the background of the Detail area.**
Make sure you do not accidentally click on a text or label box by mistake.

9 **Move the pointer to Fill/Back Color in the shortcut menu.**
A color palette appears (see Figure 3.36).

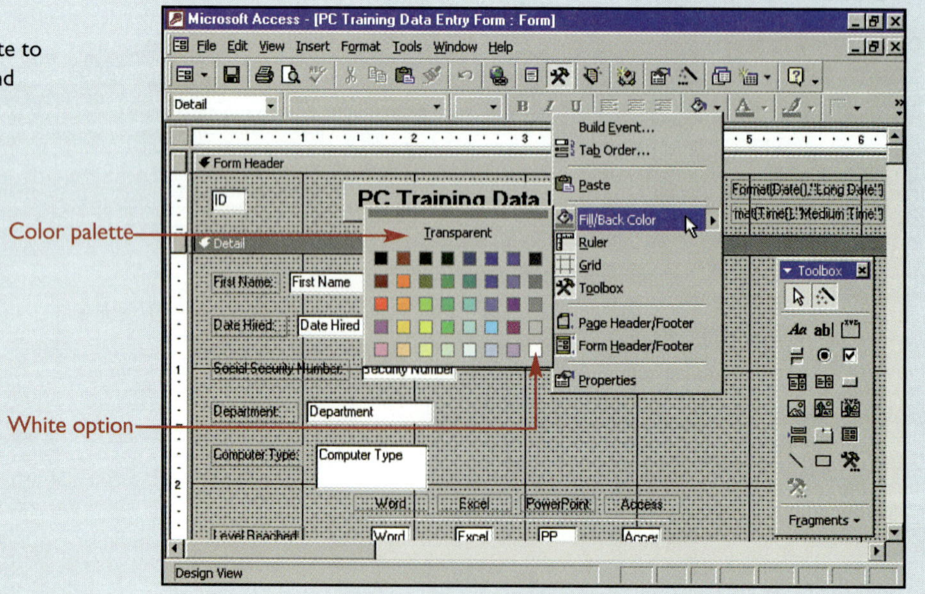

Figure 3.36
Use the color palette to choose a background color.

Color palette

White option

10 **Select white, which is located at the lower-right corner of the color palette.**
The background color of the Detail section turns white, but the Header and Footer sections remain dark gray.

11 **Repeat steps 8-10 for the Header section, and then scroll down and do the same for the Footer section.**
All three backgrounds are now white. When you print the form, the printer will use less ink.

You are almost ready to print the form, but you need to make sure you only print one form per page.

12 **Click the Toolbox button to open the toolbox, if necessary. Scroll down so that you can see the Cost of Training to Date field, and then click the Page Break button in the toolbox.**

13 **Move the cursor just below the Cost of Training to Date field in the Detail area and click the left mouse button. Click in an open area to deselect the page break.**
A page break, which is displayed as a series of six dots, is now inserted in that area (see Figure 3.37). If you want to see what your printout will look like, use the Print Preview as you did in step 5.

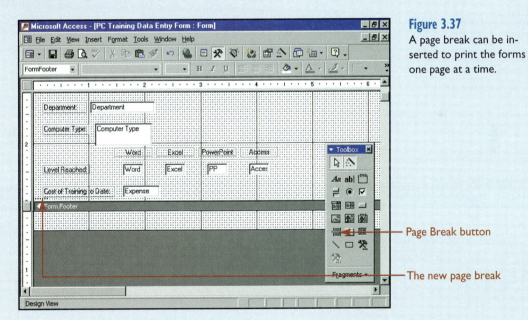

Figure 3.37
A page break can be inserted to print the forms one page at a time.

— Page Break button

— The new page break

14 **Click the View button on the toolbar to switch to Form view, and then go to the File menu and choose Print.**

15 **Click the Selected Record(s) option button in the Print Range area (see Figure 3.38).**

continues ▶

To Print the Form   (continued)

Figure 3.38
The Print dialog box
shows that a selected
record has been chosen
to print.

Selected Record(s) option ——▶

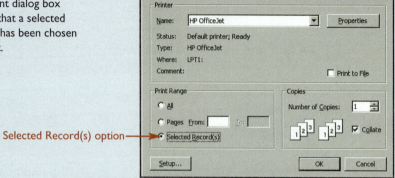

16 **Click OK to print the current record.**
This particular form does not have a lot of information on it, but you can see where the ability to print forms could be very helpful.

 Depending on the type of printer you have, the Computer Type field may be completely hidden by the highlight, making it appear that the selected value was Macintosh, when it was, in fact, Windows-based. This is one of the drawbacks of using a list box in a form.

17 **Close the PC Training Data Entry Form and save your changes when prompted. Close the database.**
If you have completed your session on the computer, exit Access and shut down Windows before you turn off the computer. Otherwise, continue with the following exercises.

Summary

In this project, you were introduced to many new techniques for improving forms. You learned some procedures that were analogous to procedures that work in tables, such as adding formats, lists, and combo boxes to forms, and filling fields automatically. You created a form/subform that is similar to the datasheet/subdatasheet concept in a table. You added the current date and time to a form header, and changed the order in which data is entered. Finally, you learned how to print a single form.

You can learn more about forms by going to the help index and typing `form`. A particularly useful topic is Sections of a form, which describes the uses of the form detail, header, and footer area, and also describes form page headers and page footers.

Checking Concepts and Terms

True/False

For each of the following statements, check *T* or *F* to indicate whether the statement is true or false.

__T __F **1.** When you create a form, any input masks you created in the underlying table appear on the form. [L1]

__T __F **2.** The formatting changes you make in Form view will also appear in the underlying Table view. [L1]

__T __F **3.** In a list box, you can type the acceptable values in the Row Source box of the List Box property sheet. [L2]

__T __F **4.** A date or time stamp is usually placed in the form Detail section. [L6]

__T __F **5.** To make a field required in a form, you must specify it as a required field in the underlying table. [L1]

__T __F **6.** To include fields from more than one table in a form, the tables must be related. [L8]

__T __F **7.** You can set up a form to look up information from a table and automatically fill in several fields when you enter the information for only one field. [L4]

__T __F **8.** If you format a field in a form to be displayed in capital letters, it does not change the appearance of that field in the table on which the form is based. [L1]

__T __F **9.** A list box allows users to enter items that are not on the list. [L2]

__T __F **10.** The Row Source Type property box tells the program where to look for the items in a list or combo box. [L2]

Multiple Choice

Circle the letter of the correct answer for each of the following questions.

1. You can use buttons from the _____ toolbar to change the appearance of the data in a form. [L1]

a. Standard

b. Formatting

c. Form Design

d. Database

2. In list and combo boxes, the _____ determines where the list values come from. [L2]

a. Expression Builder

b. Validation Rule

c. Row Source box

d. Row Source Type box

3. When you type the values for a list box, each value must be separated by _____. [L2]

a. quotation marks

b. semicolons

c. colons

d. commas

4. Automatically adding the current date to a field is done using the _____ in the Default Value area. [L5]

a. Validation Rule

b. Expression Builder

c. Row Source

d. Input Mask

5. Use the _____ menu to change the background color of a form. [L8]

a. View

b. Format

c. Shortcut

d. Tools

6. When you want a form to show all the records in one table that are related to one record in another table on one page, you can create a _____. [L8]

   a. main form/subform

   b. find matched records form

   c. form based on a query

   d. tabular form

7. A list box _____. [L2]

   a. remains visible on your screen at all times

   b. is best used when the list is short

   c. can be accessed by typing the first letter of a word on the list

   d. all of the above

8. A combo box _____. [L3]

   a. appears as a drop-down list

   b. can be overridden by typing in a field that is not available in the combo box

   c. can be set to only accept the fields showing in the combo box

   d. all of the above

9. To set a date field to the current date, you must select the _____ category in the Expression Builder. [L5]

   a. Common Expressions

   b. Date Formats

   c. Constants

   d. Operators

10. To change the Tab Order of a form, _____. [L7]

   a. choose Format, Tab Order from the menu

   b. open the detail section property sheet and select Tab Order from the Format tab

   c. choose View, Tab Order from the menu

   d. open the detail section property sheet and select Tab Order from the Data tab

Screen ID

Label each element of the Access screen shown in Figure 3.39 and Figure 3.40.

Figure 3.39

A. Tables and queries available for combo box

B. Build button

C. Combo box

D. Label box

E. Location of data for combo box

F. List box

G. Page Break button

H. Date stamp

I. Align Right button

J. Text box

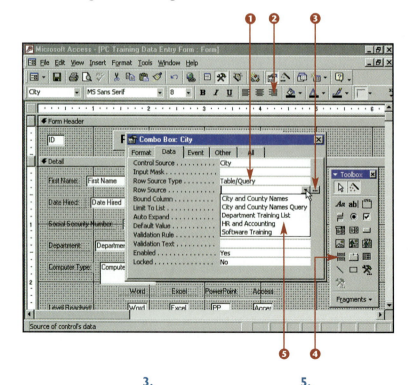

1. _____

2. _____

3. _____

4. _____

5. _____

Figure 3.40

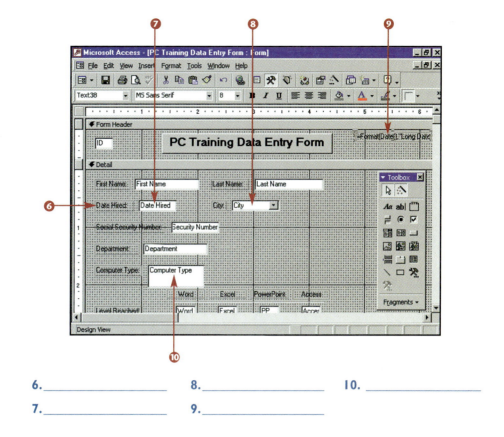

6. _____   8. _____   10. _____

7. _____   9. _____

Discussion Questions

1. You can add formats to fields in forms, but they do not translate back to the fields on which they are based. Why would you ever use form formatting when you can format the fields in tables and the formats will carry over to forms?

2. List boxes have very different characteristics from combo boxes. In what situations would list boxes be preferable, and in what situations would combo boxes be preferable?

3. In what situations might you have the current date or time automatically placed in a field?

4. Can you think of a reason why the AutoTab feature might not be adequate for setting the tab order in a form?

5. On the surface, datasheets with subdatasheets perform in much the same way as forms and subforms. Can you think of advantages to using one over the other?

Skill Drill

Skill Drill exercises reinforce project skills. Each skill reinforced is the same, or nearly the same, as a skill presented in the project. Each exercise includes a brief narrative introduction, followed by detailed instructions in a step-by-step format.

In this exercise, you have a database that has a table of information about the books in your library, a second table that tracks the books others have borrowed from you, and a third table that lists the various book categories. This is an expanded version of the database you used in the exercises in Project 2. Open the three tables to get a feel for what you'll be working with.

1. Adding a List Box to a Form

The Type of Book field has a limited number of possible entries and is a perfect candidate for a list box.

To add a list box to a form, complete the following steps:

1. Copy the file AC2-0303 from your CD. Use the shortcut menu to deselect the read-only status, and rename the copy as My Library.

2. Open the My Library database and click the Forms object button.

3. Open the Books form. Notice that there is a field called Book Type. Possible entries for this field are limited (Hardcover, Trade, and Paperback). With only three possible entries, a list box would work well.

4. Click the View button to switch to Design view.

5. Right-click on the Book Type text box and choose Change To, List Box.

6. Resize the Book Type list box so that it will hold three lines of text.

7. Right-click on the Book Type text box and select Properties. Click the Data tab and select Value List as the Row Source Type.

8. Enter Hardcover;Trade;Paperback in the Row Source box, and then close the Properties box.

9. Click the Save button to save your form.

10. Click the View button, and then click the New Record button.

11. Enter the following record, using the list box to select a book type:

    Green

    Red

    Red Green Talks Cars: A Love Story

    Humor

    Trade

    1997

12. Keep the form open for the next exercise.

2. Adding a Combo Box to a Form

In the first exercise you added a list box to the Books form. The Category field could also use a list box, but because of the number of possible categories, a combo box would work best.

To add a combo box to a form, complete the following steps:

1. Click the Design button to switch to the Books form Design view.

2. Right-click on the Category text box and choose Change To, Combo Box.

3. Right-click on the Category text box and select Properties.

4. Click the Data tab and accept Table/Query as the Row Source Type.

5. Click the drop-down arrow on the right of the Row Source box, and then select the Book Categories table.

6. Close the Properties box and click the Save button to save your work.

7. Click the View button to switch to Form view.

8. Click the New Record button and enter the following record, using the drop-down box in the Category field to select a category:

    Russell

    Eric Frank

    Somewhere a Voice

    Science Fiction

    Paperback

    1965

9. Leave the form open for use in the next exercise.

3. Changing the Tab Order

As you entered records in the first two exercises, you noticed that the insertion point jumped from field to field in an unusual order.

To change the tab order, complete the following steps:

1. Click the Design button to switch to the Books form Design view.

2. Select View, Tab Order from the menu.

3. Click the Auto Order button. Notice that the tab order now goes from left to right. It would probably be better if the order went down the left column, and then to the top of the right column and down.

4. Click the row selector for the Author First Name field. Click the row selector again and drag the field up until it is just below the Author Last Name field.

5. Close the Tab Order dialog box and click the Save button to save your changes.

6. Click the View button to switch to Form view.

7. Click the New Record button and enter the following record, watching the tab order as you enter the data:

```
Davis
Richard Harding
1903
King's Jackal, The
Fiction
Hardcover
```

8. Close the form, but leave the database open for use in the next exercise.

4. Adding the Date and Time to a Form Footer

It is relatively easy to date-stamp a form so that you know when it was printed. In this exercise, you will open the Borrowed Books form and add the date and time to the form footer.

To add a date and time to a form footer, complete the following steps:

1. Open the Borrowed Books form in Form view. Look at the layout of the form.

2. Click the View button to switch to Design view.

3. Move the pointer to the bottom of the Form Footer bar until it turns into a black, two-directional vertical arrow.

4. Click and drag down until the form footer area is about 1/2" high.

5. Choose Insert, Date and Time from the menu. Deselect Include Time and click OK. The long date is inserted into the form header area.

6. Grab the date and drag it down to the left edge of the form footer section. Center the date vertically.

7. Choose Insert, Date and Time from the menu. Deselect Include Date, select Include Time, and click OK. The long time format is inserted into the form header area.

8. Maximize the form window. Grab the time and drag it down to the right edge of the form footer section. Center the date vertically.

9. Click the Align Right button on the Formatting toolbar.

10. Click the View button to switch to Form view. Look at your changes.

11. Close the form and save your changes when prompted.

5. Creating a Form and Subform

You would like to scroll through your list of books and see the information on the borrower (if the book has been loaned out). To do this, you can create a form with a subform.

To create a form and subform, complete the following steps:

1. Click New to create a new form. Select Form Wizard and choose Books as the table from which to retrieve data.

2. Select all the fields from the Books table.

3. Select all the fields from the Borrow table except the Book Title field.

4. Choose to view your data by the Books field, and make sure Form with subform(s) is selected.

5. Select the Datasheet layout with the Standard style.

6. Name the Form `Book Information` and the Subform `Borrow Subform`.

7. Use the bottom set of navigation buttons to look at your data.

8. Leave the form open for the next exercise.

6. Printing a Copy of a Form

In this exercise, you print a copy of a single form from a database.

To print a copy of a form, complete the following steps:

1. Click the Print Preview button to see the layout of the printed page. Notice that more than one form is on each page.

2. Close the Print Preview and click the View button to switch to Design view.

3. Maximize the form window. Click the Page Break button and put a page break below the subform box, just above the Form Footer bar.

4. Right-click on the form background and select Fill/Back Color from the shortcut menu.

5. Select the White background color.

6. Click Print Preview again. Notice that the only gray background remaining is in the subform, but there is not very much.

7. Choose File, Print from the menu. Choose to print page 1 only, and then click OK.

8. Close the form and save your changes when prompted. Close the My Library database.

Challenge

Challenge exercises expand on or are somewhat related to skills presented in the lessons. Each exercise provides a brief narrative introduction followed by instructions in a numbered step format that are not as detailed as those in the Skill Drill section.

The database used for the Challenge section will continue with the literary theme used in the Skill Drill exercises. It is the list of short stories that you used in the Discovery Zone section of Project 2. There are three tables—Author Information, Book Information, and Short Stories. Browse through these tables before going on to the exercises.

1. Adding Page Numbers to the Page Footer

If you are going to print out individual records, page numbers are sometimes very helpful. Access enables you to put page numbers in the headers or footers of forms or reports in a variety of formats. The page numbers used with forms do not appear except when the form is printed.

1. Copy the AC2-0304 file from your CD. Use the shortcut menu to deselect the read-only status, and rename the copy as `Short Stories`.

2. Create a tabular AutoForm that contains all the fields in the Book Information table. Call the form `Book Information`.

3. Move to Design view and maximize the window. Make the page 6 1/2" wide, and then move the fields and adjust the width of the Editor and Publisher fields and field headings until you are satisfied with the layout. Use the Print Preview button to check your work.

4. Activate Page Header/Footer from the View menu.

5. Choose Insert, Page Numbers from the menu. Use the Page N of M format, and place it on the right side of the footer.

6. Use Print Preview to check the placement of the page number, and then print page 4.

2. Adding a Hyperlink to the Form Footer

While entering data in the Book Information table, you decide that you want to have a way to go to the Web and search for information on a book. To do this, it would be a good idea to put a link to your favorite search engine on the Web. (Search engines are programs like Yahoo or AltaVista that allow you to search millions of Web sites for information.)

Use the help provided with Access to figure out how to put a hyperlink to a search engine. Use http://altavista.digital.com or another favorite search engine of your choice. Have the text shown at the bottom of the screen say `Search for Information`. Make sure you put the hyperlink in the right place or it will never be seen while you are entering information!

3. Changing the Look of the Form

The Book Information form looks rather bland. You want to make it stand out, so you change the formatting.

1. Go to Design view of the Book Information form. Select all the header text and make it bold.

2. Select the Header and Detail text and change the color to a dark blue to match the color of the hyperlink at the bottom of the page.

3. Select all the text boxes in the Detail area and change the background color to a light blue.

4. Make the Editor field two lines high, so that the text will wrap like it does in the Book Title field. Use Format, Size to make the Editor field exactly as tall as the Book Title field.

5. Italicize the titles of the books. Use Print Preview to see the results of your changes.

6. Close the form and save your work.

4. Drawing Data from Three Tables

In earlier exercises you used two tables as the basis for a form. You are not limited to two, however. In this exercise, you use fields from all three tables to create a form. This form will be especially good for printing all the related information about a specific story.

1. Create a new form using the Form Wizard. Use the Short Stories table as the source and name the form `Three Tables`.

2. Add the Author field from the Short Stories table, and then add all the fields from the Author Information table except the Author field.

3. Add the Source field from the Short Stories table, and then add all the fields from the Book Information table except the Book Title field.

4. Add the rest of the fields from the Short Stories table.

5. Switch to Design view and put a page break at the end of the Detail area. Check Print Preview to make sure the information will fit on a vertical page. If it doesn't, go to File, Page Setup, and choose Landscape from the page tab.

6. Scroll to page 11 and print just that page. Close the form.

5. Linking Tables in a Form

In Lesson 8, "Creating Subforms," you created a Form/Subform where information from the "one" side of a one-to-many relationship was displayed at the top of the screen, and the information from the "many" table was displayed in a subform at the bottom of the screen. There is another way to display information from tables with the one-to-many relationship. It is by linking the tables and creating a button on a form that shows the same information that a subform shows. In this exercise, you will only be using the Short Stories and Book Information tables.

1. Create a new form using the Form Wizard. Use the Book Information table as the source.

2. Add all the fields from the Book Information table.

3. Add all the fields from the Short Stories table except the Source field.

4. Choose Linked forms instead of the Form with subform(s) option. Look at the preview in the preview area when you select the linking option.

5. Choose any style you want, and then name the first form **Book Information with Story Information**. Accept the default name, Short Stories, for the second form.

6. Switch to Design view and lengthen the Editor and Publisher fields to the same length as the Book Title field.

7. Click the Short Stories button at the top of the page. This is a list of all the stories in the book shown on the main form. You have just created an excellent research tool for a library or the Web!

8. Switch to Design view and make the Author field the same height as the Story Title field. Notice that there is no button to take you back to the main form from the linked form.

9. Click the Close Window button to return to the main form. Save your changes when prompted.

10. Close the form and save your changes. Close the Short Stories database.

Discovery Zone

Discovery Zone exercises help you gain advanced knowledge of project topics and application of skills. These exercises focus on enhancing your problem-solving skills. Numbered steps are not provided, but you are given hints, reminders, screen shots, and references to help you reach your goal for each exercise.

In these exercises you will be using a personnel database for an online marketing company. The database has two tables—Departments and Employee Information. You will only use one of the tables in these exercises.

1. Using Tab Control to Create Form Pages

In some situations you might want to break up your forms into separate pages for data entry. There might be too many fields to fit comfortably on one screen, there might be a natural division of data by topic, or you might want to keep confidential information (such as salary) off the screen as much as possible. In the Employee Information table, the personal information about an employee could be entered on one page, and the company information on another. You will need to copy the AC2-0305 file, remove the read-only status, and rename the file **Online Products Company**.

Goal: Create two data entry pages on a form.

The form you create should have

- Two pages
- Page tabs reading Home Information and Company Information
- An image of an address book in the Home Information tab, and a flowchart symbol in the Company Information tab
- The Name, Street, City, State, Zip, and Home Phone fields on the Home Information page, and all the other fields on the Company Information page
- Appropriate field widths for the fields

Name the form Employee Information when you are finished.

Hint #1: You will need to create the form in Design View.

Hint #2: Look for a button that might help you with this procedure.

Hint #3: If you get stuck, use help or just try double-clicking on the troublesome object.

Your figure should look like Figure 3.41.

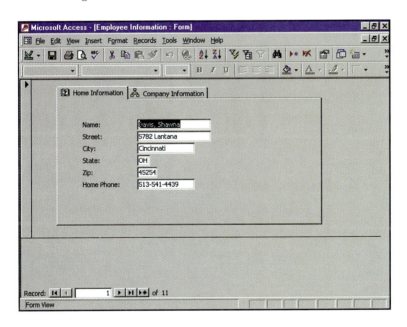

Figure 3.41
The form contains separate tabs for personal information and company information.

2. Adding an Image to a Form

Your pages for the Online Products Company form look pretty good, but you'd like to add some clip art to fill the empty spaces.

Goal: Add a clip art image to each page of the Employee Information form.

Your pages should have a clip art image on the right side of each page. The image should somehow relate to the topic. For example, you might use an image of a commercial building or a computer. The choice of images is up to you. It will also depend on which images are available on your computer. You may have to try quite a few before you find one that is on your hard drive. You may also be able to go to the Microsoft CD-ROM and install more images.

Hint #1: A couple of possible buttons in the toolbox might be useful. Place the pointer over the ones that look promising. Use the ScreenTip name to search help for information.

Hint #2: An alternative to placing the image directly into the form is to place it in another program that handles graphics better (such as PowerPoint or PhotoDraw), resize it there, and then copy and paste it into your form.

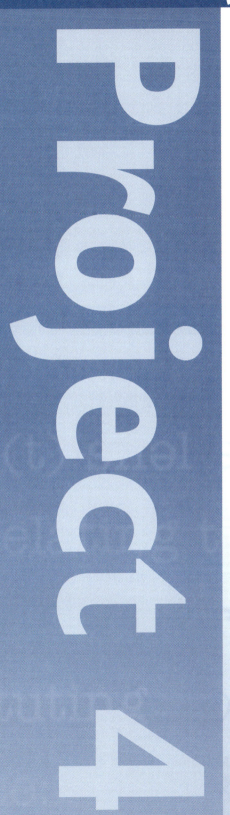

Special Purpose Reports and Advanced Report Features

Objectives

In this project, you learn how to

- ➤ **Create Labels for Mailings**
- ➤ **Create Calculated Fields in a Report**
- ➤ **Group and Sort Data in a Report**
- ➤ **Keep Grouped Data Together in Reports**
- ➤ **Add Calculated Fields to Group Headers and Footers**

Key terms introduced in this project include

- ■ sans serif
- ■ serif
- ■ unbound object

Why Would I Do This?

I f you expect to send mailings to employees, group members, customers, or any other names in your database, you can produce mailing labels with a special type of report in Access. This label report prints several fields together and includes preformatted layouts that match commercially available adhesive labels.

In many cases, you will want to display information in a report that is derived from other fields in the table or query. Access enables you to perform calculations based on existing fields to produce additional columns in your reports. Sometimes the calculations you perform provide surprising results—such as when you attempt to divide by zero. You can set conditions so that text is substituted for unusual calculation results.

A report can be made easier to read by grouping data and introducing visual breaks between the groups. You learn how to group and sub-group your data. You can also make sure that related information stays on the same page when you print your report.

Finally, you can group data to determine subtotals. In this project, you learn how to add subtotals and totals to report headers and footers.

Visual Summary

When you have completed this project, you will have created several advanced reports.

Figure 4.1
Mailing labels have been created from a customer database.

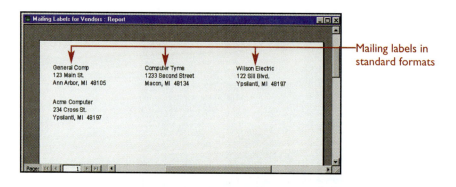

Mailing labels in standard formats

Figure 4.2
Access enables you to create new fields based on calculations using other fields.

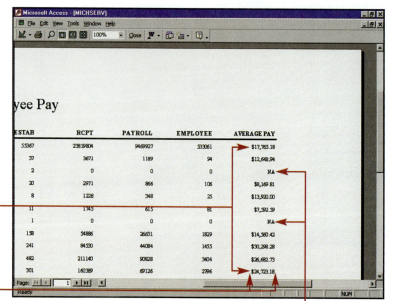

Calculated field (Payroll/Employee)

Consistent formatting

Text replaces division-by-zero errors

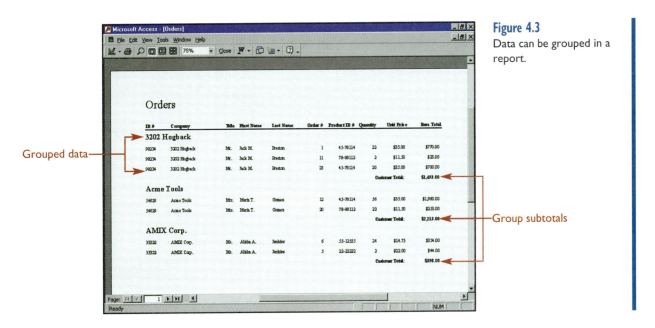

Figure 4.3
Data can be grouped in a report.

Grouped data

Group subtotals

Lesson 1: Creating Labels for Mailings

Reports are used to list many records. A mailing label report lists the records in a format that is traditionally used for addressing letters.

In this lesson, you create a report to produce labels that can be attached to envelopes or brochures for mailings. A Label Wizard helps you design your report. Creating labels, even using the Label Wizard, is a process that involves many steps. You will use the database containing the PC Hardware and Vendors tables that you used in Project 3, "Adding Useful Features to Your Forms."

To Create a Mailing Label Report

1 **Copy the AC2-0401 file to your disk, remove the read-only status, rename it** Computer Inventory 4, **and open it.**
The database window should open to the Tables area. If it does not, click the Tables object button.

2 **In the Computer Inventory 4 database, click the Vendors table to select it, and then click Open.**
Notice that this table contains data necessary to contact the vendor by mail or by phone (see Figure 4.4).

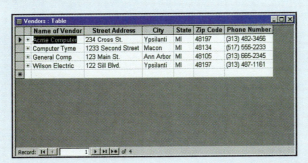

Figure 4.4
The Vendors Table includes vendor addresses and phone numbers.

continues ▶

To Create a Mailing Label Report   (continued)

3 **Close the Vendors Table. Click the Reports object button, and then click the New button.**
The New Report dialog box is displayed.

4 **Click the drop-down arrow to reveal a list of the tables and queries that are available in this database (see Figure 4.5).**

Figure 4.5
The New Report dialog box shows a list of tables and queries on which you can base your report.

Label Wizard option

List of available tables and queries

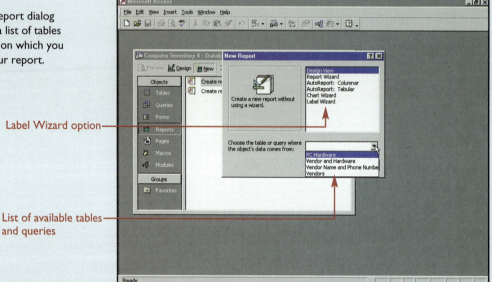

5 **Click Vendors in the list to select the Vendors Table, select Label Wizard from the list of available reports and wizards, and then click OK.**
After a short delay, the first Label Wizard dialog box is displayed (see Figure 4.6).

Figure 4.6
Select the label size and layout in the first Label Wizard dialog box.

Industry standard identification number

Unit of measure

Number of labels side-by-side on the sheet

Label manufacturer

Avery label 5160   Size of each label

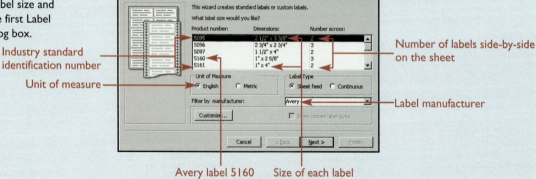

X The size of the labels may be shown in millimeters (mm). If this is the case, you can click the English option button in the Unit of Measure area to change the units to inches. For this lesson, you will also want to select the Avery label option in the Filter by manufacturer drop-down list. Select Sheet feed from the Label Type area, if necessary.

6 **Select the Avery number 5160 label.**

This is a form that prints three labels across a single 8.5" form. You will print these labels on ordinary paper for this exercise.

7 **Click Next.**

The second Label Wizard dialog box is displayed (see Figure 4.7).

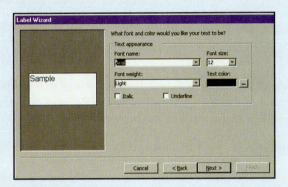

Figure 4.7
In the second Label Wizard dialog box, you select text characteristics.

8 **Change the font size to 12 and the font name to Arial, if necessary.**

Arial is a plain, easy-to-read font that is appropriate for titles or labels.

 Font Selection

The many different typefaces available can be divided into two groups—*serif* and those without serifs, or *sans serif*. Serifs are the horizontal lines at the end of each vertical letter stroke that helped earlier typesetters line up letters when they set the type. Today's reading experts find that typefaces with serifs are easier for people to read when the words are arranged in long lines. Sans serif letters are often used for short word groups such as titles or labels.

9 **Click Next to accept the settings for the font style, size, and weight.**

The third Label Wizard dialog box is displayed (see Figure 4.8). This dialog box enables you to construct your labels using existing fields and to enter other items you would like to include.

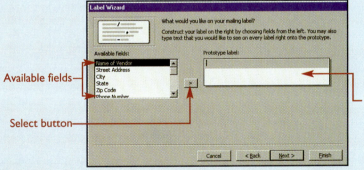

Figure 4.8
You choose what you want to include on the label in the third Label Wizard dialog box.

Available fields

Select button

Work area

10 **Click the Select button to add the Name of Vendor field to the Prototype label. Press ↵Enter to move to the next line of the label.**

continues ▶

To Create a Mailing Label Report   (continued)

 Automatic Removal of Blank Lines
When setting up an address database, you will often create a field for a person's name and a field for a company name. When you set up a label, you will create four lines—the first line will contain the name fields and the second line will contain the company field. Some of the entries in the database, however, will not have a company name. Access automatically moves the third and fourth lines up so that there is no blank line on the label.

11 **Click the Select button to add the Street Address field to the label. Press ⏎Enter to move to the next line of the label.**
If you make a mistake creating the label, you can use the Back button to undo your steps.

 Editing in the Prototype Label Box
You can also edit the sample label in the Prototype label box as if it were a normal document. You can add or edit text or punctuation marks, and you can select and delete fields that you have placed there.

12 **Click the Select button to add the City field to the label. Type a comma and a space.**

13 **Add the State field to the same line of the label. Type two more spaces and add the Zip Code field.**
You have now set up your mailing label. Curly braces {} surround each field from the Vendors table (see Figure 4.9).

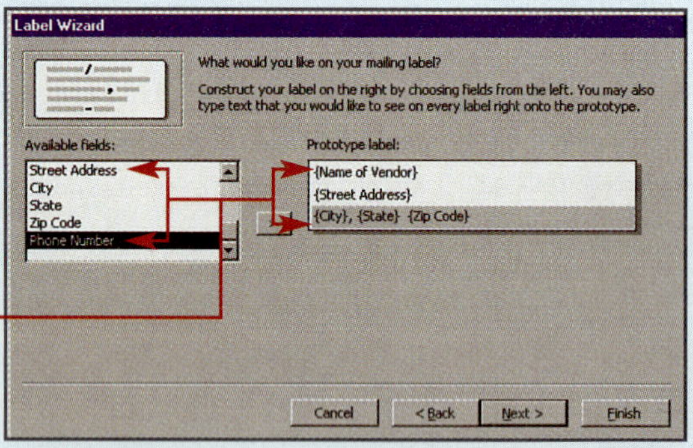

Figure 4.9
The Prototype label now includes inserted fields.

Fields from the Vendors table

14 **Click Next.**
The fourth Label Wizard dialog box is displayed. This dialog box enables you to choose the field or fields on which you want to sort. The field on which you sort does not have to be one of the fields included in the label.

15 **Click the Zip Code field to select it, and then click the Select button to add it to the Sort By list.**
Many labels are sorted by Zip Code because of postage savings for mass mailings (see Figure 4.10).

If you select more than one field, the program sorts the records by the first field listed. Then it sorts the records within that grouping by the next field listed. For example, if you had a table with many vendor names and had chosen to sort first by City and then by Name of Vendor, you would get a set of labels for each city. Within each city, the labels would be sorted alphabetically by the name of the vendor.

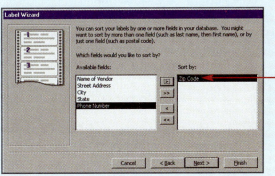

Figure 4.10
Use the fourth Label Wizard dialog box to choose the sort fields.

16 **Click Next to move to the last Label Wizard dialog box and change the name of the report to** Mailing Labels for Vendors.
Check to see that the option to preview the labels is selected and the display help option is not selected. The Display Help option has the same effect as using the Help menu to ask for help about creating reports.

17 **Click the Finish button.**
A preview of the report is displayed (see Figure 4.11).

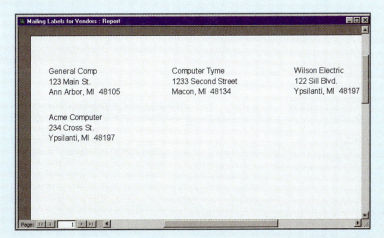

Figure 4.11
After you complete the Label Wizard, a preview of the mailing labels appears.

18 **Click the Print button on the toolbar to print a copy of the labels on a regular sheet of paper.**

19 **Click the Close Window button in the upper-right corner of the Print Preview window.**
Keep the database open for the next lesson.

Printer Requirements

Some printers require minimum margin settings that are larger than the label settings used in this example. You may get a warning message such as Some data may not be displayed. Proceed to print if you get such messages, and examine the printout to see if any characters have been left off.

For this project, it is assumed that you have a printer that uses separate sheets of paper rather than the continuous, folded paper with holes in the sides for a sprocket. If you have a printer that uses continuous feed paper, you can either select a different label that is about the same size as the one indicated in the lesson, or follow the directions as written and simply preview the labels without sending them to the printer. Ask your instructor for additional advice about the printing arrangement that is available with your computer.

 Font Sizes

The height allowed for each line of print is measured in points. This is an old typesetter's measurement that goes back to the days of manual printing presses. There are 72 points to the inch, so 1/4" would be 18 points. This is the amount of space allowed for the line of print and includes enough space above and below the letters so that the tops of the tallest letters do not touch the bottom of the previous lines. The height of the letters also affects their width.

Lesson 2: Creating Calculated Fields in a Report

You may want to display information calculated from data in one of your tables. In this lesson, you learn how to take data from two fields and display the result of dividing the contents of one field by those in another.

First you look at a tabular report that contains the fields you use to calculate the average pay per employee. You will be using the Michigan Service Businesses table that you used in Project 2, "Managing Data Using Smaller Related Tables."

To Examine the Report That Will Be Modified

1 **Copy the AC2-0402 file to your disk, remove the read-only status, rename it** Service Businesses 4, **and open it.**
The database window should open to the Reports area. If it does not, click the Reports object button. The Pay per Employee report should be selected.

2 **Click the Preview button and maximize the preview window.**
A preview of the report is displayed. The 0 ZIP code in the first row is a code used by the government to indicate totals for the entire state. Because Access sorted the report in ZIP code order, this summary line appears at the top of the report.

3 **Move the mouse pointer onto the report. It becomes a magnifying glass with a minus sign in it. Click once to decrease the magnification.**
You are able to see the entire first page of the report. Notice that there is room on the right for an additional column (see Figure 4.12). The magnifying glass pointer now has a plus in it.

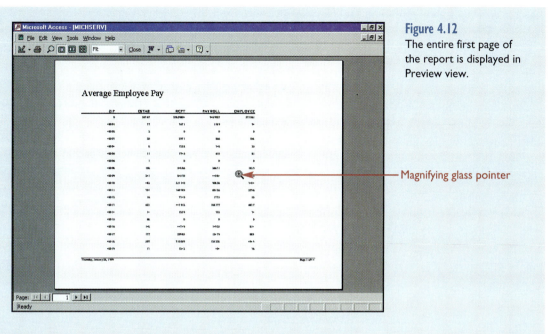

Figure 4.12
The entire first page of the report is displayed in Preview view.

Magnifying glass pointer

![icon] **4** **Click the View button on the toolbar to switch to Design view.**

![icon] **5** **Scroll the design window to the right so that you can see the right side of the report, click the Toolbox button to open the toolbox, if necessary, and then arrange the design window and the toolbox as shown in Figure 4.13.**
Close the Field list box, if necessary.

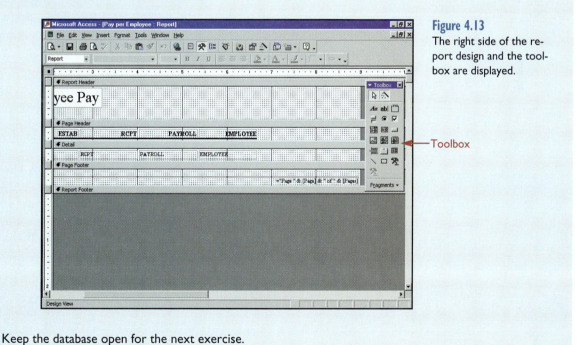

Figure 4.13
The right side of the report design and the toolbox are displayed.

Toolbox

Keep the database open for the next exercise.

You have now set up the report window to add a new field. In this next section, you add a calculated field and a field label to the report.

To Create Calculated Fields in a Report

 ① **Click the Text Box button in the toolbox.**

② **In the detail section of the report design, drag a text box that is approximately the same size as the other text boxes in the Detail section (see Figure 4.14).**

Figure 4.14
The Text Box tool enables you to add a calculated field in the detail area of the report design.

New text box —
Text Box pointer —

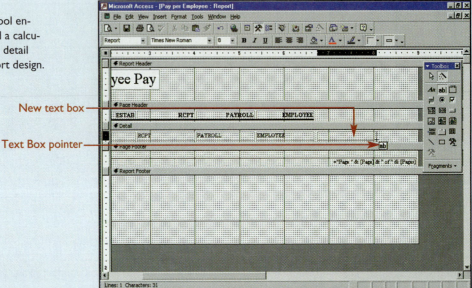

When you release the mouse button, an Unbound text box appears along with its label box (see Figure 4.15). An **unbound object** is not connected to an underlying table. The label will probably appear over the top of another field.

> ✖ When drawing a new text box, it takes some skill to get the box the size you want. You may need to turn the Snap to Grid feature off in the Format menu. If the box is not the correct size, press Del and try again. If the size is okay, but the position is not where you want it, point at the text box with your mouse until the pointer turns into a hand, and then click and drag the box to a position that is in line with the other boxes.

③ **Click an empty part of the report design to deselect the new text box, and then click in the unwanted label box to select it. Press Del.**
The label box is deleted, but the Unbound text box is unaffected.

④ **Click the new text box, and then click the word** Unbound.
The word Unbound disappears, and the insertion point is displayed on the left side of the text box (see Figure 4.16).

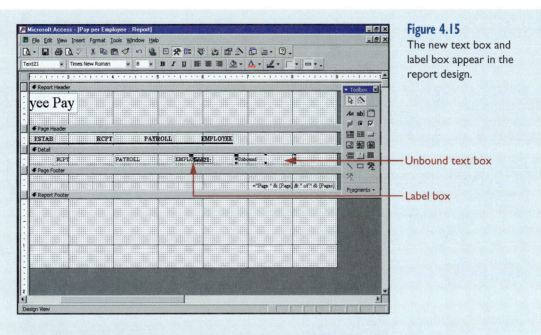

Figure 4.15
The new text box and label box appear in the report design.

Unbound text box

Label box

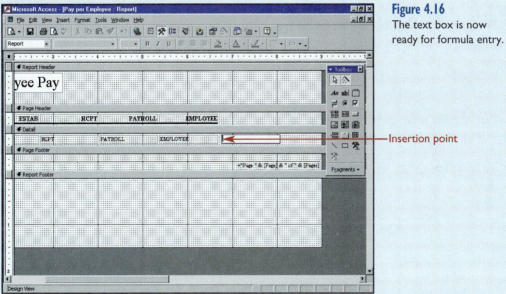

Figure 4.16
The text box is now ready for formula entry.

Insertion point

5 **Type the following formula (be sure to use square brackets):**
`=[PAYROLL]*1000/[EMPLOYEE]`

This formula takes the contents of the PAYROLL field (the amount paid to area employees in thousands of dollars), multiplies it by 1,000, and then divides by the number of employees in that Zip Code area.

The principle behind the formulas in calculated fields is the same as that of any formula. Mathematical symbols are used in the same way, but the variable names are simply the field names enclosed in square brackets.

6 **Click the Print Preview button to preview the report.**
Scroll the report to the right to see the results of the calculated field (see Figure 4.17).

continues ▶

To Create Calculated Fields in a Report   (continued)

Figure 4.17
The Print Preview of the report shows problems with the calculated field.

The new column needs to be formatted

Error messages

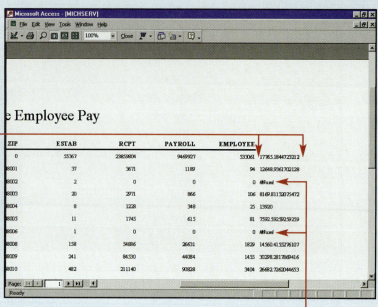

Notice that the average for the first record was approximately $17,765, but the display is showing too many decimal places. Also, there is an error message wherever the number of employees is zero. This error message is displayed when the expression tries to divide by zero.

> If you made a typographical error when typing the formula, the program will not let you go to the Print Preview window. It will tell you that you made an error, and will even tell you what type of error you made.

 7 Click the Close button on the toolbar to close the report preview.
Scroll to the right and make sure the calculated text box is still selected.

8 Click the Properties button on the toolbar to open the Properties dialog box, and then select the All tab.
The calculated field is still selected, even though it may be off the screen. The Properties dialog box shows the properties of the selected text box.

9 Click in the Format box and enter the following format:
$#,##0.00

This displays the number with commas inserted and two decimal places. Remember that the formats you learned in Project 1, "Making Data Entry Easier and More Accurate," had three parts separated by semicolons. In this case, there are no negative numbers, and the zero values will be handled in another way.

10 Replace the formula in the Control Source box with the following:
=IIF([EMPLOYEE]>0,[PAYROLL]*1000/[EMPLOYEE],"NA")

This formula uses an IIF function to test for the existence of a number of employees greater than zero. If that condition is true, it uses the same formula you used before. If it is not true, it prints the code NA for Not Applicable. You could have entered this formula directly into the text box the same way you entered the original formula.

The Properties dialog box has been widened to show you how the Control Source and Format boxes should look (see Figure 4.18).

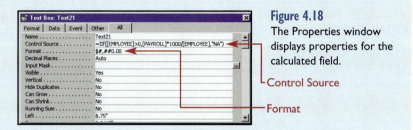

Figure 4.18
The Properties window displays properties for the calculated field.

Control Source

Format

11 Close the Properties dialog box. Click the Label tool in the toolbox, and drag a box in the Page Header section directly above the calculated field.
Make the box the same length as the text box below it and the same width as the label boxes to the left.

12 Enter the label AVERAGE PAY, and then click outside the label box to deselect it.

13 Click the new label box to select it, and then click the Align Right button on the toolbar.
The label is right-aligned.

14 Click the dark, horizontal line in the Report Header that underlines the headings to select it.
You may have to expand the Page Header section to complete this step. The pointer turns into a hand and the end of the line has a handle on it (see Figure 4.19).

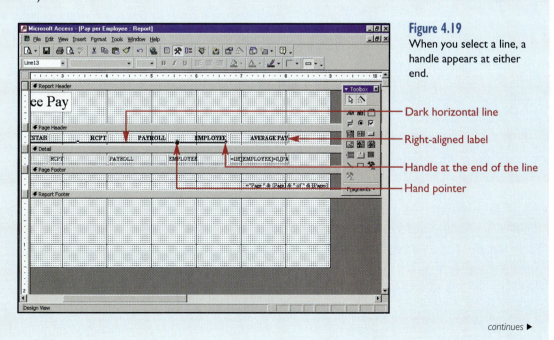

Figure 4.19
When you select a line, a handle appears at either end.

Dark horizontal line

Right-aligned label

Handle at the end of the line

Hand pointer

continues ▶

To Create Calculated Fields in a Report   (continued)

15 Move the pointer to the handle at the end of the line and drag it to the right to extend it under the new heading label.

The dark horizontal line should now extend all the way across the report.

16 Click the Print Preview button to preview the report. Scroll to the right to see the calculated field and its heading (see Figure 4.20).

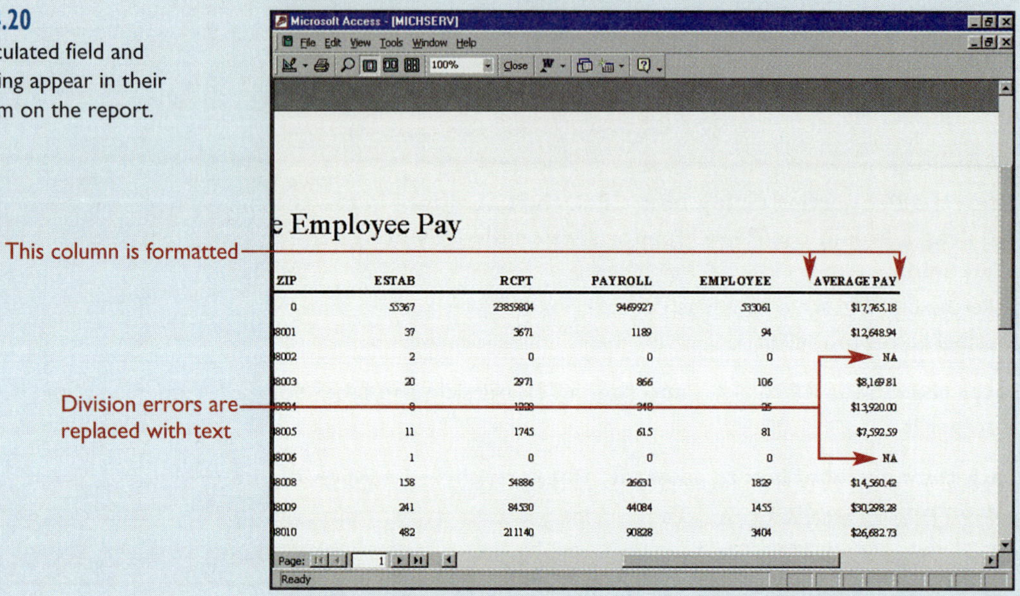

Figure 4.20
The calculated field and its heading appear in their final form on the report.

This column is formatted

Division errors are replaced with text

17 Choose <u>F</u>ile, <u>P</u>rint. In the Print Range area, enter a 1 in the <u>F</u>rom and <u>T</u>o boxes, and click OK.

This prints just page 1 of the report.

18 Click the Close Window button in the upper-right corner of the Print Preview window and save your changes. Close the database.

Lesson 3: Grouping and Sorting Data in a Report

On many occasions it is important to group records to make a report easier to read and understand. There are a couple of ways you can group data. You can run the Report Wizard and select grouping levels, and then modify the report that the wizard creates. You can also create your own report, and then create the grouping. This gives you the best control over your data.

In this lesson, you learn how to group and sort records. You will use a database that lists the orders received by a cleaning supply company, and you will set up a report to group all the orders by customer.

To Group and Sort Data in a Report

1 **Copy the AC2-0403 file to your disk, remove the read-only status, rename it** Customer Orders 4**, and open it.**

The database window should open to the Reports area. If it does not, click the Reports object button. The Orders Grouped by Customer report should be selected.

2 **Click the Preview button and maximize the Preview window.**

A preview of the report is displayed. The orders are sorted by the Product ID # (see Figure 4.21). Scroll around the report and look at the fields it contains.

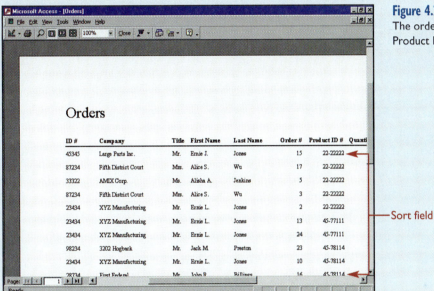

Figure 4.21
The orders are sorted by Product ID #.

3 **Click the Close button on the toolbar.**

This closes the preview and returns you to the database window with the Reports object button selected.

4 **Click Design, and then click the Sorting and Grouping button on the toolbar.**

The Sorting and Grouping dialog box is displayed (see Figure 4.22).

continues ▶

To Group and Sort Data in a Report   (continued)

Figure 4.22
The Sorting and Grouping dialog box is used to sort or group data, or both.

Field to be sorted on —

Group Header box —

Group Properties —

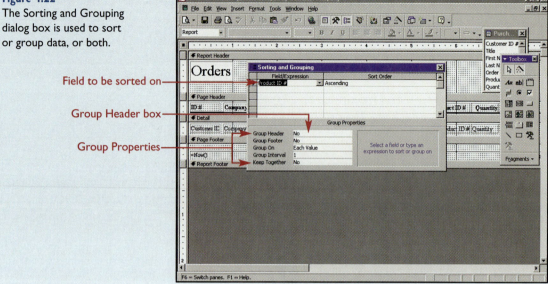

5 Click the down arrow on the right of the first line of the Field/Expression box and select Company.
The name of the new field replaces the Product ID # field.

6 Click the Group Header box, and then click the down arrow button and change the selection to Yes.

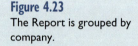 **7** Click the Print Preview button.
The new report is previewed. Notice that the records are now grouped by company, and there is a space above each of the companies (see Figure 4.23). The space was created when you selected a group header. (Note: You do not have to close the Sorting and Grouping dialog box before switching to Print Preview.)

Figure 4.23
The Report is grouped by company.

Spaces above each
company's orders

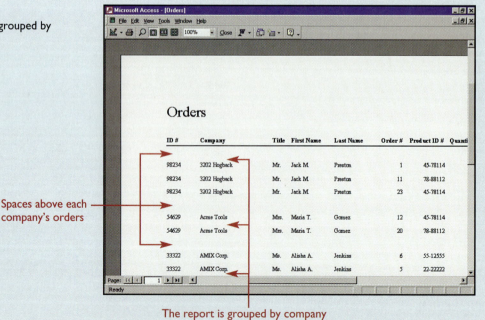

The report is grouped by company

Close ⑧ **Click the Close button on the toolbar to return to the report Design view. Close the Sorting and Grouping dialog box.**
Notice that the report design now has a section titled Company Header.

⑨ **Click the Field List button to open the field list, if it is not already open, and then drag the Company field name into the Company Header area.**
Put the new text box toward the middle of the Company Header area, so there will be room to see the text label associated with the text box. The new Company text box has its own label with the word Text plus a number (see Figure 4.24). Click an empty part of the design to deselect the text box.

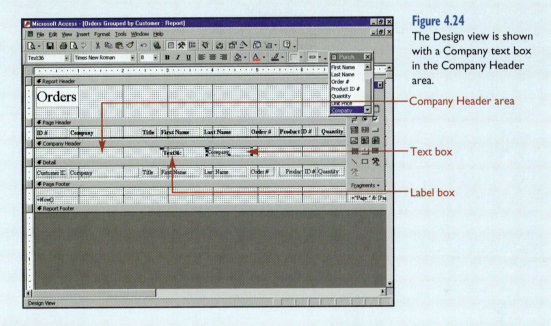

Figure 4.24
The Design view is shown with a Company text box in the Company Header area.

Company Header area

Text box

Label box

⑩ **Click the text box label to select it, and then press Del to delete the label.**
The Company text box remains, but without a label.

⑪ **Click the Print Preview button to preview the report.**
Notice that the headers are too small and not positioned correctly.

Close ⑫ **Click the Close button on the toolbar to return to Design view, and then move the Company text box to the left so that it lines up with the left side of the report.**
The Company text box should line up with the left edge of the Company ID # text box in the Detail area.

⑬ **Use a handle on the bottom-right of the Company text box to enlarge the box so that it is twice as high and about 3" long.**
You can drag the bottom downward to enlarge the box, but it will not work if you try to drag the top of the box upward.

⑭ **Use the Font Size drop-down list on the Formatting toolbar to change the font size to 16 points, and click the Bold button to change the typeface to bold (see Figure 4.25).**

continues ▶

To Group and Sort Data in a Report (continued)

Figure 4.25
The Header text box is shown after it has been enlarged.

The header text box has been enlarged

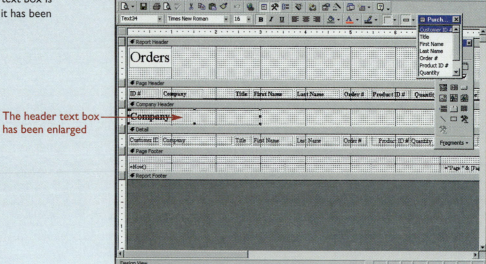

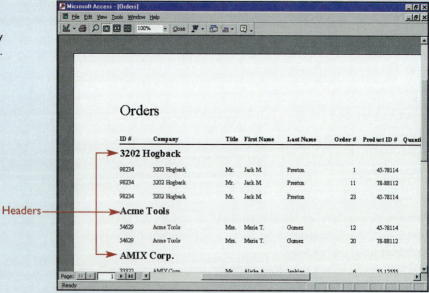

15 Click the **Print Preview** button to preview the report.

Notice that the header contains the same information as the Company field (see Figure 4.26).

Figure 4.26
The final report is grouped on the Company field and displays headers.

Headers

16 Click the **Print** button on the toolbar to print the report.

17 Close the **Print Preview** window, close the **Design** window, and save your changes.

Keep the database open for the next lesson.

Removing Duplicate Fields

In this exercise, you have a header that duplicates the company name field. It is a good idea to remove the duplicate field from the Detail area.

Lesson 4: Keeping Grouped Data Together in Reports

In most cases grouped data should be kept together on the same printed page. Access gives you the option of starting a new group at the top of the next page instead of over-lapping. This feature works dynamically as you add records to your database.

In this lesson, you designate where to break a page of grouped records.

To Keep Grouped Data Together

1 Click the **P**review button in the Customer Orders 4 Database window to open the report in Preview view.

2 Maximize the Preview window, and then scroll to the bottom of the page.

Notice that the First Federal heading is detached from its records (see Figure 4.27). (Note: Your preview may include one record under the First Federal Heading.) You will also often see records from a group split between two pages.

Figure 4.27
The header has been separated from its records.

This header is separated from its records

3 Click the **C**lose button on the toolbar.

This closes the preview and returns you to the database window with the Orders Grouped by Customer selected.

4 Click the **D**esign button in the Database window to open the report in Design view.

continues ▶

To Keep Grouped Data Together   (continued)

5 Click the Sorting and Grouping button on the toolbar.
The Sorting and Grouping dialog box is displayed.

6 Click the down arrow in the Keep Together text box in the Grouping Properties area.
A drop-down list is displayed (see Figure 4.28).

Figure 4.28
The Keep Together drop-down list has three options.

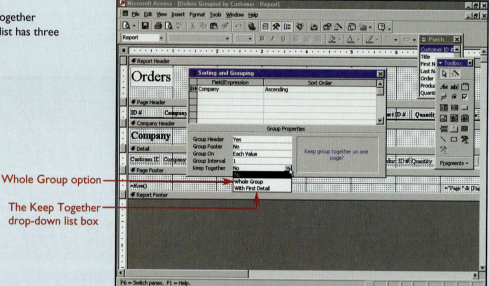

Whole Group option

The Keep Together drop-down list box

7 Select the Whole Group option, and then close the Sorting and Grouping dialog box.

8 Click the Print Preview button and scroll to the bottom of the page.
Notice that the page ends at the end of a group (see Figure 4.29).

Figure 4.29
The page breaks at the end of a group.

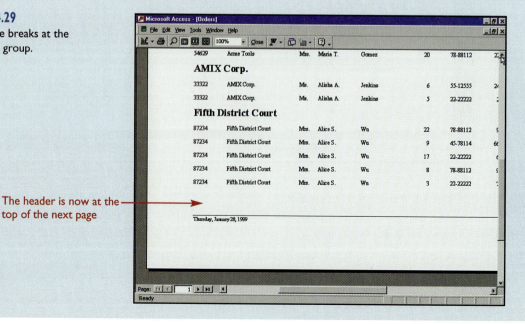

The header is now at the top of the next page

9 Click the Next Page button and look at the top of page 2 to verify that the page break worked correctly.

Close **10** Click the **Close** button on the toolbar to return to the report Design view. Close the Design view window and save your changes.
Leave the database open for the next lesson.

Lesson 5: Adding Calculated Fields to Group Headers and Footers

If you have a report with grouped records, it is often useful to place calculated information in a header or footer for that group. The values of a number field may be totaled or subtotaled in a footer by using a summation expression. If it is used in a group footer, you see the subtotal for that group. Similarly, if the expression is used in a page or report footer, you see the total for the page or report respectively. Grouping records is of particular importance if you use page subtotals. If groups were allowed to split over two pages, the subtotals at the bottom of each page would be meaningless.

In this lesson, you add an expression to a group footer to show totals for each group.

To Add a Group Total Using an Expression

1 Click the **Design** button in the Customer Orders 4 Database window to open the Orders Grouped by Customer report in Design view.

2 Click the Sorting and Grouping button on the toolbar. Choose Yes from the Group Footer drop-down list box, and then close the dialog box.
A Company Footer area is created (see Figure 4.30).

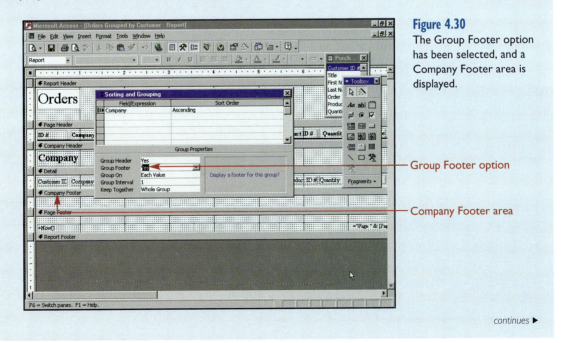

Figure 4.30
The Group Footer option has been selected, and a Company Footer area is displayed.

continues ▶

To Add a Group Total Using an Expression   (continued)

3 Click the Text Box button from the toolbox. Drag a text box near the right edge of the Company Footer area.
The text box and a label are displayed.

4 Click the attached label box to select it. Click it again to turn on the Text Edit mode. Delete the current label and replace it with the following:
```
Customer Total:
```

5 Click the text box to select it. Click it a second time to enable the Edit mode and enter the following expression:
```
=sum([Quantity]*[Unit Price])
```

Your screen should look like Figure 4.31.

Figure 4.31
An expression has been added to the text box and the label has been changed.

New expression

New label

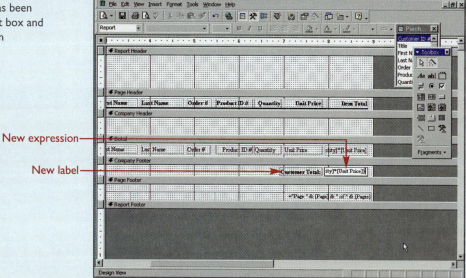

6 Click in an open area, and then click on the text box again to select it. Click the Properties button, and then select the Format tab, if necessary.

7 Scroll to the bottom and select Right in the Text Align box.
This should line up the numbers in this field with those in the detail line above if the right edges of both boxes are lined up. If it does not, select the Text Box and adjust the right edge as necessary.

8 While still in the Properties box, scroll up to the Format option.

9 Type $#,##0.00 in the Format box.
This matches the format of the subtotals with the numbers in the Detail section.

10 Close the Properties box. With the text box still selected, choose 10 from the Font Size box, and click the Bold button.
This will make the group totals stand out.

⓫ Click the Print Preview button to preview the report. Scroll across the report to reveal the Item Total column.

Your report preview should look like Figure 4.32. If you need to touch up the formatting, go back to Design view and make your changes.

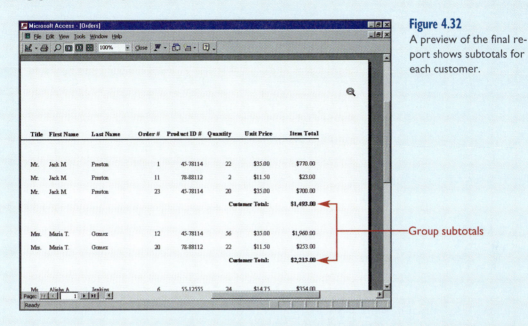

Figure 4.32
A preview of the final report shows subtotals for each customer.

Group subtotals

⓬ Click the Print button on the toolbar to print the report.

⓭ Close the Print Preview, close the report, and save your changes when prompted.

⓮ Close the database.

If you have completed your session on the computer, exit Access and shut down Windows before you turn off the computer. Otherwise, continue with the exercises for this project.

Using Expressions

Standard expressions start with the equal sign. The SUM function adds all the prices for this group. Functions like SUM, AVERAGE, and COUNT are applied according to the section they are in. For example, if the SUM function is in a Group Footer, it sums the field in that group. If the SUM function is in a report footer, it sums that field for the entire report. Be careful with the square brackets and parentheses.

Summary

In this project you were introduced to many new techniques for improving reports. You created mailing labels from a customer table. You added calculated fields to the records in a report and to group footers. You learned how to group and sort records in a report, and how to break the pages at logical points.

You can learn more about forms by going to the Help index and looking for information on expressions. Start with "Examples of expressions" to see some of the things you can do.

Checking Concepts and Terms

True/False

For each of the following statements, check *T* or *F* to indicate whether the statement is true or false.

__T __F **1.** Mailing labels can have only one field per line of the label. [L1]

__T __F **2.** Labels can be customized with additional text and a variety of font types and sizes. [L1]

__T __F **3.** Calculated fields are usually used in the Detail section of a report. [L2]

__T __F **4.** When field names are used in calculated fields, they must be enclosed by curly braces ({}). [L2]

__T __F **5.** To select the fields to be used for grouping, you use the Properties dialog box. [L3]

__T __F **6.** If you put two fields on the same line of a label, the program will automatically insert a comma and a space between them. [L1]

__T __F **7.** Some reports have horizontal lines in the headers with lengths that need to be adjusted if you add a new field. [L2]

__T __F **8.** If you add a text box with a calculated field in the Group Header section of a report, the program automatically adds a label box in the report header using the name of the first field used in the calculation. [L5]

__T __F **9.** You can keep grouped data together on a printed page using the Sorting and Grouping dialog box. [L4]

__T __F **10.** The operator IIF may be used in a property box to make sure that division by zero error messages are not displayed. [L3]

Multiple Choice

Circle the letter of the correct answer for each of the following questions.

1. If a label has fields in four individual lines, what happens if some of the labels have no data in the field on the second line? [L1]

a. The labels will be printed with an empty second line.

b. The third and fourth lines will be automatically moved up.

c. Those labels will not be printed.

d. An error message warns you that you must at least enter spaces in those fields so that they can be printed.

2. If a report is grouped on a field named Expense, what would the report look like if the following formula were placed in a text box in the Detail section? [L2]

`=[Expense]*.10`

a. Ten percent of the total of all the expenses would be displayed in the footer.

b. Ten percent of the expense shown in each record would be printed in each record.

c. The word `Expense` would be printed in the header of that section.

d. both a and b

3. If a table contained the field Last Name and the report was grouped on that field, what effect would it have on the report if the following expression were placed in a text box in the Group Header? [L3]

[Last Name]

a. Each record would start with the last name.

b. Each group would begin with the last name for that group.

c. The words `Last Name` would appear at the beginning of each group.

d. An error message would be displayed because you forgot to start the expression with an equal sign.

4. If a currency value is calculated, it may be displayed with too many decimal places. To control the appearance of the calculated value, _____. [L2]

a. click the Currency button on the toolbar

b. choose Format, Currency from the menu bar

c. use the following form in the calculated field:

   ="$ "+[expression]

d. click the Properties button and type in the format you want

5. When you create a Labels report, the Avery number _____. [L1]

a. is used to designate industry standard label sizes

b. indicates the number of labels per page

c. represents the width of the label in centimeters

d. indicates which tray of the printer to select from

6. If you were sending a letter to the parents of each member of a children's group, the easiest way to add the phrase, `To the Parents of:`, to each mailing label would be _____. [L1]

a. adding a field to the table and placing this phrase in it for each student. You could then use that field in the label.

b. ordering pre-printed labels with this phrase already printed on them and then creating a custom label format to print the first line further to the right.

c. writing the phrase on each envelope by hand.

d. typing the phrase directly into the label design in the Label Wizard.

7. If you use an operator such as IIF in a calculated field, you must _____. [L2]

a. begin the calculation with an equal sign, =

b. place the formula within <>

c. place the formula within {}

d. place the formula between three asterisks

8. A Group Header or Footer _____. [L3]

a. must contain a calculated field

b. may contain label boxes, text boxes, and calculations

c. will automatically contain a text box that displays the contents of the first column

d. cannot contain the same fields as any of the boxes used in the detail section without producing an error message

9. What is wrong with the following calculated field? [L2]

=IIF([PAYROLL]<0,0,PAYROLL)

a. The IF function is misspelled.

b. Both zeros should be enclosed by quotation marks.

c. The field name, PAYROLL, should be enclosed by [].

d. The field name, PAYROLL, should be enclosed by {}.

10. To show subtotals for each group in a grouped report, you can _____. [L5]

a. use a calculated field with a formula in the Detail section

b. use a calculated field with a formula in the Report Header section

c. use a calculated field with a formula in the Page Header section

d. use a calculated field with a formula in the Group Footer section

Screen ID

Label each element of the Access screens shown in Figure 4.33 and Figure 4.34.

Figure 4.33

A. Expression

B. Group subtotal

C. Sorting and Grouping button

D. Next Page button

E. View button

F. Group Footer label

G. Group Header

H. Text button

I. Group Header area

J. Label button

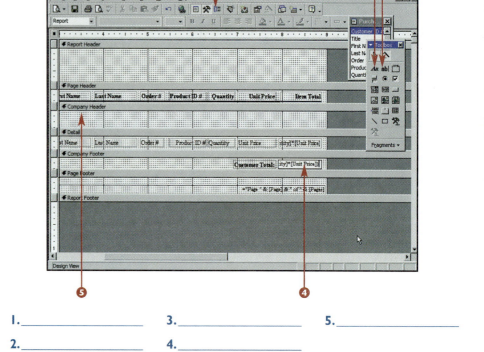

1. _____   3. _____   5. _____

2. _____   4. _____

Figure 4.34

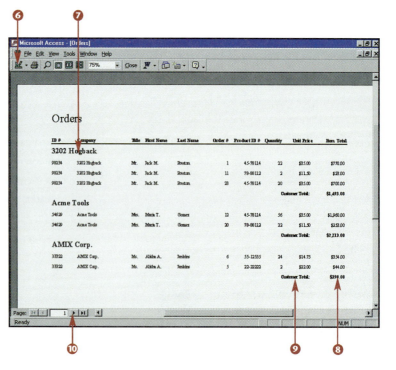

6. _____   8. _____   10. _____

7. _____   9. _____

Discussion Questions

1. In the first lesson of this project you created mailing labels. The label tool can be used to make labels for many different purposes. What other kinds of labels might you want to create?

2. You created a group subtotal in the third lesson. Subtotals can also be used in page footers and report footers. In what situations might you use these kinds of subtotals?

3. Can you think of an instance where you might want to create a group, and then create subgroups for each group?

4. You created a logical page break in the fourth lesson. When might you want to avoid using these?

5. You used a calculated field in the Detail and the Group Footer areas. How does this procedure compare to doing the same tasks in a worksheet? If you could transfer records to an Excel worksheet easily, would that help you analyze data?

Skill Drill

Skill Drill exercises reinforce project skills. Each skill reinforced is the same, or nearly the same, as a skill presented in the project. Each exercise includes a brief narrative introduction, followed by detailed instructions in a step-by-step format.

In this exercise, you will work with a database you created to track your accounts payable for your plumbing company.

1. Creating a Mailing Label Report

The company pays its bills once a month. With the names and addresses of the vendors in the Vendors table, you can make the job a little easier by creating mailing labels.

To create a mailing label report, complete the following steps:

1. Copy the file AC2-0404 from your CD. Use the shortcut menu to deselect the read-only status, and rename the copy **Accounts Payable**.

2. Open the Accounts Payable database and click the Reports object button, if necessary.

3. Click the <u>N</u>ew button in the Reports window. Select the Label Wizard option and choose the Vendors table from the drop-down list. Click OK.

4. Select the Avery manufacturer, and then select label number 5160. Make sure the units of measure are inches and the Sheet feed option is selected. Click <u>N</u>ext.

5. Choose the Arial font and a 12-point font size. Click <u>N</u>ext.

6. Click the Select button to select the Vendor field, and then press ⏎Enter.

7. Select the Street field, and then press ⏎Enter.

8. Select the City field, and then type a comma and a space. Select the State field, add three spaces, and then select the Zip Code field. Click <u>N</u>ext.

9. Click the Select button to sort on the Name field, and then click <u>N</u>ext.

10. Name your report **Vendor Mailing Labels**, and then click <u>F</u>inish.

11. Look at your new report, and then close the report preview. Leave the database open for the next exercise.

2. Grouping Data in a Report

The Accounts Payable report shows the purchases that your company hasn't paid for yet. It would be a good idea to group the bills together by vendor.

To group the accounts payable by vendor, complete the following steps:

1. Select the Accounts Payable report and click the Preview button to examine the report and see how it is set up. Click the View button to switch to Design view.

2. Click the Sorting and Grouping button on the toolbar.

3. Click in the first empty row of the Sorting and Grouping dialog box. Click the arrow and select the Vendor field from the drop-down list. You should now have two fields showing.

4. With the Vendor field selected, choose Yes in the Group Header drop-down list.

5. Close the Sorting and Grouping dialog box. Click the Field List button, if necessary, and drag the Vendor field from the field list to the Vendor Header area.

6. Select the label text and press Del. Drag the Vendor text box to the left of the Vendor Header area.

7. Click the handle in the lower-right corner of the Vendor text box and drag down and to the right. The text box should be about double the original height and about 3" long.

8. Click the Font Size button to change the font size to 16 points, and then click the Bold button.

9. Click the Print Preview button to preview the report. Scroll down the report. The vendor name appears in both the header and the records. Also notice that there are duplicate entries for the vendors based on the date of purchase. You will correct this in the next exercise.

10. Click the View button to return to Design view. Click and delete the Vendor heading in the Page Header area, and then delete the Vendor text box in the Detail area.

11. Move the headers and text boxes for the Number, Description, and Cost fields to the left, next to the PO# text box and header. (Hint: You can move all six items by holding down ◆Shift and clicking on each one. This selects all six, which can then be moved as a group.) Leave the Billing information on the right edge of the report.

12. Click the Print Preview button to preview the report. Go back to Design view, if necessary, to make any necessary changes. Leave the report open for the next exercise.

3. Changing the Sort Order in a Report

In the previous exercise, you noticed that the grouping was not working properly. This is because the report is sorted on the wrong field.

To change the sort order in a report, complete the following steps:

1. Click the View button to switch to Design view of the Accounts Payable report.

2. Click the Sorting and Grouping button on the toolbar. Notice that the Date field is above the Vendor field, meaning that the Date field sort comes before the Vendor field sort.

3. Click the row selector to the left of the Date field. The entire Date row should be highlighted.

4. Click the row selector again, and drag the Date row below the Vendor row.

5. Close the Sorting and Grouping dialog box, and then click the Print Preview button on the toolbar. Notice that all orders for each vendor are now grouped together.

6. Click the Next Page button to move to page 2. Scroll to the top, if necessary. Notice that some of the fields from the Brother-in-Law Fittings vendor have overlapped from page 1.

7. Leave the report open for the next exercise.

4. Forcing Logical Page Breaks

Since records will be added and deleted from the Accounts Payable table as bills are received or paid, you can't anticipate whether the pages will break in the right place. You can add a logical page break to your report so that you won't have to worry about this.

To force a logical page break, complete the following steps:

1. Click the View button to switch to Design view of the Accounts Payable report.

2. Click the Sorting and Grouping button on the toolbar.

3. Select the Vendor field, if necessary.

4. Select Whole Group from the Keep Together drop-down list.

5. Close the Sorting and Grouping dialog box.

6. Click the Print Preview button on the toolbar. Notice that the Brother-in-Law Fittings vendor records have all been moved to the top of page 2.

There is a fairly large gap at the bottom of the first page, which is one of the drawbacks of using this feature (although it is still best to keep related information together).

7. Leave the report open for the next exercise.

5. Adding Calculated Fields to a Record

You can calculate the total cost for each item by multiplying the number of items purchased by the cost of a single item. By moving the fields in exercise 2, you have even created a space for this extra column!

To add calculated fields to a record, complete the following steps:

1. Click the View button to switch to Design view of the Accounts Payable report.

2. Click the Text Box button and draw a box in the Detail area between the Cost field and the Billing field.

3. Click the label box and press Del.

4. Click the Label button and draw a label box in the Page Header area above the Unbound text box. Type **Total Cost** in the box.

5. Click outside the new label box, and then click it again and click the Font Size button to change the font size to 9 points. Click the Align Right button to right-align the label.

6. Right-click on the label, choose Properties from the shortcut menu, and then scroll down and select

Heavy from the Font Weight drop-down list. Close the Properties box, and then make sure all the Page Header labels are consistent.

7. Click the Unbound text box and click the Align Right button.

8. Right-click on the box, choose Properties from the shortcut menu, select the Format tab, and then click in the Format box. Click the down arrow and select Currency from the drop-down list.

9. Click the Unbound text box again and type

   `=([Number]*[Cost])`

10. Click the Print Preview button to see your new calculated field. Leave the report open for the next exercise.

6. Adding Calculated Fields to a Group Footer

You have taken a plain database report and made it very usable and readable. The last thing you need to do to the report is add an expression to show how much is owed to each supplier.

To add calculated fields to a group footer, complete the following steps:

1. Click the View button to switch to Design view of the Accounts Payable report.

2. Click the Sorting and Grouping button on the toolbar. Make sure the Vendor field is selected, and then choose Yes in the Group Footer box in the Group Properties area. Close the Sorting and Grouping dialog box.

3. Click the Text Box button and draw a box in the Vendor Footer area underneath the expression you entered in the last exercise.

4. Click the label box, erase the default label, and then type **Total Charges:**.

5. Click the Unbound text box and click the Align Right button and Bold button on the toolbar.

6. Right-click on the Unbound box, choose Properties from the shortcut menu, select the Format tab, and then click in the Format box. Click the down arrow and select Currency from the drop-down list.

7. Scroll down to the Font Weight box and select Heavy. Close the Properties box.

8. Click the Unbound text box again and type

   `=sum([Number]*[Cost])`

9. Click the Print Preview button to see your new calculated field. Page 2 of your report should look like Figure 4.35.

10. Make sure your formatting is the way you want it, and then click the Print button to print out your report.

11. Close the report and save your changes when prompted. Close the Accounts Payable database.

Figure 4.35
Calculated fields have been added to the report.

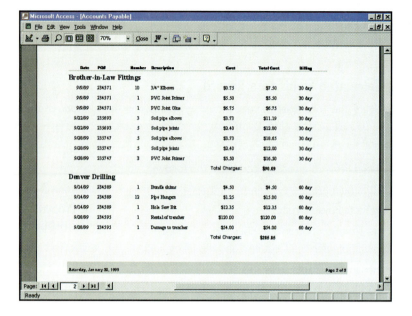

Challenge

Challenge exercises expand on or are somewhat related to skills presented in the lessons. Each exercise provides a brief narrative introduction followed by instructions in a numbered step format that are not as detailed as those in the Skill Drill section.

The database used for the Challenge section is a subset of an historical database. It contains the names of the 123 Haynes Township women listed as having had children in the 1900 U.S. census. The data comes from a transcription, by the authors, of the 1900 Alcona County, Michigan census. These records have been filtered from a database containing about 6,000 entries. Also, only seven of the more than 30 fields have been included.

1. Creating File Folder Labels

You are doing some anthropological research, and you want to print out a form for each of the records. You want to group the records by place of birth, so you'd like to print out a file folder label for each place of birth in these records.

1. Copy the file AC2-0405 from your CD. Use the shortcut menu to deselect the read-only status, and rename the copy `Haynes Township 4`.

2. Use the Label Wizard to create file folder labels for 5-tab file folders. Your labels should be 1/2" x 1 3/4" and the font should be Times New Roman 12 point. You will use the Place of Birth table as the source of information for this report.

3. Name your report `Place of Birth File Folder Labels`.

4. Close the report, but leave the database open for the next exercise.

2. Grouping Data Using the Report Wizard

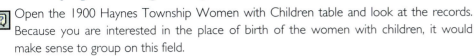

Open the 1900 Haynes Township Women with Children table and look at the records. Because you are interested in the place of birth of the women with children, it would make sense to group on this field.

Use the available help to figure out how to use the Report Wizard to group data on the Birth Place field. Show all the fields. Sort on the number of children, and then the number of children still living. Choose your favorite layout and style, and call the report **1900 Haynes Township Women with Children**.

Edit the layout so that the fields are spaced properly and the labels are all readable. You may have to shorten the labels to make the report design more attractive. You will also want to make the places of birth bold.

3. Using the Average Function

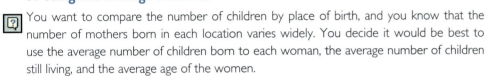

You want to compare the number of children by place of birth, and you know that the number of mothers born in each location varies widely. You decide it would be best to use the average number of children born to each woman, the average number of children still living, and the average age of the women.

Use the skills you learned in Lesson 5, "Adding Calculated Fields to Group Headers and Footers," to insert a place for group subtotals, and then use the available help to learn how to insert averages for the # of Children, Children Living, and Age fields.

Place a field label called **Avg.** on the left side of the group footer area. Format the three averages so that they display one decimal place. The decimal point should be displayed to the right of the numbers in the columns above. Make the new numbers the same color as the rest of the label text. (Hint: You can find out the color number in the Properties box of any of the label fields.)

Your report should look like Figure 4.36.

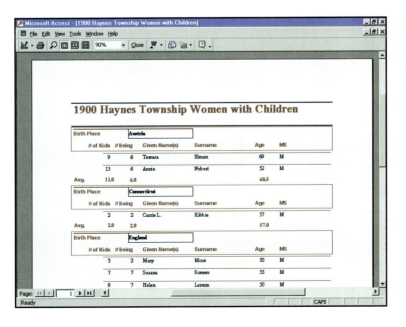

Figure 4.36
The new group subtotal area contains a label and an average value for three numeric fields.

4. Creating a Summary-Only Report

1. Create a new report. Use the Report Wizard and base the report on the 1900 Haynes Township Women with Children table.

2. Select the Age, # of Children, Children Living, and Birth Place fields and group on Birth Place.

3. In the third Report Wizard dialog box, click Summary Options.

4. Select Avg for all three numeric fields, and select the Summary Only option.

5. Choose the Outline 1 layout and the Corporate style. Call your report Averages by Place of Birth.

6. Examine the report in Preview view. Notice that the report is difficult to read and understand, and needs formatting. This will be done in the next exercise.

5. Formatting a Summary-Only Report

The summary report that you just created contains some good information, but it is difficult to read and interpret. In this exercise, you will change some of the Access default formats.

1. Move to Design view of the new report.

2. Select the Age, # of Children, and Children Living fields in the Birth Place Footer area and make them all one decimal place.

3. Select the long expression at the top of the Birth Place Footer area and delete it.

4. Select the four items in the Birth Place Footer area and move them up to the top of the footer.

5. Reduce the size of the Birth Place Footer area so that it is just slightly longer than the text boxes.

6. Add a text box to the right of the Birth Place text box in the Birth Place Header. Rename the label Number=.

7. Type =count(*) into the new text box. This function counts all the records in the grouped field; in this case it counts all the records for each birth place.

8. Move the Birth Place text box closer to its label in the Birth Place Header area. Do the same for the count function you just added. Make the text labels and text boxes in the new count function match those of the birth place label and text boxes.

9. Move the field labels from the Birth Place Header area to the Report Header area. You will need to make room and move the gray lines down.

10. Move the line at the top of the Birth Place Footer area to the bottom of the same area. You may not be able to see the line to select it. Instead, move the pointer to the ruler on the left of the Birth Place Footer area. When it turns into a black right arrow, click and hold down, and then drag up to the gray Birth Place Footer bar. When you let go, you can move everything in this area down so that you can see the line.

11. Your final report should look like Figure 4.37. Print page 1 of the report, and then close the report and the database.

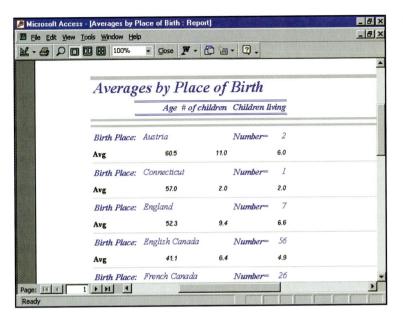

Figure 4.37
Several formatting
changes in the group
subtotal area make the
data easier to read and
interpret.

Discovery Zone

Discovery Zone exercises help you gain advanced knowledge of project topics and application of skills. These exercises focus on enhancing your problem-solving skills. Numbered steps are not provided, but you are given hints, reminders, screen shots, and references to help you reach your goal for each exercise.

The database you will be using for these exercises contains tornado data for the state of Arizona. These records cover a 45-year time span, and include all the confirmed sightings during that period. The records are an abbreviated form of records produced by the National Oceanic and Atmospheric Administration (NOAA). The fields included in this sample table include the year, date, time of day, number of people killed, number of people injured, a damage scale, the county, and the F-scale (a measure of tornado intensity). Many of the fields are blank because there were no casualties or damage, or because the F-scale was not recorded.

I. Grouping on Multiple Fields

In this database, you have data from several different counties and many different years. Some of the years saw multiple tornadoes. You will use the AC2-0406 database, renamed `Arizona Tornadoes 4`.

Goal: Create a report using the Report Wizard that groups the data first on the county, and then on the year. You will also use an expression to make a two-digit year code into a standard year format.

The report you create should

- Use the County field as the main group field.
- Use the Year field as the secondary group field.
- Include all but the Damage field.
- Change the 2-digit year code to a 4-digit year code in the Year Header area.
- Be formatted to look like Figure 4.38.

Figure 4.38
The Arizona tornado data has been grouped according to county and year.

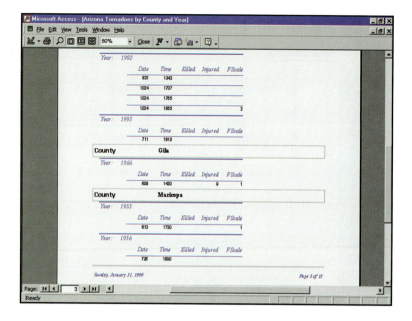

Name the report `Arizona Tornadoes by County and Year` when you are finished.

Hint #1: Changing the year code to a standard 4-digit format is rather tricky. If you use the =SUM function, it will work when there is only one record for that year, but will add the numbers together when there are multiple entries. Think about what the formula actually does, and you may be able to come up with a way to make this procedure work.

2. Adding Subtotals and Grand Totals

Subtotals for each year would probably be unnecessary, but subtotals for the county and state would be very helpful in the Arizona Tornadoes 4 database.

Goal: Add subtotals for each county, and a grand total for the entire database.

The report you create should

- Add a subtotal for each county, but not each year.
- Add a grand total for the entire state. This should be displayed at the end of the report.
- Be formatted to look like Figure 4.39.

Figure 4.39
Subtotals and a grand total have been added to the Arizona tornado report.

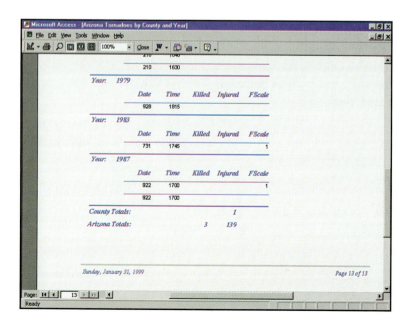

Project 5

Automating Your Database with Macros

Objectives

In this project, you learn how to

- ➤ Create a Macro to Open a Form in the Edit Mode
- ➤ Create a Macro to Open a Form in the Add Mode
- ➤ Create a Macro to Open a Form in the Read Only Mode
- ➤ Create a Macro to Open a Report in Preview View
- ➤ Create a Macro to Close a Form
- ➤ Run a Macro from a Button on a Form
- ➤ Create Switchboard Forms
- ➤ Create a Macro to Automatically Launch the Main Switchboard Form

Key terms introduced in this project include

- ■ actions
- ■ macros
- ■ arguments
- ■ switchboard

Why Would I Do This?

Ｏne of the functions that computers are best suited for is automating repetitive tasks, and **macros** are the mechanisms that enable you to perform this automation. Access macros make your database applications more productive. A few simple macros can automate mundane, repetitive procedures.

Almost any action in Access can be assisted or completely performed by a macro. You can create a form with buttons that activate macros. You can also create an automated menu, referred to as a **switchboard**, that enables the user to preview and print reports, review table or query contents using forms, enter new records into tables, close windows, or complete any other task that a macro can perform by simply clicking on a button.

This project covers how to create a macro and how to enter **actions** and **arguments** that control the macro, as well as comments that describe the function of the macro. Actions are Access-defined functions that perform database tasks, whereas arguments are values needed for a macro to perform its function. You learn how to work with the Macro Design window and toolbar. You also learn how to name, save, and run macros. In some of the lessons, you create additional macros that are used to create a customized form to serve as a switchboard.

Visual Summary

When you have completed this project, you will have created a switchboard that launches automatically when you launch the database.

Figure 5.1
A button that activates a Close macro has been added to a form.

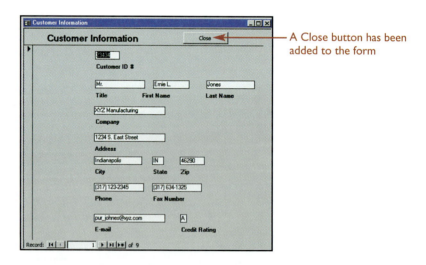

A Close button has been added to the form

Figure 5.2
The switchboard acts as a button-activated menu to help automate your database.

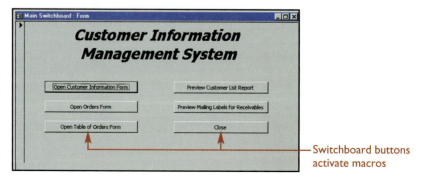

Switchboard buttons activate macros

Lesson 1: Creating a Macro to Open a Form in the Edit Mode

You create Access macros by starting with an empty Macro Design window, and then adding the actions and arguments that make your macro do its work. In this lesson, you create a macro that automatically opens a form allowing you to edit the records in a table or query.

To Create a Macro to Open a Form in the Edit Mode

1 **Copy the AC2-0501 file to your disk, remove the read only status, and rename it** Customer Orders 5.

2 **Open the Customer Orders 5 database, and select the Macros object button.**

3 **Click the New button.**
The Macro dialog box is displayed.

4 **Click the drop-down arrow in the first Action box and then scroll down and select the OpenForm option from the list of possible actions (see Figure 5.3).**
OpenForm is a macro instruction that automatically opens the form you select in the following steps. Scroll through the list of actions to see what is available.

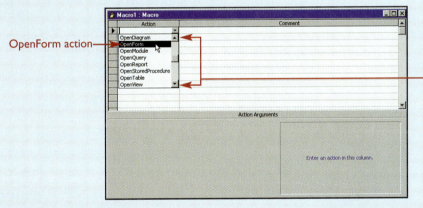

OpenForm action ──

Figure 5.3
The Macro window drop-down list shows available actions.

── Action drop-down menu

5 **Move the cursor to the Action Arguments section of the window and click the Form Name box.**
This box is used to select the form opened by the macro. After you click the box, a drop-down arrow appears at the right side of the box.

6 **Click the drop-down arrow and select Customer Information.**
The Form Name list shows all the forms in the database (see Figure 5.4).

continues ▶

To Create a Macro to Open a Form in the Edit Mode   (continued)

Figure 5.4
The Form Name drop-down list shows all available forms.

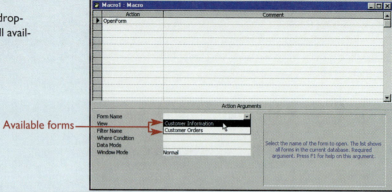

Available forms —

(i) When to Create Macros

You can create macros at any point while you are developing your database. It is usually best, however, to work on your macros after you have created all the other database objects.

---

7 Click the Data Mode box and use the drop-down list to choose Edit.
This enables you to edit or add records.

8 Click the Close button in the upper-right corner of the window, and save the macro with the name Open Customer Information Form.
Macro names can be used as command buttons on forms. When you name a macro, consider how its name would look on a command button in a form (see Figure 5.5).

Figure 5.5
The name you give a macro can be used on a command button in a form.

New macro

Run button —

(i) Renaming the Macro Button

If you don't like the way the text looks on a macro button, you can easily change it. In Design view, right-click on the button and select Properties from the shortcut menu. Click the Format tab and type the new text in the Caption box.

---

9 Click the Run button in the Database window to test the macro.
The Customer Information form opens automatically.

10 Close the Customer Information form.
Leave the database open for the next lesson.

A Quick Way to Select an Action in the Macro Window
A quick way to select an action in the macro window is to type the first letter of the action that is needed. The list scrolls automatically to the first action that begins with that letter. You can then click the drop-down arrow if needed, and select the specific action. For example, OpenDataAccessPage is the first action under O. By typing an O in the action box, OpenDataAccessPage is automatically filled in. Pressing Tab⇵ or ↵Enter then activates the argument section of the window.

Lesson 2: Creating a Macro to Open a Form in the Add Mode

When you open a form in Edit mode, you see the data from one of the existing records filling the form. If your intent is to add a new record, you must click the new record button to move to the next available empty record. It is possible to open the form directly to the next available empty record. This option is useful when you want to create a data entry form that allows the addition of records, but not the viewing of existing records.

To Create a Macro to Open a Form in the Add Mode

1 **In the Customer Orders 5 database window, click the Macros object button, if necessary, and click New.**
The Macro design window is displayed.

2 **Click the drop-down arrow in the first Action box, scroll down the list, and click OpenForm.**
The Action Arguments section of the window is displayed.

3 **Click in the Form Name box, click the drop-down arrow, and then select Customer Orders.**
The Customer Orders form is displayed in the Form Name box.

4 **Click the Data Mode box, click the drop-down arrow to show the list of data mode options, and select Add.**
The Macro design window should look like Figure 5.6.

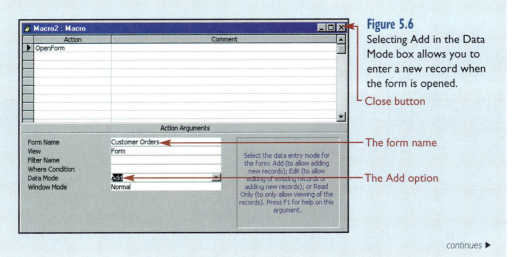

Figure 5.6
Selecting Add in the Data Mode box allows you to enter a new record when the form is opened.

Close button

The form name

The Add option

continues ▶

To Create a Macro to Open a Form in the Add Mode   (continued)

5 **Click the close button in the upper-right corner of the Macro dialog box.**

You are asked if you want to save the changes to the design of Macro1.

6 **Click Yes, and then save the macro as** Open Orders Form.

The database window appears with the new macro shown (see Figure 5.7).

Figure 5.7
The second macro is
displayed.

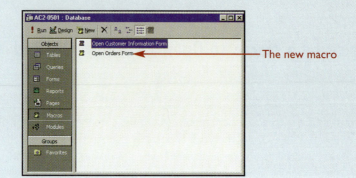

The new macro

7 **Select the Open Orders Form macro and click Run to test the macro.**

The Customer Orders form is displayed, ready to receive new data.

8 **Close the Customer Orders form.**

Leave the database open for the next lesson.

  Testing Your Macros

It is always a good idea to run each macro after it has been created to make sure it works the way you intended. You can run a macro by double-clicking on the macro name. You can also run a macro from the Design window by clicking the Run button.

Lesson 3: Creating a Macro to Open a Form in the Read Only Mode

In some cases, you may want to allow people to read the data in a table, but you do not want them to be able to change it. Access enables you to create a macro to open a form in the Read Only mode for this purpose.

To Create a Macro to Open a Form in the Read Only Mode

1 **Click the Macros object button, if necessary, and click New.**

This opens the Macro design window.

2 **Click the drop-down arrow in the first action box, scroll down the list, and click OpenForm.**

The Action Arguments section of the window is displayed.

3 **Click in the Form Name box, click the drop-down arrow, and then select Orders in Row-and-Column Format.**

The list disappears and the Orders in Row-and-Column Format form is displayed in the Form Name box.

4 **Click the drop-down arrow to show the list of data mode options, and then select Read Only.**

The Data Mode is now shown as Read Only (see Figure 5.8).

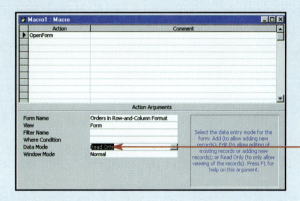

Figure 5.8
Selecting Read Only in the Data Mode box allows the user to look at the data, but not make changes when the form is opened.

— The Read Only option

5 **Click the Close button in the upper-right corner of the Macro window.**

You are asked if you want to save the changes to the design of Macro1.

6 **Click Yes, and then type the name** Open Table of Orders Form **in the Save As dialog box.**

The database window is displayed with the new macro shown.

7 **Select the Open Table of Orders Form macro and click Run.**

The Table of Orders form opens in Datasheet view and in Read Only mode (see Figure 5.9).

The title bar does not — indicate the form is Read Only

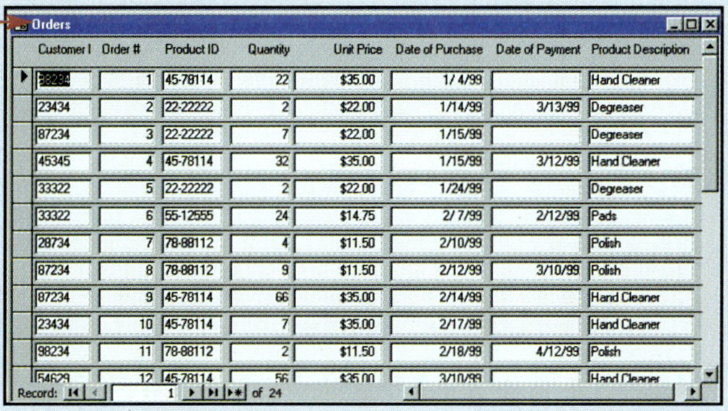

Customer I	Order #	Product ID	Quantity	Unit Price	Date of Purchase	Date of Payment	Product Description
23224	1	45-78114	22	$35.00	1/4/99		Hand Cleaner
23434	2	22-22222	2	$22.00	1/14/99	3/13/99	Degreaser
87234	3	22-22222	7	$22.00	1/15/99		Degreaser
45345	4	45-78114	32	$35.00	1/15/99	3/12/99	Hand Cleaner
33322	5	22-22222	2	$22.00	1/24/99		Degreaser
33322	6	55-12555	24	$14.75	2/7/99	2/12/99	Pads
28734	7	78-88112	4	$11.50	2/10/99		Polish
87234	8	78-88112	9	$11.50	2/12/99	3/10/99	Polish
87234	9	45-78114	66	$35.00	2/14/99		Hand Cleaner
23434	10	45-78114	7	$35.00	2/17/99		Hand Cleaner
98234	11	78-88112	2	$11.50	2/18/99	4/12/99	Polish
15462	12	45-78114	55	$35.00	3/10/99		Hand Cleaner

Record: 1 of 24

Figure 5.9
The table is opened in Read Only mode, even though the title bar does not indicate it.

8 **Try to change an existing record.**

Notice that no error message is displayed; Access does not allow any changes to be made.

9 **Close the Orders form.**

Leave the database open for the next lesson.

Lesson 4: Creating a Macro to Open a Report in Preview View

It is possible to open forms or reports in different data modes. Forms are usually opened in Edit, Add, or Read Only mode. Reports are opened in Preview view or sent directly to the printer. Because it is possible to print from the Preview view, it is a good idea to preview before you print to catch mistakes.

To Create a Macro to Open a Report in Preview View

1 **Click the Macros object button, if necessary, and click the New button.**
The Macro1 dialog box is displayed.

2 **Click the Action box and its drop-down arrow. Scroll down and click the OpenReport action.**
The OpenReport action is displayed in the Action column.

3 **Click the Report Name box in the Action Arguments section, and then click its drop-down arrow. Select the report named Customer List by City.**
The Report Name box now shows Customer List by City.

4 **Select Print Preview in the View box if it is not already selected.**
The Macro window should now look like Figure 5.10.

Figure 5.10
The Action Arguments are different for a Report action than for a Form action.

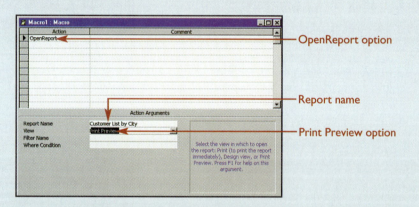

5 **Close and save the macro with the name** Preview Customer List Report.

6 **Follow steps 1–5 to create a macro that previews the Label for Each Receivable report. Name it** Preview Mailing Labels for Receivables.

7 **Run each of the new macros to see that they work.**
Keep the database open for the next lesson.

Lesson 5: Creating a Macro to Close a Form

It is possible for some macros to perform a generic function, such as closing a form, query, or table. The Close action closes whatever object it is attached to. This macro can be attached to a button that can be used by those who are less familiar with Access. In this lesson, you add this type of macro to the database you have been working on in the previous lessons. Later, this macro is added to several forms, so it can be used to close those particular forms.

To Create a Macro to Close a Form

 Click the Macros object button, if necessary, and click the New button.

2 **Click the Action box and select Close from the list of actions.**

Do not specify an Object Type or Object Name in the Action Arguments section of the design window (see Figure 5.11).

> ⚠️ **Creating a Generic Macro**
>
> By not specifying a form or report name in the Action Arguments area, you are creating a generic macro that you can use over and over again. You can attach this macro to many buttons throughout your database to close whatever window is active.

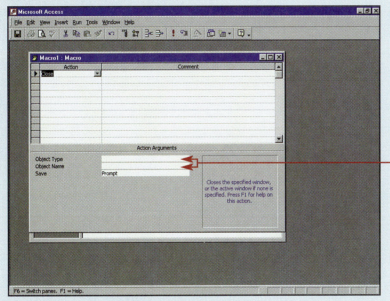

Figure 5.11
For a general action such as Close, no Object Type or Object Name needs to be selected.

The Object Type and Object Name boxes are left empty

3 **Close and save this macro with the name** `Close`.

> **Accidentally Closing the Database**
>
> You can accidentally close the database by using the button you created in this lesson. If you double-click the button while you are in the form, or double-click the macro from the Macros window, the database will close. You will not lose information if this happens—just reopen the database.

Keep the Customer Orders 5 database open for the next lesson.

Lesson 6: Running a Macro from a Button on a Form

Simple macros can be run from the database window. They are much more valuable, however, when they are attached to buttons on a form. This process creates the equivalent of a command button on a form that performs the action designated by the macro. A form can contain several types of command buttons. When you want to create command buttons specific to a particular form, it is better to use the Command Wizard in the

Form design window toolbox. In this lesson, you add the generic Close macro to several forms. This creates a command button on the form that will be used to close the form.

To Run a Macro from a Button on a Form

1 **In the** `Customer Orders 5` **database, click the Forms object button in the database window to display the existing forms.**

2 **Open the Customer Information form in Design view.**

3 **Choose Window, Tile Vertically to arrange the Database window and the form Design window so they do not overlap.**
This step enables you to see both windows clearly without overlap (see Figure 5.12). This is not a necessary step in the following process, but it is faster than dragging and resizing windows to see what you are doing.

Put the Close
Form window   macro button here   Database window

Figure 5.12
The Database and form Design windows are shown side-by-side.

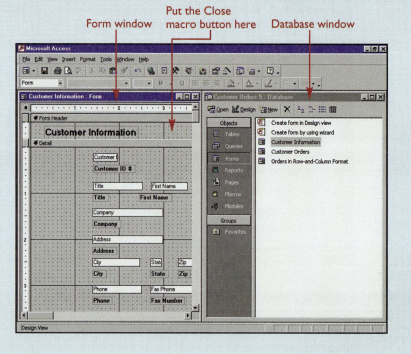

4 **Close the toolbox and properties windows, if they are open.**

5 **Scroll the form Design window so that you can see the right side of the form.**

6 **Select the Macros object button on the Database window to show a list of available macros.**

7 **Move the pointer to the Close macro. Click and drag it to the header in the form design window.**
A button is placed on the form when you release the mouse. It has the name of the macro on the button (see Figure 5.13).

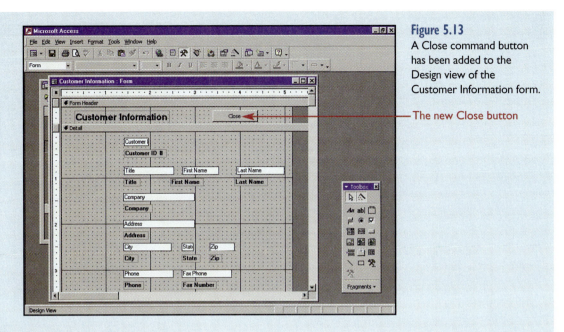

Figure 5.13
A Close command button has been added to the Design view of the Customer Information form.

— The new Close button

8 **Close the form and save the changes.**

9 **Click the Forms object button to display the names of available forms. Select the Customer Information form and click the Open button.**
Notice the new button in the form header (see Figure 5.14).

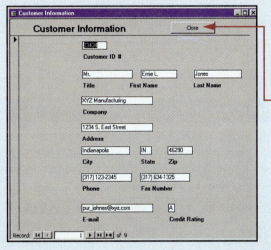

Figure 5.14
The Close command button has been added to the header of the Customer Information form.

— The Close button

10 **Close the form by clicking the new Close button.**

11 **Follow steps 2–8 to add a Close button to the header of the Customer Orders form.**

12 **Follow steps 2–8 to add a Close button to the header of the Orders in Row-and-Column Format form.**
Place the Close button to the right of the Product Description label in the form header (see Figure 5.15). If necessary, decrease the length of the button. Make sure the button and the right edge of the form do not extend past the 6 1/2" mark or the button will not fit on the page if you choose to print it in portrait mode, which is the default print setting.

continues ▶

To Run a Macro from a Button on a Form   (continued)

Figure 5.15
The Close command button is displayed on the Orders in Row-and-Column Format form.

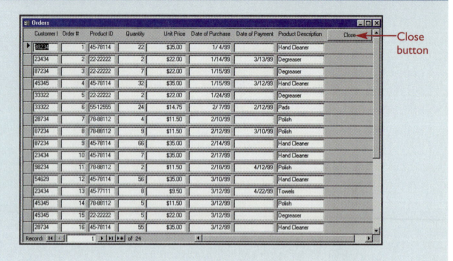

Close button

Keep the database open for the next lesson.

Lesson 7: Creating Switchboard Forms

It is possible to create a switchboard form that links all parts of the database. This allows part-time workers or others who are unfamiliar with Access to enter data and produce reports easily and conveniently. After you have created a new form, the process of creating the switchboard is broken down into three parts: creating a title, creating command buttons, and testing the switchboard.

The first step in creating a switchboard is to build a form to hold the buttons and labels you will need to make use of the database easier.

To Create a Switchboard and Add a Title

1 **In the Customer Orders 5 database, click the Forms object button, and then click New to create a new form.**
Do not select a table or query.

2 **Click Design view and click OK.**

3 **Open the toolbox by clicking the Toolbox button on the toolbar.**

4 **Click the Label button on the toolbox. Click and draw a rectangle near the top of the form.**
You can draw the box wider than the light gray work area. The work area will expand to accommodate the label box (see Figure 5.16).

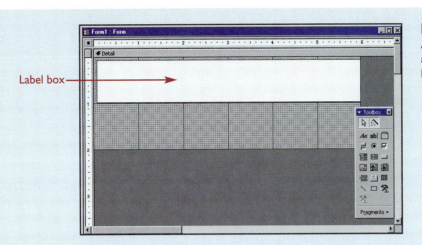

Figure 5.16
A label box has been added for the switchboard title.

Label box

5 **Type** Customer Information Management System **and press** ⏎Enter.
Handles appear on the edges of the label box. You can now format the label.

6 **Use the Font Size button on the toolbar to change the font size to 24.**

7 **Use the Center button on the toolbar to center-align the text.**

8 **Use the Italic and Bold buttons to enhance the text.**

9 **Adjust the size of the box to fit the title, if necessary.**
The new title should have two words on each line (see Figure 5.17).

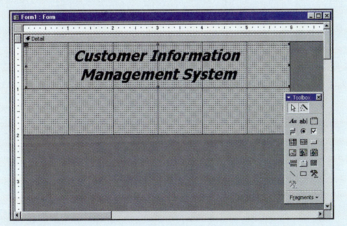

Figure 5.17
A title has been added to the form.

10 **Close the toolbox.**
Keep the form open for the next procedure.

The second step in creating a switchboard is to create buttons on the form to activate the macros that open and close the forms and reports.

To Create Command Buttons on the Switchboard Form

1 With the new form still open in the Design view, open the **W**indow menu and choose **T**ile Vertically to place the Database window and the form Design window side-by-side.

2 Click the Macros object button in the database window to reveal the available macros.

These are the macros you created earlier in this project.

3 Click and drag the **Open Customer Information Form** macro from the Database window to the form.

4 Click and grab the middle handle on the right edge of the button, and then adjust the size so that the whole macro name fits.

Your screen should look like Figure 5.18.

Figure 5.18
The Switchboard form is shown with a title and one button.

Switchboard button source macro ——

New switchboard button ——

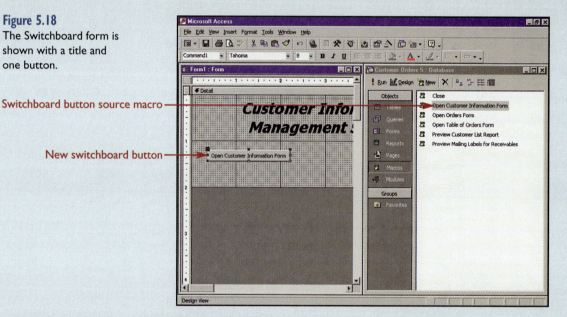

 If you didn't place the button where you wanted it, you can easily move it. Deselect the button, and then point to the button and click with your mouse pointer. When the pointer changes into a hand, you can drag the button to a new location. This is the same technique that is used to move text boxes around in a form.

5 Drag the following macros onto the form:
Open Orders Form
Open Table of Orders Form
Preview Customer List Report
Preview Mailing Labels for Receivables
Close

You will need to drag the macros into a column because you can't see the entire work area. You can drag a macro onto a dark gray section of the form if you want. The boundary of the form automatically expands to include the new button.

6 **Widen the design window. Adjust the position and size of the buttons so that their names fit on the buttons.**

> **Formatting Switchboard Buttons**
> To move more than one button at a time, you can click one button and then press ◆Shift+click to select additional buttons. After you have selected the buttons, you can move them as a group, or use the Format menu options to adjust size, alignment, and horizontal and vertical spacing.

When you are finished, your form should look like Figure 5.19.

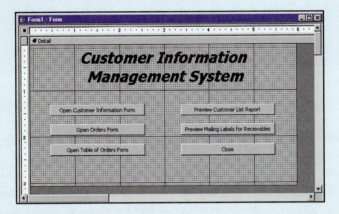

Figure 5.19
The Switchboard form is shown with all the buttons added.

7 **Select the entire form by choosing Edit, Select Form.**
By selecting the entire form, you can adjust the form's properties.

8 **Click the Properties button to open the Properties box. Find the Navigation Buttons property in the Format tab and change it to No.**
Switchboard forms are not used to scroll through records.

9 **Close and save the form with the name** Main Switchboard.
Keep the database open for the next procedure.

> **An Alternative Way to Create a Switchboard**
> A switchboard can also be created using the Switchboard Manager Wizard found under Tools, Add-Ins, if this wizard has been installed.

The final step in the development of a switchboard is to test it to see if it works.

To Test the Switchboard

1 **In the Customer Orders 5 database, click the Forms object button, if necessary.**

2 **Click the Main Switchboard form, and then click Open.**
The Main Switchboard opens (see Figure 5.20). Notice that the switchboard is not centered on your screen. You can always go back and adjust the location of the title and buttons in Design view.

continues ▶

To Test the Switchboard   (continued)

Figure 5.20
The Main Switchboard
form is displayed.

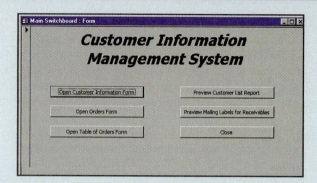

3 **Click the Open Customer Information Form button.**
The Customer Information Form opens.

4 **Click the Close button to close the form.**
The program returns to the Main Switchboard.

5 **Test each of the other forms in that column of buttons.**
Use the Close buttons you added to these forms to return to the Main
Switchboard.

6 **Click the Preview Customer List Report button.**

7 **Click the Close button on the menu bar to close the report.**
You did not add the Close button to the headers of the reports because you
view the reports in Preview view. This is not an interactive view, but an image
of how the printed report will look. Use the Close button on the menu bar
when previewing reports.

8 **Click the Preview Mailing Labels for Receivables button.**
Scroll through the report to view it. You may want to maximize the window.

9 **Click the Close button on the menu bar.**

10 **Click the Close button on the Main Switchboard form.**
Keep the database open for the next lesson.

Lesson 8: Creating a Macro to Automatically Launch the Main Switchboard Form

The Main Switchboard form now performs most functions needed for everyday use of
the database. You could turn the maintenance of the database and production of routine
reports over to a staff person with much less training on Access. It would be convenient if
the Main Switchboard form came up automatically whenever this database opened.
Fortunately, there is a special macro name that is reserved for this purpose.

To Create a Macro to Automatically Launch the Main Switchboard Form

1 **In the Customer Orders 5 database, click the Macros object button
and click the New button.**

2 **Select the OpenForm action.**

3 **Select the form named Main Switchboard in the Action Arguments area.**

4 **Click the second Action box and select Maximize from the drop-down list.**

This action maximizes the Switchboard form to fill the screen (see Figure 5.21).

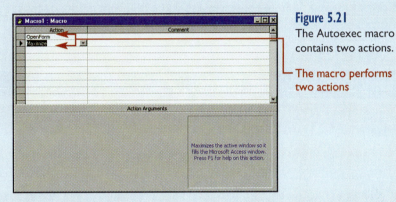

Figure 5.21
The Autoexec macro contains two actions.

The macro performs two actions

 Using More Than One Action in a Macro
You can use more than one action in a macro—in fact, you can build a macro that performs several functions or many complex activities.

5 **Close the macro and name it** Autoexec.
Do not include the period. This name means "automatically execute" and is recognized as a macro that is run whenever the database is opened.

6 **Close the database.**

7 **Open the database to test this feature.**
The Main Switchboard appears automatically.

 If your switchboard does not open automatically, it almost always means that you have misspelled the word "autoexec." If this is the case, click the Macros object button, right-click on the filename, and select rename from the shortcut menu. Correct the spelling of the filename and try it again.

8 **Close the Main Switchboard form.**
This takes you back to the usual Database window.

9 **Close the database.**
If you have completed your session on the computer, exit Access and shut down Windows before you turn off the computer. Otherwise, continue with the exercises.

 Closing Access with a Macro
You can also create a macro to close the database and Access at the same time. The action for that macro is Quit, with the Save All argument.

Summary

In this project, you created macros to open forms in Edit, Add, and Read Only modes. You opened a report in Preview view, and created a generic macro that can be used to close any form. You placed macros on buttons on several forms, and created a switchboard to act as a menu for your database. Finally, you made the switchboard appear automatically every time you open the database by adding an Autoexec form.

You can enhance your knowledge of macros by using the available help to examine other types of arguments you can use. You might also find out if there are ways to run macros other than attaching them to buttons.

Checking Concepts and Terms

True/False

For each of the following statements, check *T* or *F* to indicate whether the statement is true or false.

__T __F   **1.** Read Only mode is a macro option that prevents changes when previewing reports. [L3]

__T __F   **2.** A switchboard can be a form with macro buttons. [L7]

__T __F   **3.** Actions in a macro can be chosen from a drop-down list. [L1]

__T __F   **4.** If you name a macro Autorun, it will run each time the database is opened. [L8]

__T __F   **5.** One way to create a command button on a form is to drag a macro from the list of macros in the database window onto the form. [L6]

__T __F   **6.** In the Action box of the Macro window, you can type the first letter of the desired action to quickly scroll to the actions that begin with that letter. [L1]

__T __F   **7.** If you use the Add mode for an OpenForm macro, the form that is opened can be used to add new records or to edit existing ones. [L2]

__T __F   **8.** Each macro can perform only one action. [L8]

__T __F   **9.** A generic Close macro does not have to specify an object name. [L5]

__T __F **10.** A switchboard is a useful tool for a database that will be maintained by someone who does not know much about Access. [L7]

Multiple Choice

Circle the letter of the correct answer for each of the following questions.

1. An easy way to automate repetitive tasks is to use _____. [Intro]
   a. a macro
   b. the drag-and-drop procedure
   c. the Automate command
   d. the Repeat button

2. A value needed for a macro to continue its action is called a(n) _____. [Intro]
   a. action
   b. macro
   c. function
   d. argument

3. Which of the following data modes would enable the user to enter new records in a form without scrolling to the next empty record? [L2]
   a. Read Only
   b. New Record
   c. Edit
   d. Add

4. The form that is used as a switchboard _____. [L7]
   a. is always based on a select query
   b. is not directly based on any table or query
   c. must always be opened from the database window under the forms object button
   d. should only be used by advanced users

5. Immediately after creating a macro, you should _____. [L2]
   a. copy it to a working directory
   b. save it in a special macro directory
   c. sort the arguments alphabetically
   d. run it to test it

6. You can open a form using a macro in _____ mode. [L2]
   a. Preview
   b. Print
   c. Add
   d. all of the above

7. To make a form that is opened by a macro fill the screen, choose _____ as the second action in the macro. [L7]
   a. Expand
   b. Maximize
   c. Fill screen
   d. Optimize

8. To see the Switchboard form and the macro list at the same time, go to the Design view of the switchboard and choose _____ from the Window menu. [L7]
   a. Show Macros
   b. Cascade, and then click the Macros object button
   c. Tile Vertically, and then click the Macros object button
   d. Display List

9. After a macro has been created, it should be run to _____. [L2]
   a. make sure it works as intended
   b. set the macro
   c. establish a macro program
   d. clear the macro path for a new macro

10. When you name a macro, it is best to use a name that _____. [L1]
   a. is one word
   b. includes the word "macro"
   c. is no longer than 10 letters or spaces
   d. would make sense if it were on a button

Screen ID

Label each element of the Access screens shown in Figure 5.22 and Figure 5.23.

Figure 5.22

A. Source object

B. Macro window Run button

C. Data entry/edit option

D. Switchboard button

E. Macro action

F. Click here to create a macro

G. Action view

H. Switchboard title

I. Macro design Run button

J. Macro on which button is based

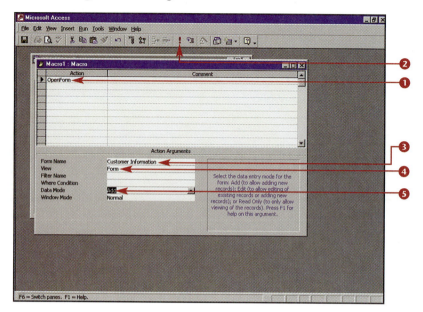

1._____   3._____   5._____

2._____   4._____

Figure 5.23

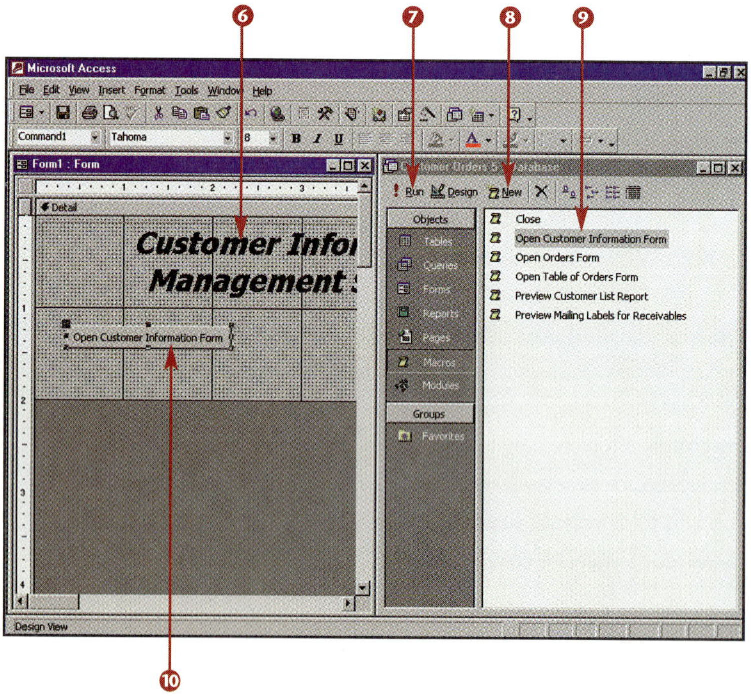

6._____   8._____   10._____

7._____   9._____

Discussion Questions

1. You created macros for forms and reports, but not for tables and queries. In a well-designed database, would there ever be a reason to use a macro in a table or query?

2. Buttons can be placed in a switchboard to go to a report print preview and also to directly print the document. Would it be a good idea to use both buttons on the switchboard, or just one? Why?

3. You can add buttons to both add and edit records in a form. Wouldn't the edit option suffice for both tasks? Why might you want to add both macros to your switchboard?

4. What are some of the things you might consider when creating buttons for a switchboard? Include macro names, button sizes and shapes, and switchboard layout. Might you want to add text boxes to the switchboard to give instructions to users? How would you do this?

5. If many different people are going to use a database, why would it be a good idea to use an autoexec form to run a switchboard? Could there be disadvantages to using this feature?

Skill Drill

Skill Drill exercises reinforce project skills. Each skill reinforced is the same, or nearly the same, as a skill presented in the project. Each exercise includes a brief narrative introduction, followed by detailed instructions in a step-by-step format.

In these exercises you use the Computer Inventory database you have used in earlier projects. In the Skill Drill section, you will create several macros, put them together in a switchboard, then set up the switchboard to run automatically.

1. Creating Add Macros for Forms

The people who use this database will be entering information into two of the forms—the Vendors form, and the Vendor and Hardware form. The third form is the PC Hardware Subform, for which you will create a Read Only macro in the next exercise.

To create add macros for forms, complete the following steps:

1. Copy the file AC2-0502 from your CD. Use the shortcut menu to deselect the Read Only status, and rename the copy Computer Inventory 5.

2. Click the Macros object button and click New.

3. Select OpenForm from the Action drop-down list.

4. Select the Vendor and Hardware form from the Form Name box in the Action Arguments area.

5. Select Add from the Data Mode box in the Action Arguments area.

6. Close the Macro window and save your changes as Add New PCs when prompted.

7. Repeat steps 2-6 to create a macro to open the Vendors form in the Add mode. Name the macro Add a New Vendor.

8. Leave the database open for use in the next exercise.

2. Creating Read Only Macros for a Form

In this exercise, you will create a Read Only macro for a subform. This will open the sub-form to show one record at a time. When you are finished creating a switchboard in Exercise 5, you will want to test this macro to see if it makes sense to open a subform independently of the main form.

To create a Read Only macro for a form, complete the following steps:

1. Click the Macros object button, if necessary, and click <u>N</u>ew.

2. Select OpenForm from the Action drop-down list box.

3. Select the PC Hardware Subform from the Form Name box in the Action Arguments area.

4. Select Read Only from the Data Mode box in the Action Arguments area.

5. Close the Macro window and save your changes as `Look at Current PCs` when prompted.

6. Leave the database open for use in the next exercise.

3. Creating Macros to Open Reports in Print Preview View

Three reports need macros so that the user can preview them.

To create macros to preview reports, complete the following steps:

1. Click the Macros object button, if necessary, and click <u>N</u>ew.

2. Select OpenReport from the Action drop-down list.

3. Select the Folder Labels by Processor from the Report Name box in the Action Arguments area.

4. Select Print Preview from the View box in the Action Arguments area.

5. Close the Macro window and save your changes as `Preview Folder Labels` when prompted.

6. Repeat steps 1-5 to create a macro called `Preview Mailing Labels` for the Mailing Labels for Vendors report.

7. Repeat steps 1-5 to create a macro called `Preview Vendors & Hardware Report` for the Vendor and Hardware report.

8. Leave the database open for use in the next exercise.

4. Creating a Close Macro and Attaching It to Forms

The next step in automating your database is to create a generic Close macro that can be used to close your forms.

To create and attach a Close macro, complete the following steps:

1. Click the Macros object button, if necessary, and click <u>N</u>ew.

2. Select Close from the Action drop-down list.

3. Close the Macro window and save the macro as `Close` when prompted.

4. Click the Forms object button and open the PC Hardware Subform form in Design view.

5. Move the pointer to the bottom of the Form Footer bar. When it turns into a black two-sided arrow, click and drag down about 1/2".

6. Choose <u>W</u>indow, <u>T</u>ile Vertically from the menu. Click the Macros object button in the Database window half of the screen.

7. Click and drag the Close macro onto the left side of the Form Footer area.

8. Close the PC Hardware Subform and save your changes when prompted.

9. Click the Forms object button and open the Vendor and Hardware form in Design view.

10. Choose <u>W</u>indow, <u>T</u>ile Vertically from the menu, and then follow the above procedure (steps 5-8) to add a Close button to the bottom of the Vendor and Hardware form.

11. Repeat the same procedure to add a Close button to the bottom of the Vendors form.

12. Leave the database open for use in the next exercise.

5. Creating a Switchboard

Now that you have created seven macros, you can put them together on a form to create a switchboard. This will act as a menu for people who use this database.

To create a switchboard, complete the following steps:

1. Click the Forms object button, if necessary, and then click New. Select Design View and click OK.

2. Click the Toolbox button to turn on the toolbox, if necessary. Click the Label button and create a label box that goes from the 1" mark to the 6" mark in width. Position the box near the top of the work area, and make it about 3/4" high.

3. Type Computers and Computer Vendors Menu in the box, and then press ⏎Enter). Use the toolbar buttons to make the text Arial, 24 point, bold, and centered.

4. Choose Window, Tile Vertically from the menu. Click the Macros object button in the Database window half of the screen.

5. Drag all the macros to the form Design window.

6. Maximize the form Design window. Increase the size of the Preview Vendors and Hardware Report button until you can read all of the text. Select all seven buttons and choose Format, Size, To Widest from the menu.

7. Align the three form buttons on the left and the three report buttons on the right. Center the Close button below the two columns.

8. Use the Align and Size options from the Format menu to align your buttons.

9. Click the View button to look at your switchboard. It should look like Figure 5.24.

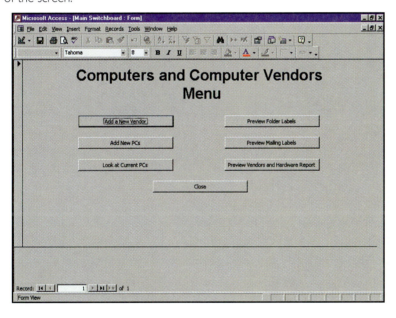

Figure 5.24
Your new switchboard should contain seven equal-size buttons.

10. Close the form and save your changes as Main Switchboard.

11. Click the Forms object button. Select the Main Switchboard and click Open. Try your switchboard buttons. Use the Close button on the toolbar to close the reports. Close the forms using the Close buttons you added.

12. Leave the database open for use in the next exercise.

6. Running Your Switchboard Automatically

The last step in your automation project is to run the switchboard when the database is launched.

To run your switchboard automatically, complete the following steps:

1. Click the Macros object button, if necessary, and then click <u>N</u>ew.

2. Select the OpenForm action.

3. Select Main Switchboard from the Form Name box in the Action Arguments area.

4. Click in the second action box row and select the Maximize option.

5. Close the window and save the macro as `Autoexec` when prompted.

6. Close the database, and then re-open it. It should run your new switchboard automatically.

7. Close the database. If you are not going to do the Challenge exercises, exit Access.

Challenge 💡

Challenge exercises expand on or are somewhat related to skills presented in the lessons. Each exercise provides a brief narrative introduction followed by instructions in a numbered step format that are not as detailed as those in the Skill Drill section.

The database you will use for the Challenge exercises is a slightly modified version of the Computer Inventory 5 database in the Skill Drill exercises.

1. Editing a Macro

When you opened the Add a New Vendor form and the Add New PCs form using the switchboard, you probably noticed that both forms opened in fairly small windows. In this exercise, you will have the macro maximize the forms when they are opened.

1. Copy the file AC2-0503 from your CD. Use the shortcut menu to deselect the Read Only status, and rename the copy as `Computer Inventory 5-2`.

2. When you open the database, close the switchboard.

3. Open the Add a New Vendor macro and add a Maximize action. Close and save your changes.

4. Open the Add New PCs macro and add a Maximize action. Close and save your changes.

5. Test your new macros to make sure both forms that open are maximized. Leave the database open for the next exercise.

2. Deleting a Macro and Its Macro Button on the Switchboard

When you ran your switchboard after completing Exercise 5 of the Skill Drill section, you probably noticed that creating a macro to open a subform was of little use. In this exercise, you will delete the macro, and then remove the button from the switchboard.

1. Display your list of macros on the screen and select the Look at Current PCs macro.

2. Press Del and click Yes when asked if you really want to do this.

3. Click the Forms button and open the Main Switchboard in Design view.

4. Select and delete the Look at Current PCs button. Don't bother rearranging the buttons at this point—you will be adding a few more in the following exercises.

5. Close the window and save your changes when prompted.

3. Creating a Macro to Run a Query

Most buttons on switchboards open forms or reports. There are also times when you will want to open queries from your switchboard.

Use the available help to discover how to create a macro to run a query. You will also need to find out if you can add the Close button to the query window, and if not, how you will get back to the switchboard from the query. Create the macro for the Vendor Name and Phone Number for each PC query. Call the query `Vendor Name and Number Query`. Have the query open in Datasheet view and in the Edit mode.

When you are through creating the macro, add it to the switchboard.

4. Dragging an Object into the Query Design Window

There is another way to quickly set up a macro. You can drag an object into the macro Design window. This will create an action and fill in various Action Argument options.

In the Skill Drill exercises, you created macros to let you add records to the Vendors form and the Vendor and Hardware form. You will use the drag-and-drop feature to create two macros that will enable the end-user to edit records in these forms.

Use the available help to find out how to drag objects into the macro Design window. Create two new macros to edit the Vendors and the Vendor and Hardware forms. Call them `Edit Vendor Information` and `Edit Hardware Information` respectively. Make sure you select the Edit mode.

When you have created the new macros, add them to your switchboard.

5. Copying, Pasting, and Editing a Macro

You will probably print the mailing labels fairly often, so it would be a good idea to have a button that will send the labels directly to the printer. You could create a new macro, but in this exercise you will use a shortcut.

1. Select the Preview Mailing Labels macro.
2. Click the Copy button, and then click the Paste button. Give the new macro the name `Print Mailing Labels`.
3. Open the Print Mailing Labels macro in Design view and change the View argument from Print Preview to Print. Close the macro and save your changes.
4. Add the Print Mailing Labels macro to your switchboard. Your switchboard is getting pretty messy.
5. Make all the buttons the same size, and change the font on the new buttons to Comic Sans MS.
6. Rearrange the menu so that it looks like Figure 5.25.
7. Save your changes, and then close the database. Open the database again and test the new buttons.
8. Close the database. If you are not going to do the Discovery Zone exercises, close Access.

Figure 5.25
A new button has been
added to the switchboard,
and the buttons have
been rearranged.

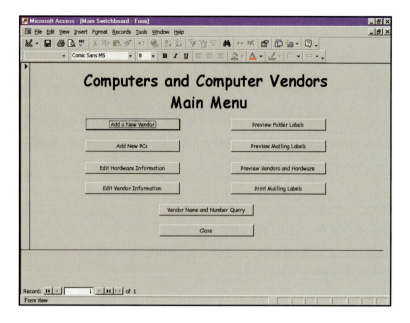

Discovery Zone

Discovery Zone exercises help you gain advanced knowledge of project topics and application of skills. These exercises focus on enhancing your problem-solving skills. Numbered steps are not provided, but you are given hints, reminders, screen shots, and references to help you reach your goal for each exercise.

The database you will be using is a modified version of the Computer Inventory database you have used in the Skill Drill and Challenge sections.

1. Setting Macro Conditions

Access enables you to set conditions when you write a macro. For example, you can have a report print only the equipment purchased between two dates, or print just those items that have an entry in a particular field. You will use the AC2-0504 database, renamed `Computer Hardware 5-3`.

Goal: Edit the Preview Mailing Labels macro to print only those vendors in a particular city.

- The macro you create should print mailing labels only for those vendors located in `Ypsilanti`.
- You should rename the macro `Ypsilanti Mailing Labels`.
- The button on the switchboard should match the macro name.

Hint #1: You can find help by clicking in the Where Condition box in the Action Arguments area and pressing F1.

Hint #2: Remember the requirements for identifying a field name in an expression!

2. Adding a New Option to the Menu

You can add menu options to your Access database. Some people prefer this feature rather than a switchboard, although you can have a switchboard and custom menu options in the same database. Adding a menu option seems a little tricky at first, but once you get the hang of it, you will be able to create one in seconds (assuming that all the database objects you need, such as forms, reports, and macros, have been created).

In some ways, customized menu options do not work quite the way you might expect. For example, if you create a custom menu option in a database and then move that database to another computer, the menu will not go along with the database file. After you have created the option, it will remain for every database opened on Access on that machine. It will, however, display whatever menu options have been displayed for each database. If you have not identified menu options in a particular database, this custom menu choice will not have options.

Note: If you are working in a lab environment, ask your instructor how to handle this situation. You may need to show your work, and then delete the new menu option.

Goal: Create a new choice on the menu bar and add nearly all the macros as menu options (see Figure 5.26).

In this exercise, you should

- Create a new menu choice called **Reports and Forms**.
- Add all your macros except Autoexec.
- Delete the new menu choice when instructed, if necessary.

Hint #1: Don't use help. Try the following hints first.

Hint #2: You will find a New Menu option in the Commands section of the Customize dialog box, which is activated by choosing View, Toolbars, Customize. Drag the New Menu in the Commands area to the toolbar.

Hint #3: Close the dialog box and drag all your macros into an open area on the menu bar. Open the Customize dialog box again, and then drag the macro icons to the new menu option and down.

Hint #4: When you are done, you can click and move the menu options up or down into a meaningful order.

Good luck! This one is tricky, but very useful once you get the hang of it.

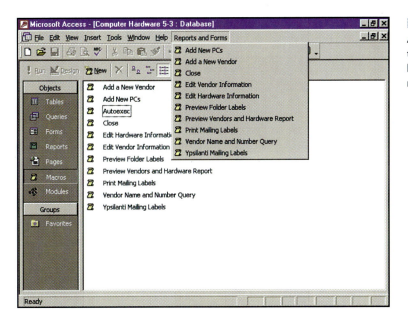

Figure 5.26
A new menu option, containing all your macros, has been added to the menu bar.

Project 6

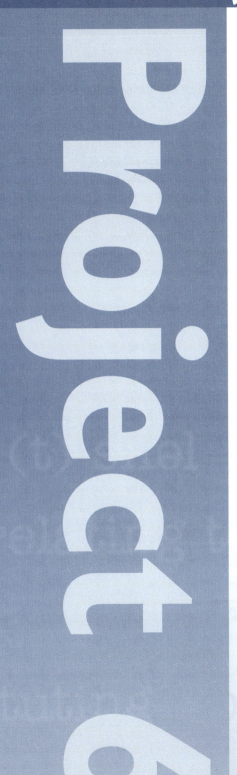

Managing Your Databases with Special Action Queries and Database Utilities

Objectives:

In this project, you learn how to

> **Make Backup Copies of Your Data**

> **Save an Access 2000 Database as an Access 97 Database**

> **Compact and Repair Files for Efficient Storage**

> **Use Detect and Repair to Fix Access Problems**

> **Generate a Query That Creates an Archive Table**

> **Modify the Archive Setup Query to Delete Records from a Table**

> **Create a Query to Append Records to an Archive Table**

> **Create a Macro to Run Two Queries**

Key terms introduced in this project include

- archive table
- compact
- delimiter
- Detect and Repair
- encrypt
- MDE file
- text qualifier

Why Would I Do This?

 atabases, particularly those used regularly, require some upkeep. This is true of a database for a user on a single machine or for a database used by many people on a network.

One of the first things every database user will learn, often the hard way, is to make regular backups of frequently used database files. Accidents do happen, particularly when more than one person uses the database. Files can become damaged or accidentally erased. If you have a regular backup plan, you can minimize the disruption that a file problem could cause. There are several ways to back up your data. You can use the copy-and-paste procedure to duplicate the file, or you can export the data in the tables into text files. You might also try backing up your data with either a commercial file backup program or with the Backup program that comes with Windows.

You may need to share a database with a colleague who is using the previous version of the program, Access 97 (also called Access 7.0). For the first time, Access enables you to save a database to be used with an older version.

When you delete and add many records to one or more tables in a database, the database file can become fragmented. This can cause the database to take up more room than necessary on your disk drive and can slow database operations. Access has a feature that loads the database into memory and puts the file back into a single block of information. This will speed up the program and save disk space.

Occasionally databases become corrupted, or damaged, and need repair. Sometimes Access detects the damage and prompts you to repair it. Sometimes you can repair the damage even if Access does not recognize that damage has occurred.

Another common problem is the proliferation of records in some tables. When a great deal of data is added to a table, the amount of time needed to do such things as search and sort can increase greatly. In some cases, older, "completed" records don't belong in a table. For example, a business that records customer orders in a table might want to remove them when a transaction is completed. Access enables you to move completed records from an active table to an archive table, and then delete the records from the original table. After the queries have been created to archive and delete completed data, you can create a macro and attach it to a button in the switchboard.

Visual Summary

When you have completed this project, you will have created a text file to back up your data.

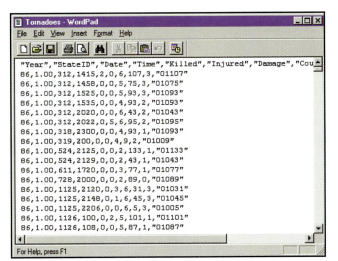

Figure 6.1
A large Access table has
been saved as a text file.

Lesson 1: Making Backup Copies of Your Data

One method of backing up your information is to export your tables into text files. This method will allow you to save the data in your tables without saving the design of your queries, forms, reports, macros, or modules.

There are several benefits of saving your data into text files. First, you reduce the file size by up to 90%. Second, you can read this type of text file directly into other databases, spreadsheets, and word processors. Finally, you can give the data set to someone using an earlier version of Access, such as Access 2.0 or Access 95. The other objects, such as reports and forms, will not be saved, but at least the user of an older version of the software can access the data.

In this exercise, you save the data from three tables as text files. The database you will be using is a record of the 10,845 tornadoes recorded in the United States over a ten-year period (1986-1995). The information was compiled from National Oceanic and Atmospheric Administration records.

To Make Backup Copies of Your Data Using the Export Feature

1 **Copy the AC2-0601 file to your disk, remove the read-only status, rename it** Ten Year Tornado Records, **and open the database.**

2 **If necessary, select the Tables object button and highlight the Tornadoes table.**
You must use the following procedure for each table you want to back up; Access only backs up the highlighted table.

3 **Choose Export from the File menu. Select the destination for your data file, accept the default File name, and select Text Files from the Save as type drop-down list.**
The Export Table dialog box should look like Figure 6.2.

continues ▶

To Make Backup Copies of Your Data Using the Export Feature (continued)

Figure 6.2
The Export As dialog box enables you to choose the data type of the new data file.

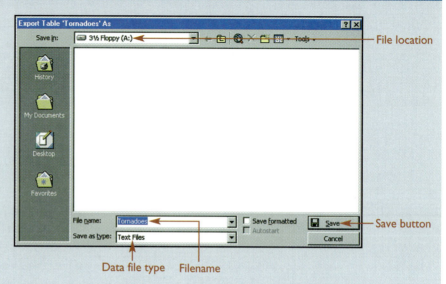

File location

Save button

Data file type   Filename

4 **Click the Save button in the Export Table dialog box.**
The first Export Text Wizard dialog box is displayed (see Figure 6.3).

> ⚠ **Field Delimiters**
> By default, the Delimited option is selected. A *delimiter* is an ASCII character, such as a tab, comma, semicolon, or space, that separates fields in a text file. This means that the contents of each field can be of variable length. The Delimited option saves disk space when the widths of field entries vary.

Figure 6.3
The Export Text Wizard dialog box enables you to choose an export format.

Delimited option

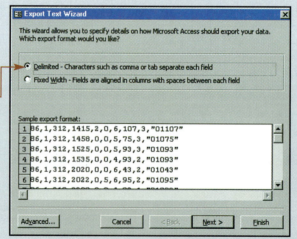

> ℹ **Filenames of Text Files**
> The default filename is the same as the table name. When the data is saved as a text file, the program adds a .txt extension, which will help you identify the types of the files on your disk.

5 **Make sure the <u>D</u>elimited option is selected, and then click <u>N</u>ext. Accept the defaults, but click the <u>I</u>nclude Field Names on First Row check box (see Figure 6.4).**

The type of delimiter used may depend on the application to which you are exporting the file. In this case you will use commas, which are the default choice. The default *text qualifier* is quotation marks. This means that every text field entry will be exported surrounded by quotation marks.

A comma is the
default delimiter

Include Field Names
on First Row option

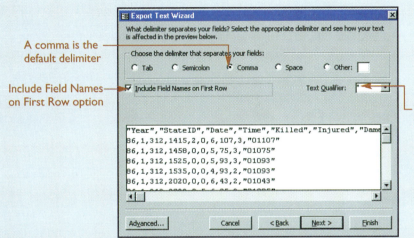

Figure 6.4
The second Export Text Wizard dialog box gives you the option of choosing a delimiter and a text qualifier.

The default text qualifier
is quotation marks

6 **Click <u>N</u>ext.**

The final Export Text Wizard dialog box is displayed (see Figure 6.5). This dialog box enables you to rename the file, if you wish.

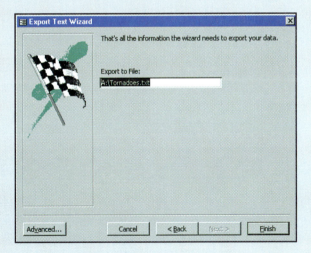

Figure 6.5
The final Export Text Wizard dialog box enables you to rename the file.

7 **Click <u>F</u>inish.**

A dialog box tells you that the text file was successfully created (see Figure 6.6). It also gives you the name of the file, including the extension.

continues ▶

To Make Backup Copies of Your Data Using the Export Feature   (continued)

Figure 6.6
A dialog box tells you that your data has been exported to a text file.

8 **Click OK, and then highlight the County Names table. Repeat steps 3 through 7 to export the data in the County Names table as text.**

9 **Click OK, and then highlight the State Names table. Repeat steps 3 through 7 to export the data in the State Names table as text.**

10 **Go to the Windows Explorer and look at the file sizes of the original file and the three table text files.**
   Notice that the text files, which contain all the data in this database, total about 450KB, whereas the original file is 1052KB. (Note: Your numbers may vary depending on which version of Windows you are using.)

11 **Double-click the Tornadoes text file.**
   The file opens up in WordPad (see Figure 6.7). Notice that the text field is surrounded by quotation marks, whereas numbers are not. The field names are displayed in the first row.

Figure 6.7
The exported text viewed in WordPad has quotation marks around the text field, with commas separating all fields.

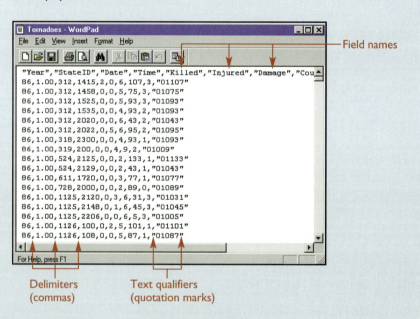

12 **Close the WordPad window and return to the Ten Year Tornado Records database. Close the database.**

 Backing Up Entire Files
In this lesson, you backed up only the data. If you want to make backups of your entire database, use the Windows Explorer (or My Computer) to copy the file and send it to a floppy disk, zip disk, or network drive.

Lesson 2: Saving an Access 2000 Database as an Access 97 Database

You may be working with a colleague who does not have access to Access 2000, or you may want to take the database home or to a lab that still has Office 97 installed. Access now provides a procedure for saving an Access 2000 database as an Access 97 database. It does not, however, allow you to save it in any of the earlier versions.

In this lesson, you take a database created in Access 2000 and save it as an Access 97 file.

To Save an Access 2000 Database as an Access 97 Database

1 **Copy the AC2-0602 file to your disk, remove the Read Only status, and open the database.**

2 **Choose Tools, Database Utilities, Convert Database, To Prior Access Database Version from the menu.**
The Convert Database Into dialog box is displayed.

3 **Type** PC Training-Access 97 **in the File name box.**

4 **Click the Save button.**
The new file is saved to your disk, but you are returned to the original AC2-0602 database.

5 **Close the AC2-0602 database. Open the PC Training-Access 97 database.**
Access no longer recognizes the database as an Access 2000 file. Instead, the Convert/Open Database dialog box is displayed (see Figure 6.8).

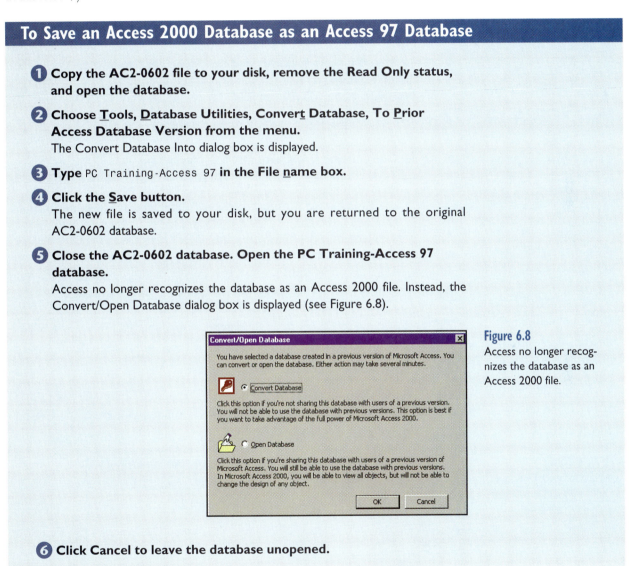

Figure 6.8
Access no longer recognizes the database as an Access 2000 file.

6 **Click Cancel to leave the database unopened.**

Lesson 3: Compacting and Repairing Files for Efficient Storage

After you use your database for a while, it is likely that some fragmentation will occur. This will cause the database to use more disk space than necessary and may cause the program to perform poorly. Access reserves room on the disk for tables, queries, forms, and reports that have been deleted. In this lesson, you will use one of the Access database tools to *compact* and repair the AC2-0602 database, which will strip out the extra blank space saved with the database. While it is compacting the file, Access will look for possible problems and fix them.

When you delete data or database objects from your hard disk, you create areas of un-used space of varying sizes that are scattered about the disk. The computer's operating system will try to use these spaces when you add new data. If the new data will not fit into one of the unused spaces, the system will divide the new data into segments and fit them into the available spaces. When you need to list your database, the computer must search the disk to find the segments and reassemble them. Also, when Access deletes objects from a file, it does not free up the area where the data was stored, but simply marks it as having been deleted.

To Compact and Repair Files for Efficient Storage

1 Go to the Windows Explorer and check the file size of the AC2-0602 database.
The database should be about 264KB.

2 Switch to Access and close any open database.

> **⚠ Compacting Databases Used On Networks**
> If you are running Access on a network, you must make sure that no one else is using the database file you want to compact. If the file is open at even one location, the compacting procedure will not work. One way to be sure you are the only one using the database is to select the filename in the Open dialog box, click the arrow on the right of the Open button, and select Open Exclusive.

3 In the Tools menu, choose Database Utilities, and then select Compact and Repair Database.
The Database to Compact From dialog box is displayed. This is the basic Office Find Files dialog box.

4 Find the AC2-0602 database and select it.

5 Click the Compact button.
The Compact Database Into dialog box is displayed (see Figure 6.9). This is similar to the basic Office Save As dialog box.

Figure 6.9
The Compact Database Into dialog box asks you for a new filename.

Type filename here

The Compact and Repair procedure creates a second database file. If you are using a floppy disk that is nearly full, you will get an error message. Remove some of the files from your floppy disk, or use a new one.

6 **Enter** AC2-0602 Compacted **as the new filename and click** **S**ave.

Access compacts the database with the new name. If you try to save the file as AC2-0602, a message box appears telling you the filename already exists and asking if you want to replace it. It is a good idea to use a different filename and use the old version as a backup.

7 **Switch to the Windows Explorer and check the new file size.**

The database should now be about 188KB (it may vary slightly). You may have to use the **V**iew, **R**efresh option from the menu to update the display. The compacting procedure reduced the file size by about a third.

 Compacting Files to Fit on Floppy Disks

If you have to transport your database files on floppy disks, this procedure can be extremely helpful. In many cases, you can take a database that is too large for a floppy and reduce it in size so that it will fit. If you have a very large database (up to 5 or 6 megabytes), you can use one of the commercial zip programs, which reduce file size by up to 80%.

Lesson 4: Using Detect and Repair to Fix Access Problems

When you install Access 2000 on your computer, many files are also installed. Over time, and with heavy use, some of these files can become corrupted or accidentally deleted. Office keeps track of the necessary files and offers a **_Detect and Repair_** feature to detect problems and repair them by copying them from the installation source. The source could be the installation CD or the installation source on your network. This feature is included in nearly all the Office applications. (The lone exception is PhotoDraw, which is a graphics program included with the Office Premium edition.)

To Detect and Repair Access Problems

1 **Launch Access (if necessary), but do not open any databases.**

2 **Choose** **H**elp, Detect and **R**epair from the menu.

The Detect and Repair dialog box is displayed (see Figure 6.10). Make sure the **R**estore my shortcuts while repairing option is selected.

continues ▶

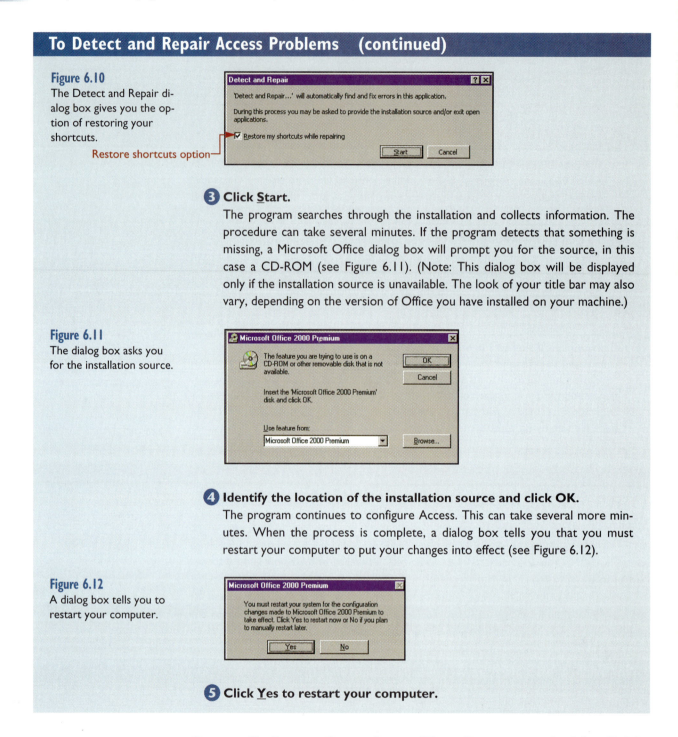

To Detect and Repair Access Problems   (continued)

Figure 6.10
The Detect and Repair dialog box gives you the option of restoring your shortcuts.

Restore shortcuts option

3 **Click Start.**

The program searches through the installation and collects information. The procedure can take several minutes. If the program detects that something is missing, a Microsoft Office dialog box will prompt you for the source, in this case a CD-ROM (see Figure 6.11). (Note: This dialog box will be displayed only if the installation source is unavailable. The look of your title bar may also vary, depending on the version of Office you have installed on your machine.)

Figure 6.11
The dialog box asks you for the installation source.

4 **Identify the location of the installation source and click OK.**

The program continues to configure Access. This can take several more minutes. When the process is complete, a dialog box tells you that you must restart your computer to put your changes into effect (see Figure 6.12).

Figure 6.12
A dialog box tells you to restart your computer.

5 **Click Yes to restart your computer.**

Lesson 5: Generating a Query That Creates an Archive Table

Setting up an archive of old records and removing them from the active table is a three-step process and is done with three queries. First, you generate a query to create an **archive table**. Then you create a query to append records to the archive table in the future. Finally, you create a query to remove the archived records from the active table.

The first step in creating an archive system for your database is to create the archive table. This archive table can be created in either the active database or another database. You will create the archive table and then either delete the query or change and rename it (as you will do in the next lesson). Running the query again would cause Access to write over the old archive table.

To Generate a Query That Creates an Archive Table

1 **Copy the AC2-0603 file to your disk, remove the Read Only status, rename it** Customer Orders 6, **and open the database.**

2 **Click the Close button to close the switchboard, click the Queries object button, and click New.**
The New Query dialog box is displayed.

3 **Select Design View from the New Query dialog box, and then click OK.**
The Show Table dialog box is displayed (see Figure 6.13).

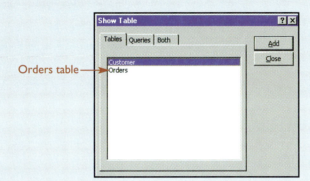

Orders table ——▶

Figure 6.13
The Show Table dialog box lists the tables available for your query.

4 **Select the Orders table, click Add, and then Close the Show Table dialog box.**

5 **Select all the fields and add them to the Field row.**

6 **Use the scrollbar to move to the right until you can see the Date of Payment field, and then type** >0 **in the Date of Payment Criteria box.**
The >0 (greater than zero) identifies those records that have an entry in the Date of Payment field. Those that have been paid will be sent to the archive table. Your Query dialog box should look like Figure 6.14.

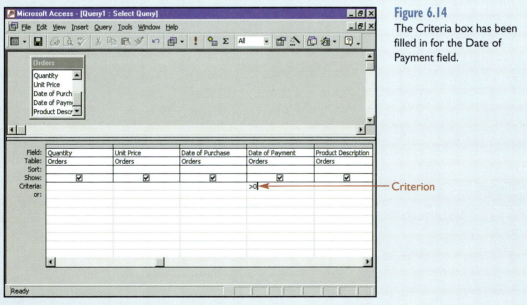

Criterion

Figure 6.14
The Criteria box has been filled in for the Date of Payment field.

continues ▶

To Generate a Query That Creates an Archive Table   (continued)

> ⚠️ **Problems with the Date Search Expression**
> Using >0 in the Criteria box for a date field works well if the dates you are looking for all occur on or after 01/01/1900. If you are working with historical data, you need to know that this procedure will not find dates before 1900.

 7 **Click the arrow on the right of the Query Type button, and then select the Ma̲ke-Table Query option.**
A Make Table dialog box appears, asking you what you want to call the table.

8 **Enter the table name** `Completed Orders`.
Accept the default of C̲urrent Database (see Figure 6.15). If your database is getting too large, you can use the A̲nother Database option in the Make Table dialog box to send the table to another database file.

Figure 6.15
The Make Table dialog box enables you to add the table to the current database or to another database.

Name of the archive table

9 **Click OK, and then close the query and name it** `Archive Setup`.
At this point, the query has been designed, but it has not created the table.

10 **Select the Archive Setup query and click O̲pen.**
A dialog box is displayed, warning that you will be modifying data in your table (see Figure 6.16).

Figure 6.16
The dialog box tells you that you will be modifying data in your table.

11 **Click Y̲es.**
Another message box appears, telling you how many records will be added to the new table, and warning you that you will not be able to undo this action (see Figure 6.17).

Figure 6.17
The message box warns that you will not be able to undo this action.

This warning is not as dire as it sounds in this instance. If you want to delete the new table, it is easy to do so. This message is more important when you are removing data.

⓬ Click Yes.
The table is created. Select the Tables object button to make sure a new table has been created. Open the new table. You will notice that only the records that have a date in the Date of Payment field have been copied. Close the table and open the Orders table. Notice that those records have not been removed from the Orders table.

⓭ Close the Orders table.
Leave the database open for the next lesson.

Defusing a Potential Make Table Query Problem
When you have confirmed that the appropriate records have been copied to the archive table, it is a good idea to remove the query that created the table. You can do this by deleting or changing the function of the query. This will ensure that no one will accidentally create a new table that writes over the archive file.

Lesson 6: Modifying the Archive Setup Query to Delete Records from a Table

In the previous lesson, you created a query to archive those records that have an entry in the Date of Payment field. That query is now of no use; in fact, it is dangerous to leave it in your database, especially if more than one person has access to the file.

The Archive Setup query copied records to the Orders with Payment Received table, but did not remove them from the Orders table. In this lesson, you will change the function of the query you created in the previous lesson from a Make Table query to a Delete query, which will delete the records that have been archived from the original table.

To Modify the Archive Setup Query to Delete Archived Records from a Table

❶ Click the Queries object button in the Customer Orders 6 database, if necessary, and right-click the Archive Setup query.
The shortcut menu is displayed.

❷ Choose Rename, and then type Delete Archived Records from the Orders Table.

❸ Click the Design button.
The Make Table Query dialog box is displayed.

 ❹ Click the arrow on the right of the Query Type button and select Delete Query from the drop-down list.

❺ Close the query window and save the changes when prompted.
Your Queries window should look like Figure 6.18.

continues ▶

To Modify the Archive Setup Query to Delete Archived Records from a Table (continued)

Figure 6.18
The Queries window contains the renamed query.

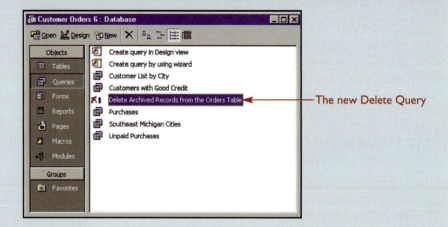

The new Delete Query

6 Click Open.
A dialog box appears, warning you that you are about to make a change to your table. This message is similar to one you saw in the last lesson (refer to Figure 6.16).

7 Click Yes.
Another dialog box appears, telling you that you are about to delete 7 rows and that you will be unable to undo these changes. This message is also similar to one in the previous lesson (refer to Figure 6.17).

8 Click Yes to delete the records from the Orders table.

9 Click the Tables object button, select the Orders table, and click Open.
Notice that there are only 17 records in the table now. The other 7 have been deleted.

10 Close the table.
Leave the database open for the next lesson.

Lesson 7: Creating a Query to Append Records to an Archive Table

You have now created an archive table and built a query to delete records after they have been copied from the Orders table to the archive. The last step is to create a Query you can use on a regular basis to move records from the active table to the archive table you just created.

You can create a new query following the same procedure used in Lesson 5, "Generating a Query That Creates an Archive Table." In this lesson, however, you learn how to save much work by copying the existing query and making one minor modification to it.

To Create a Query to Append Records to an Archive Table

1 **Click the Queries object button in the Customer Orders 6 database and right-click the Delete Archived Records from the Orders Table query.**
A shortcut menu is displayed.

2 **Select Copy from the shortcut menu.**

3 **Right-click an open spot in the window and select the Paste command.**
The Paste As dialog box is displayed (see Figure 6.19).

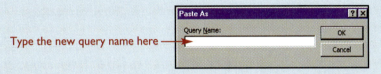

Type the new query name here

Figure 6.19
The Paste As dialog box enables you to give the new query a name.

4 **Type the name** `Append Paid Orders`, **and then click OK.**
You have copied the Delete Query and renamed it; now all you need to do is change the function of this new query.

5 **Highlight the Append Paid Orders query, if necessary, and click Design.**

6 **Click the arrow on the right of the Query Type button and select Append Query.**
An Append dialog box is displayed, asking you to which table to send the records.

7 **Click the drop-down list arrow in the Table Name box.**
A list of available tables is displayed (see Figure 6.20).

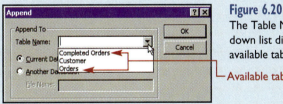

Figure 6.20
The Table Name drop-down list displays all available tables.

Available tables

8 **Choose the Completed Orders table, click OK, and then close the query. Save your changes when prompted.**
You are now ready to move paid orders to the archive regularly and to delete them from the Orders table.

9 **Click the Tables object button, open the Orders table and add dates to the Date of Payment field for Orders 7 and 12, and then close the table.**

10 **Click the Queries object button and open the Append Paid Orders query.**
This will run the query and append the records that meet the criteria to the specified table. You will again be warned twice that you are about to make irrevocable changes to your tables.

continues ▶

To Create a Query to Append Records to an Archive Table (continued)

11 **Open the Delete Archived Records from the Orders Table query to delete the records that meet its criteria.**

Once again, you are warned twice that you will not be able to undo your changes. Make sure that you use the queries in the correct order. If you delete the records first, they will be permanently lost.

12 **Move to the Orders table to make sure that order numbers 7 and 12 are gone.**

13 **Check the Orders with Payment Received table to make sure that order numbers 7 and 12 are there. Close the database.**

Lesson 8: Creating a Macro to Run Two Queries

In Lessons 6 and 7 you created queries to append completed records to an archive table, and then deleted the completed records from the original table. The problem with running these queries is that someone who doesn't understand the program might run them in the wrong order, deleting the completed records before they have been appended to the archive table. You can solve this problem by creating a macro to run the queries in the correct order. You can then attach the macro to a button on your switchboard.

To Create a Macro to Run Two Queries and Attach It to a Switchboard Button

1 **Click the Macros object button and click New.**

2 **Choose Window, Tile Vertically from the menu.**

3 **Click the Queries object button and drag the Append Paid Orders query to the first Action row. Drag the Delete Archived Records from the Orders Table to the second Action row.**

Your Macro window should look like Figure 6.21. Make sure the delete query is in the second row.

4 **Close the macro and save it as** Update Completed Orders**.**

5 **Click the Forms object button, select the Main Switchboard, and click the Design button.**

The Main Switchboard opens in Design view.

6 **Choose Window, Tile Vertically from the menu. Click the Macros object button.**

7 **Drag the Update Completed Orders macro to the Main Switchboard and maximize the window.**

8 **Resize the Update button, move the Close button, and move the Update button to the position the Close button previously occupied. Click the View button.**

Your switchboard window should look like Figure 6.22.

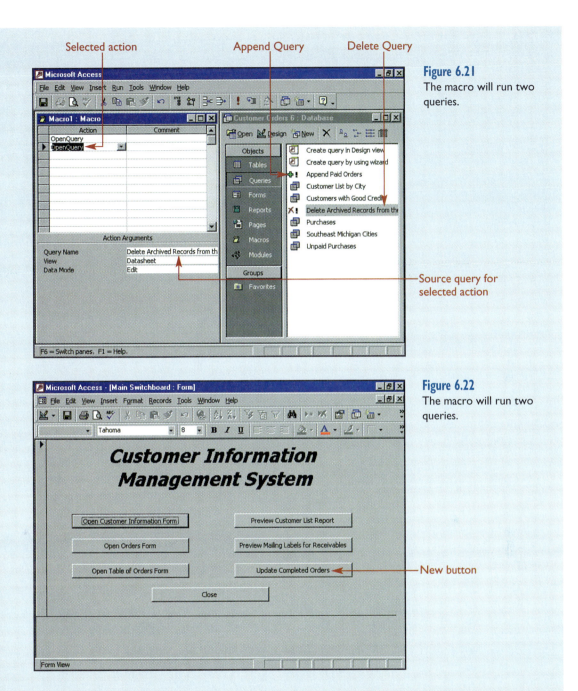

Selected action   Append Query   Delete Query

Figure 6.21
The macro will run two queries.

Source query for selected action

Figure 6.22
The macro will run two queries.

New button

9 **Close the switchboard. Click the Tables option button, open the Orders table, put a date in the Date of Payment field for the first order, and close the table.**

10 **Click the Forms object button and run the Main Switchboard. Click the Update Completed Orders button.**
Notice that you still have to respond to the confirmation dialog boxes.

continues ▶

To Create a Macro to Run Two Queries and Attach It to a Switchboard Button (continued)

 Turning Off Confirmation Dialog Boxes
You can turn off the confirmation dialog boxes by selecting Tools, Options and clicking the Edit/Find tab. In the Confirm area, you can turn off confirmation on record changes, deletions, and action queries.

⑪ **Close the switchboard and click the Tables object button. Check the Orders table to verify that there are fourteen records. Check the Completed Orders table to verify that it contains ten records.**

⑫ **Close the database and close Access unless you are going to proceed with the exercises.**

Summary

In this project, you looked at various ways to manage your database. You backed up data from tables to text files, and you converted an Access 2000 database to Access 97. You used Access and Windows tools to compact and repair databases and repair the program. Finally, you learned a three-step procedure for moving completed records to an archive table, and then you automated the procedure by adding a button to a switchboard.

You can enhance your knowledge of Access utilities by looking at the Tools, Security options in the menu, and then looking up these security features using the Office Assistant.

Checking Concepts and Terms

True/False

For each of the following statements, check T or F to indicate whether the statement is true or false.

__T __F **1.** When data from a table is archived as a text file, Access adds a .txt extension to the filename. [L1]

__T __F **2.** You can compact and repair a damaged file even if others are using the file on your network. [L3]

__T __F **3.** You can send records to an archive table in another database by using the Make Table Query option. [L5]

__T __F **4.** Once you have updated an archive table with an Append Query, it is a good idea to delete or change the query so that you won't accidentally write over your archive table. [L5]

__T __F **5.** You can save a database created in Access 2000 as an Access 2.0 file. [L2]

__T __F **6.** A text qualifier is a set of single or double quotation marks that surround text fields in a text file. [L1]

__T __F **7.** When you compact a database, it is a good idea to write the compacted version over the old version. [L3]

__T __F **8.** It is a good idea to keep the Make Table Query available in case you need to back up your data again. [L5]

__T __F **9.** If you use a Delete Query and decide you didn't really want to delete the records, you can recover them by clicking the Undo button. [L6]

__T __F **10.** You can turn off the confirmation dialog boxes that appear when you run a query to append or delete records. [L8]

Multiple-Choice Questions

Circle the letter of the correct answer for each of the following questions.

1. The <u>E</u>xport command from the <u>F</u>ile menu saves _____. [L1]

   a. only the highlighted table

   b. all the tables in the database

   c. the highlighted table and any associated forms, queries, and reports

   d. all tables, forms, queries, and reports

2. If you enter >0 in a date field's criteria box, you are asking the query to show _____. [L5]

   a. any records containing dates after the current date

   b. any records containing dates before the current date

   c. any records containing dates with only the year entered

   d. all records with any date (after 1900) in that field

3. The process of creating an effective archive table for storing completed records involves the _____ query types. [L5–7]

   a. Make Table Query, Update Query, and Append Query

   b. Make Table Query, Append Query, and Delete Query

   c. Make Table Query, Update Query, and Delete Query

   d. Update Query, Append Query, and Delete Query

4. You can convert Access 2000 databases to _____. [L2]

   a. Access 1 and 2 only

   b. Access 2 only

   c. Access 7 only

   d. all older versions of Access

5. To reduce the size of the database, it is a good idea to use the _____ command occasionally. [L3]

   a. <u>C</u>ompact and Repair Database

   b. <u>C</u>ompress and Repair Database

   c. <u>R</u>educe and Repair Database

   d. <u>P</u>ack Database

6. One reason to back up your tables as text files is to _____. [L1]

   a. save space

   b. read the file into other programs

   c. use with earlier versions of Access

   d. all of the above

7. A delimiter is _____. [L1]

   a. a set of quotation marks around text in a text file

   b. ASCII characters such as tabs or spaces used to separate fields in a text file

   c. a restriction as to how long a text file field can be

   d. a fixed-length field size in a text file

8. The Detect and Repair feature _____. [L2]

   a. finds problems with the Access program and fixes them

   b. is included with most Office 2000 applications

   c. replaces missing or damaged files from the installation source

   d. all of the above

9. The Detect and Repair option is found in the _____ menu. [L2]

   a. <u>F</u>ile

   b. <u>T</u>ools

   c. <u>H</u>elp

   d. F<u>o</u>rmat

10. The quickest way to create a macro that runs two or more queries is to _____. [L2]

   a. start a new macro, split the screen vertically, and drag the query names into the action column

   b. start a new form, split the screen vertically, and drag the query names into the action column

   c. select both queries, right-click on either one, and then select <u>C</u>reate Macro from the shortcut menu

   d. none of the above

Screen ID

Label each element of the Access screens shown in Figure 6.23 and Figure 6.24.

Figure 6.23

A. Delimiter

B. Text qualifier

C. Append Query

D. Run button

E. Action query source

F. Delete Query

G. Data record in text format

H. Query object button

I. Macro action

J. Field names

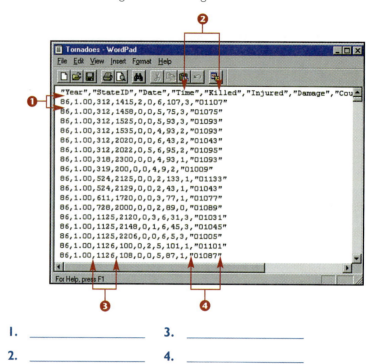

1. _____   3. _____

2. _____   4. _____

Figure 6.24

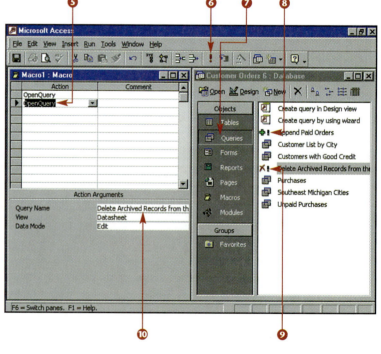

5. _____   7. _____   9. _____

6. _____   8. _____   10. _____

Discussion Questions

1. You learned several procedures to fix Access and repair and compact Access files. If you are working in a lab or network setting, which of these procedures might you want to use, and which should probably be left to the lab/network administrator?

2. It was mentioned in Lesson 8, "Creating a Macro to Run Two Queries," that you can turn off confirmation messages when using queries to append or delete data. When might that be helpful? What possible harm could come from doing this?

3. If you want to automatically confirm that completed records are removed from the Orders table when you run the update button on your switchboard, what might you do to the macro?

4. If you were to add the Close action to the update button you added in this project, what would happen?

5. Can you think of a way to append data to a table in the current database, and also to send the data to a backup database at the same time?

Skill Drill

Skill Drill exercises reinforce project skills. Each skill reinforced is the same, or nearly the same, as a skill presented in the project. Each exercise includes a brief narrative introduction followed by detailed instructions in a step-by-step format.

In these exercises you will use two databases that you have seen before. The first is the short story database, and the second is the video store database.

1. Creating a Data File from a Table

The short story table has an extensive list of short stories that you want to send to someone in text format. You will need to export the data to a text file.

To create a data file from a table, complete the following steps:

1. Copy the AC2-0604 file to your disk, remove the Read Only status, rename it **Short Stories 6**, and open the database.

2. Click the Tables object button, if necessary, and select the Short Stories table.

3. Select File, Export from the menu.

4. Accept the default name, **Short Stories**, and select Text Files from the Save as type drop-down list box.

5. Click the Save button in the dialog box.

6. Choose Delimited from the first Export Text Wizard dialog box.

7. Choose Comma as the delimiter, and quotation marks as the text qualifier. Also, choose to include the field names in the first row.

8. Click Finish to finish your text file.

9. Go to the Windows Explorer, find the Short Stories text file, and open it in WordPad or Microsoft Word to make sure the procedure worked.

2. Compacting and Repairing Files

Because you have added and deleted many records and database objects in this database, it probably includes a lot of wasted space.

To compact and repair a file, complete the following steps:

1. Close the Short Stories 6 database.

2. Choose Tools, Database Utilities, Compact and Repair Database from the menu.

3. Find and select the Short Stories 6 database.

4. Click the Compact button in the Database to Compact From dialog box.

5. Type **Short Stories 6 Compacted** in the File name box of the Compact Database Into dialog box.

6. Go to the Windows Explorer window and compare the size of the original database to the compacted one. The file size should be reduced from about 1160KB to 750KB.

3. Saving an Access 2000 Database as an Access 97 Database

Now you want to save the Short Stories 6 database in Access 97 format so that a colleague can use the file.

To save an Access 2000 database as an Access 97 database, complete the following steps:

1. Open the Short Stories 6 database.

2. Choose Tools, Database Utilities, Convert Database, To Prior Access Database Version from the menu.

3. Type Short Stories 6-Access 97 in the File name box of the Convert Database Into dialog box.

4. Click the Save button. A duplicate of the file in the Access 97 format is created, but you are left in the current database.

5. Close the Short Stories 6 database.

4. Generating a Query That Creates an Archive Table

The next three exercises repeat the archive creation lessons (Lessons 5-7). This time, you will be dealing with a small database of videos rented and returned from a video store. Take a look at the Rental Activity table to get a feel for the table with which you will be working.

To generate a query that creates an archive table, complete the following steps:

1. Copy the AC2-0605 file to your disk, remove the read-only status, rename it Video Store 6, and open the database.

2. Click the Queries object button, click New, and select Design View from the New Query dialog box.

3. Select the Rental Activity table, click Add, and then Close the Show Table dialog box.

4. Select all the fields and add them to the Field row.

5. Type >0 in the Date Returned Criteria box.

6. Click the arrow on the right of the Query Type button, and then select the Make-Table Query option. Call the new table Returned Videos.

7. Close the query and name it Archive Setup.

8. Select the Archive Setup query and click Open. Click Yes in both dialog boxes.

9. Click the Tables object button and open the Returned Videos table. It should contain three records. Close the table.

5. Creating a Query to Delete Records from a Table

Now that you have created an archive table and moved the completed records to it, it is time to modify the Make-Table Query to delete the completed records in the Rental Activity Table.

To create a query to delete records from a table, complete the following steps:

1. Click the Queries object button in the Video Store 6 database and right-click the Archive Setup query.

2. Choose Rename, and then type Delete Archived Records from the Rental Activity Table.

3. Click the Design button.

4. Click the arrow on the right of the Query Type button and select Delete Query from the drop-down list.

5. Close the query window and save the changes when prompted.

6. Click Open, and then click Yes in each of the warning dialog boxes.

7. Click the Tables object button, select the Rental Activity table, and click Open. The table should now contain five records.

8. Close the table.

6. Creating an Append Query

The last step in the process is to create an Append Query to append records to the archive table from the Rental Activity table for videos that have been returned.

To create an Append Query, complete the following steps:

1. Click the Queries object button in the Video Store 6 database, and right-click the Delete Archived Records from the Rental Activity Table query.

2. Select Copy from the shortcut menu.

3. Right-click on an open spot in the window and select the Paste command. Type the name **Append Returned Videos**, and then click OK.

4. Click Design, click the arrow on the right of the Query Type button, and select Append Query.

5. Click the drop-down list in the Table Name box.

6. Choose the Returned Videos table, click OK, and then close the query. Save your changes when prompted.

7. Click the Tables object button, open the Rental Activity table, add a date to the Date Returned field for Video ID 001, and then close the table.

8. Click the Queries object button and open the Append Returned Videos query. Answer Yes to both dialog boxes.

9. Open the Delete Archived Records from the Rental Activity Table query to delete the records that meet its criteria. Once again, answer Yes to both dialog boxes.

10. Open the Rental Activity table and the Returned Video table to make sure that the video was moved from the active table to the archive table.

11. Close the database.

Challenge

Challenge exercises expand on or are somewhat related to skills presented in the lessons. Each exercise provides a brief narrative introduction followed by instructions in a numbered step format that are not as detailed as those in the Skill Drill section.

The database you will use for the Challenge exercises is a slightly modified version of the Customer Orders 6 database that you used in this project. In these exercises, you will transfer data and use a couple of Access utilities to improve the database security.

1. Exporting Data to Excel

In Lesson 1, "Making Backup Copies of Your Data," you exported data from a table to a text file. In this exercise, you will transfer data to an Excel worksheet.

1. Copy the AC2-0606 file to your disk, remove the Read Only status, and rename it **Customer Orders 6-2**.

2. Open the database and close the switchboard.

3. Select the Orders table and choose File, Export.

4. Accept the default name **Orders**, select Microsoft Excel 97-2000 as the file type, and save the new worksheet.

5. Open Excel and open the Orders worksheet. Notice that the field names are automatically transferred to the worksheet, and you didn't need to use delimiters or text qualifiers.

6. Close Excel, but leave the Customer Orders 6-2 database open for the next exercise.

2. Creating a Text File from a Query

In the first lesson, you backed up your data from a table to a text file. You can use the same procedure to export the information from two or more tables at the same time by using the Export command with a Query.

1. Click the Query object button and select the Purchases query. This query contains fields from both the Orders and the Customer tables.

2. Choose File, Export from the menu. Use the default **Purchases** filename. Choose Text as a file type.

3. Delimit the data with tabs, and use quotation marks as text qualifiers. Add field names to the data.

4. Check your new text file in WordPad or Microsoft Word. Notice how different a file that contains mainly text looks from those that contain mainly numbers.

5. Close the word processor, but leave the database open for the next exercise.

3. Sending a Database Object to Another Database

There might be times when you need to develop a database that contains tables that are similar, if not identical, to tables that you have already created. Access enables you to send an entire table to another database, or just the underlying table structure with no data. You also can export other Access database objects, such as queries, forms, and reports, to other databases. Because these objects contain no data, you are not given a structure-only option.

In this exercise, you will need to use the available help to set up a database with an empty table, a query, a form, and a report. Create a new, blank database and call it **Customers**. Send the Customer table from the Customer Orders 6-2 database to the Customers database, but without data. Then send the Customer List by City query, the Customer Information form, and the Customer List by City report to the new database.

When you are finished, close the Customer Orders 6-2 database and open the new Customers database to examine the results of your database object exports. Close the Customers database when you are finished.

4. Adding a Password to a Database File

Earlier in this project you learned to use some of the Access utilities to manage files. Utilities are also available to help you maintain database security. One of the easiest things you can do to secure a database is to add password protection. This is very useful when you are using a database that contains sensitive or confidential information. You must be careful using passwords, however. If you forget your password, you cannot get into the database either!

1. Choose File, Open from the menu. You need to open the database in a special way to add password protection.

2. Select the Customer Orders 6-2 file, and then click the arrow on the right of the Open button.

3. Select Open Exclusive from the Open drop-down list. This ensures that you are the only one using this database, even if it is a shared database on a network.

4. Close the switchboard and choose Tools, Security, Set Database Password from the menu.

5. Type the word **Sunset** in the <u>P</u>assword box, type it again in the <u>V</u>erify box, and click OK. Make sure you type it exactly the same—passwords are case-sensitive, so "Sunset" and "sunset" are not the same!

6. Close the database, and then reopen it. Notice that the Password Required dialog box is displayed.

7. Type your password and click OK. (You can remove a password by choosing <u>T</u>ools, Securi<u>t</u>y, Unset <u>D</u>atabase Password from the menu.) Leave the database open for the next exercise.

 ## 5. Encrypting a File for Data Security

Sometimes your data is very confidential in nature. Even if your database is password-protected, someone who knows how could open your database with a word processor. Much of what appears will look like junk, but the data itself will be readable. There is a way to **encrypt** data so that even the text in the database is unreadable in a word processor.

Use the available help to figure out how to encrypt the Customer Orders 6 database. Save the encrypted file as **Customer Orders 6-2 Encrypted**. If you want to test the results, open Word, choose All Files from the Files of <u>t</u>ype box, and open both database files. Scan through them to see if you can find any of the database text in the encrypted file.

Discovery Zone

Discovery Zone exercises help you gain advanced knowledge of project topics and application of skills. These exercises focus on enhancing your problem-solving skills. Numbered steps are not provided, but you are given hints, reminders, screen shots, and references to help you reach your goal for each exercise.

1. Reading a Text File into an Access Table

In Project 2, "Managing Data Using Smaller, Related Tables," you saved the data from several tables into text files. The format you saved them in is very common, and if you download data files from the Web, they will often use comma delimiters, quotation text qualifiers, and have the field names in the first row. In this exercise, you are going to create a table using the data file you created in Project 2.

Goal: Create a table from the Short Stories text file.

In this exercise, you should

- Create a blank database and call it **Stories from a Text File**.
- Bring the data into a new table in your new database.
- Make sure the field names are defined during the process.
- Call the new table **Short Stories**.

Hint #1: You can find help in the <u>H</u>elp menu if you think about what type of data you are trying to bring into your database.

2. Creating an MDE File to Protect Your Database Objects from Being Changed

If you have designed a database that you are distributing, you might want to change the file to an MDE format. This enables users to run the database and manipulate data, use forms and queries, and print reports, but stops them from making changes to the structure of the forms and reports. Also, if you have done any programming in VBA (Visual Basic for Applications), your program code will be unavailable to the user. This procedure works well in some instances, but you must keep an original copy of the database in MDB (normal) format in case you want to make any changes (you cannot make changes in the MDE version either). Make sure you read the help information on **MDE files**!

Goal: Change an Access database to MDE format.

In this exercise, you should

- Copy and remove the Read Only property from the AC2-0607 file and rename it `Customers database in MDE format`.

- Change the file type to MDE. (Note: You will have two files named Customers database in MDE format. One will have an .mde extension and one will have an .mdb extension.)

- Close the database, go to Windows Explorer, and open the version of the database with the little lock in the icon.

- Attempt to change the form or report included with this database.

Hint #1: Read the Office Assistant help on MDE files before you begin.

Project 7

Using Access on the Web and Linking to Other Documents

Objectives

In this project, you learn how to

➤ **Add Hyperlinks from Forms to Word Documents**

➤ **Add Hyperlinks from Forms to Excel Worksheets**

➤ **Save Database Objects as Static HTML Pages**

➤ **View HTML Pages on a Local Drive Using a Browser**

➤ **Edit an HTML Document in WordPad**

Key terms introduced in this project include

- FTP
- HTML
- hyperlink
- Internet
- intranet
- LAN
- static HTML pages
- tag
- title
- UNIX
- URL
- Web browser
- Windows NT
- World Wide Web

Why Would I Do This?

Internet technology is changing the way people communicate within a company. Many companies are setting up private internets called **intranets**. These intranets use the same **Web browsers** that are used on the Internet, but are limited to company networks. For the purpose of brevity, the term "Net" is used in this project to refer to either the Internet or a company intranet.

The advantage of using the Internet or a company intranet to disseminate information is that you retain control of the data. Formerly, you made copies of your data and distributed them to the intended users. This method has two significant drawbacks: 1) the data may become out of date, and 2) some people in the company may need the information, but may not be on the distribution list.

If you publish your data on the Net, anyone may visit the site whenever they need the information, and you can make sure the information is current. Similarly, you can insert links from your forms, documents, worksheets, or presentations to sites provided by others.

Visual Summary

When you have completed this lesson, you will have created links from Access to other documents, and you will have created static Web pages.

Figure 7.1
A hyperlink has been added to connect a form to a Word document.

A hyperlink has been added to the form

A ScreenTip has been attached to the hyperlink

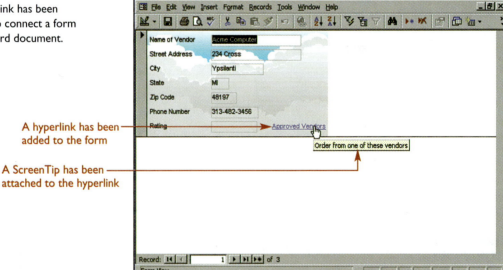

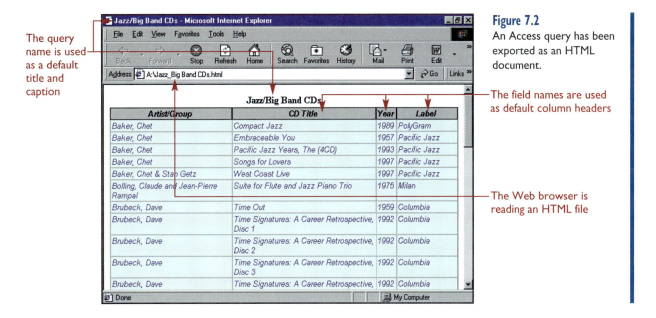

The query name is used as a default title and caption

Figure 7.2
An Access query has been exported as an HTML document.

The field names are used as default column headers

The Web browser is reading an HTML file

Lesson 1: Adding Hyperlinks from Forms to Word Documents

In this lesson, you use two files. The AC2-0701 file is a word processing document, and AC2-0702 is an Access database. Both are located on your CD-ROM. You create a link from a form in Access to a document written in Word. Access forms can contain **hyperlinks** that connect the user directly to documents stored on the user's personal computer, local area network (**LAN**), or the **World Wide Web**. Hyperlinks to other documents can be added to either forms or reports.

The database used in this lesson illustrates the kind of data that a department may keep for tracking purchases of personal computers. The Vendors table contains a list of vendors that can be used for corporate purchases. In this example, you assume that the purchasing department keeps a current list of approved vendors and makes that list available to other departments as a Word document. The vendor rating can change, and it is important that the user's purchase request reflect the current vendor rating. Access enables you to place a hyperlink in the Vendor Information form that allows you to check the current rating from the Purchasing department document.

To Create a Hyperlink Between an Access Form and a Word Document

1 Find the AC2-0701 file on your CD-ROM and open it in Microsoft Word.

A list of approved vendors is displayed (see Figure 7.3).

continues ▶

To Create a Hyperlink Between an Access Form and a Word Document (continued)

Figure 7.3
The Word document contains a rated list of vendors.

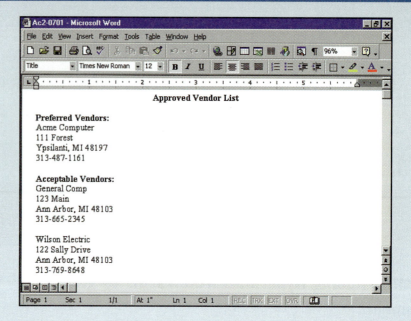

❷ Choose **File, Save As**, and save the document to drive A as Approved Vendors.

❸ Close the document and close Word.

❹ Copy the **AC2-0702** file to your disk, remove the Read Only status, rename it PC Purchases, **and open the database.**

❺ Click the Forms object button to reveal the available forms.

❻ Select the **Vendor Information** form and click the **Design** button to reveal the design of the form. Maximize the window for convenient editing (see Figure 7.4).

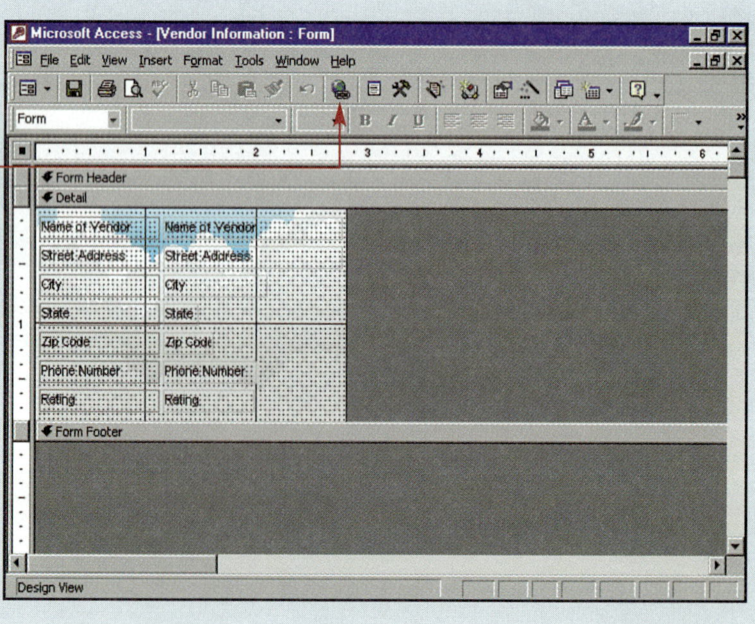

Figure 7.4
Hyperlinks may be placed in a form using Design view.

Insert Hyperlink button—

7 **Click the Insert Hyperlink button on the toolbar.**

The Insert Hyperlink dialog box is displayed (see Figure 7.5). The Inserted Links list will be active (as shown), although the Recent Files list or the Browsed Pages list could be displayed if someone used one of those options recently.

The link goes here →

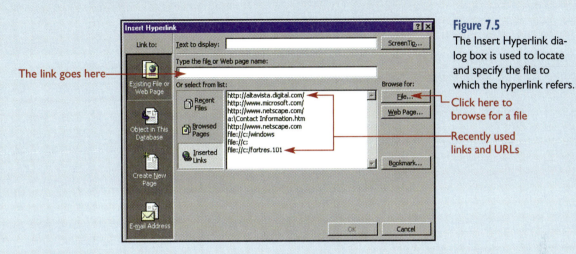

Figure 7.5
The Insert Hyperlink dialog box is used to locate and specify the file to which the hyperlink refers.

└ Click here to browse for a file

Recently used links and URLs

You can type the path to the file or the **URL** (Uniform Resource Locator) in the Type the file or Web page name box. A URL is also known as an Internet address. In this example, the file is on a disk, and the File button to the right of the box helps you find the Approved Vendors file that you opened earlier in this lesson.

8 **Click the File button in the Insert Hyperlink dialog box. Use the buttons on the toolbar of this dialog box to find the Approved Vendor document used in the previous lesson.**

9 **Click the Approved Vendors document and click OK.**

The filename and location on the disk are added to the dialog box. Notice that the filename is also displayed in the Text to display box at the top of the Insert Hyperlink dialog box, and that it shows the file extension. This is the text that will be displayed on your form.

10 **Remove the .doc extension from the Text to display text box.**

Your hyperlink will now say Approved Vendors instead of Approved Vendors.doc. You still need to remove the file extension from the ScreenTip.

11 **Click the ScreenTip button in the upper-right corner of the Insert Hyperlink dialog box. Type** Order from one of these vendors **in the ScreenTip text box.**

The hyperlink will now say Approved Vendors and the ScreenTip will give further instructions (see Figure 7.6).

continues ▶

To Create a Hyperlink Between an Access Form and a Word Document (continued)

Figure 7.6
The text for the hyperlink has been changed using the ScreenTip button.

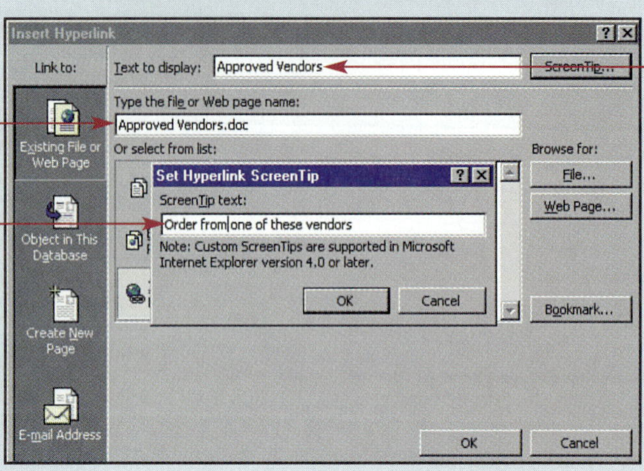

File to be hyperlinked to —

ScreenTip text —

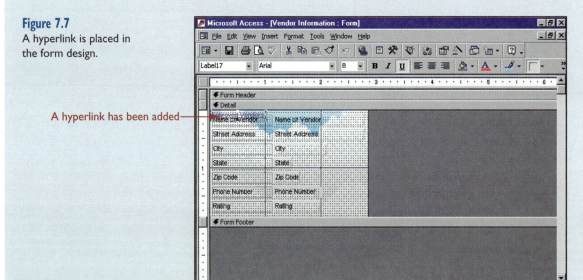

Text for the hyperlink

12 **Click OK to close the Set Hyperlink ScreenTip dialog box, and then click OK again to close the Insert Hyperlink dialog box.**
A link is placed on the form in the upper-left corner (see Figure 7.7).

Figure 7.7
A hyperlink is placed in the form design.

A hyperlink has been added —

13 **Deselect the hyperlink, and then click and drag the hyperlink to a new location to the right of the Rating field.**
You can drag the hyperlink and drop it in the gray area to the right of the current right edge of the form. The form widens to accommodate the hyperlink (see Figure 7.8).

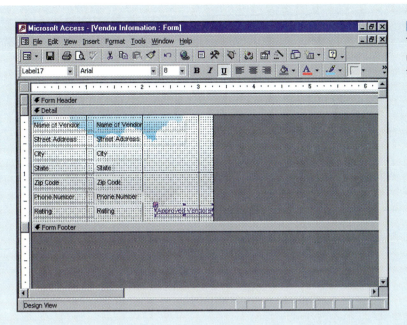

Figure 7.8
The hyperlink can be moved to another location in the form.

Formatting the Hyperlink

You might want to change the format of the hyperlink so that it stands out more. You can use bold or italic, or change the font or font size, but it is recommended that you not change the font color. Blue has become almost universally recognized as the color of a hyperlink, or "hot" spot on the screen.

14 **Click the View button on the toolbar to change to Form view.**
The hyperlink is displayed on the form in dark blue with underlined text.

15 **Move the pointer to the hyperlink on the form.**
The pointer changes into a small hand, indicating that this text represents a hyperlink. The ScreenTip is also displayed (see Figure 7.9).

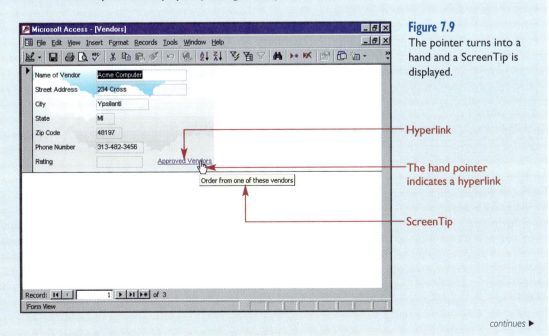

Figure 7.9
The pointer turns into a hand and a ScreenTip is displayed.

Hyperlink

The hand pointer indicates a hyperlink

ScreenTip

continues ▶

To Create a Hyperlink Between an Access Form and a Word Document (continued)

16 **Click the hyperlink to the Approved Vendors document.**

The Word program is launched, if necessary, and the Approved Vendors document is opened. The Web toolbar is turned on so you can move back to your original location (see Figure 7.10).

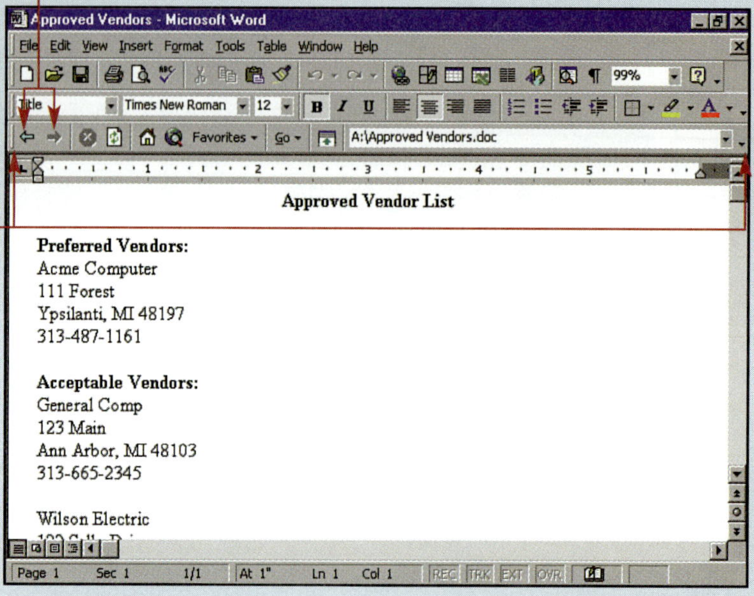

Navigation buttons

Figure 7.10
The Web toolbar is automatically turned on in the hyperlinked application.

Web toolbar

(i) **Displaying Only the Web Toolbar**

You will probably not edit the Word document that you have linked to, so it is often a good idea to close all the toolbars except the Web toolbar. You can do this easily by clicking the Show Only Web Toolbar button on the Web toolbar. The only time this might be an inconvenience is if you want to copy information from the linked document. If you have turned off all the other toolbars, the Copy and Paste buttons will be hidden, and you will need to use the menu or the keyboard shortcuts to perform these functions.

Leave the document open for use in the next section.

You can copy information from one file and paste it into another. You can also use navigation buttons on the toolbar to quickly jump back and forth between the files once the link is established.

To Copy Information and Move Between Linked Files

In this example, the address of the Acme Computer Company has changed since the last time it was used in the database, as shown in the Approved Vendors document. Because you are updating the database of computer orders for your division, you will want to update the Vendors table of the PC Purchases database.

1 **Select and copy the new address, 111 Forest, into the Approved Vendors document.**

> ❌ If the Show Only Web Toolbar button has been clicked, the Copy button will not be available on your toolbar. You can use the menu or keyboard shortcuts to copy the text, or you can click the Show Only Web Toolbar button again to turn on the Standard and Formatting toolbars.

2 **Click the Back button on the Web toolbar.**
This button returns you to the Access Form.

> ❌ The Web toolbar should open automatically when you use a hyperlink to move between applications. If for some reason you do not see the Web toolbar, go to View, Toolbars and click the Web option to turn on this toolbar. If the Back button does not work, you can still move between applications using the Windows taskbar.

3 **Select the old address for the Acme Computer Company and click the Paste button to paste in the new one.**

4 **In the Rating box, type** Preferred **(see Figure 7.11).**

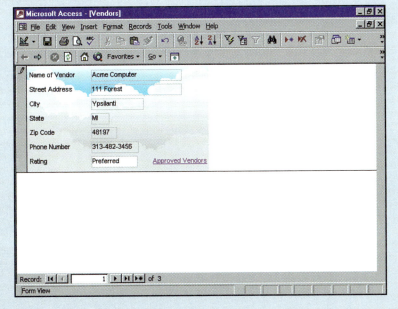

Figure 7.11
The information from the Approved Vendors document has been used to update the Vendors table.

5 **Click the Forward button on the Web toolbar to return to the Approved Vendors document.**

continues ▶

To Copy Information and Move Between Linked Files (continued)

6 **Close the document and close Word.**
The Vendor Information form should be displayed after you close the Word document. If not, use the taskbar to return to Access.

7 **Close the form and save the changes, if necessary.**
Leave the database open for the next lesson.

Lesson 2: Adding Hyperlinks from Forms to Excel Worksheets

You can establish links from Access forms to Excel worksheets in the same way you linked to a Word document in Lesson 1. In this lesson, you will connect an Access form in the PC Purchases database to a budget worksheet in an Excel worksheet.

To Link a Form and Worksheet

1 **Launch Excel and click the Open button. Find the AC2-0703 file on your CD-ROM and open it in Microsoft Excel. Save the file as** Computer Budget**.**
This will remove the Read Only status. This Excel worksheet represents the budget for computer purchases for three departments. It consists of a separate sheet for each of three departments—Sales, Marketing, and Engineering, plus a summary sheet showing computer purchases for all three departments.

2 **Return to Access and open the Orders form in Design view. Maximize the window if necessary (see Figure 7.12).**

Figure 7.12
Hyperlinks to worksheets may be placed in a form in Design view.

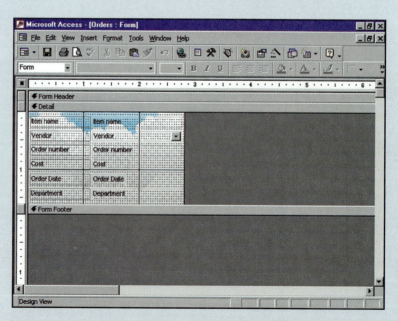

This form is used to enter computer purchase requests.

3 **Click the Insert Hyperlink button on the toolbar.**

The Insert Hyperlink dialog box is displayed.

4 **Click the File button and locate the Computer Budget file.**

5 **Select Computer Budget and click OK.**

The location of the file is entered in the Type the file or Web page name box (see Figure 7.13).

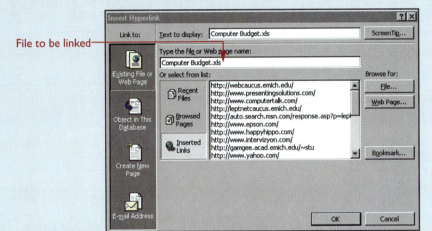

File to be linked

Figure 7.13

In the Insert Hyperlink dialog box, enter the name of the worksheet and its location using the Browse button.

6 **Change the name in the Text to display text box to** Computer Budget.

7 **Click OK to place the link in the form.**

The link is placed in the form in the upper-left corner.

8 **Drag the hyperlink to a position to the right of the Department field (see Figure 7.14).**

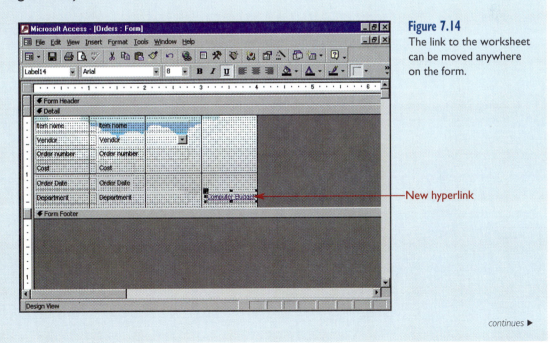

New hyperlink

Figure 7.14

The link to the worksheet can be moved anywhere on the form.

continues ▶

To Link a Form and Worksheet   (continued)

▣ ➒ **Click the View button on the toolbar to switch to Form view (see Figure 7.15).**

Figure 7.15
The hyperlink is displayed in the form.

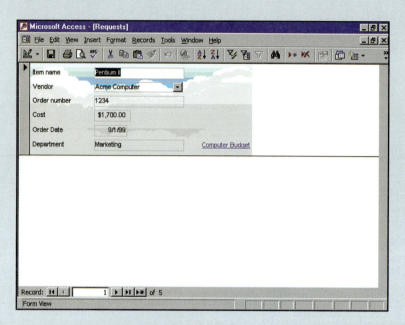

➓ **Click the hyperlink to move directly to the budget sheet to see if there is adequate funding for further computer purchases.**

The hyperlink launches Excel and opens the worksheet (see Figure 7.16).

Figure 7.16
The hyperlink launches Excel and opens the worksheet.

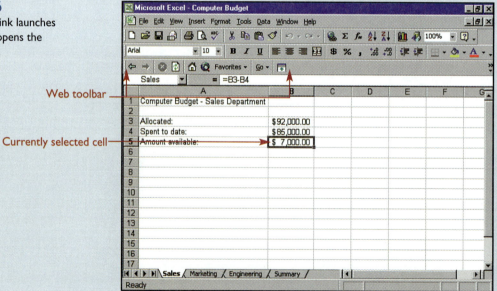

⬅ ⓫ **Click the Back button to return to your Access form.**

⓬ **Close the form and save the changes.**

You may want to use the taskbar to return to Excel and close the program.

⓭ **Close the database and close the Excel worksheet.**

Lesson 3: Saving Database Objects as Static HTML Pages

The World Wide Web is designed to be used by a variety of different computers that share a common way of sending documents to each other and a common way of viewing those documents. These documents are created with a special set of codes that tell the browser program how to display the text. This set of codes is called **HTML**, the Hypertext Markup Language. It is used to create a basic document that has a limited set of formatting features. Some browsers support additional features that are not common to all browsers. These browsers use additional HTML codes called extensions that handle features such as columns, tables, and animation.

In *Access 2000 Essentials Basic*, you created data access pages that enabled the user to interact with the data on the Web. Sometimes you will want to put information on a Web site that can be read, but not manipulated. In this lesson, you save a table and a query as **static HTML pages** that may be viewed by an Internet Web browser, but that are not interactive. These pages are also no longer linked to the database they were created from.

To Save a Table as an HTML Document

1 **Copy the AC2-0704 file to your disk, remove the Read Only status, rename it** CD Collection**, and open the database.**
This database is a compilation of music CDs, with the name of the artist, the CD title, and other information about each CD.

2 **Click the Tables object button, if necessary, and select the CD Collection table.**

3 **Choose File, Export from the menu.**
The Export Table 'CD Collection' To dialog box is displayed.

4 **Use the Save in box to select the disk to which you want to send the file, and choose HTML Documents from the Save as type drop-down list.**
The Export dialog box should look like Figure 7.17. The Export dialog box now reads Export 'CD Collection' As, indicating that you have selected a file type.

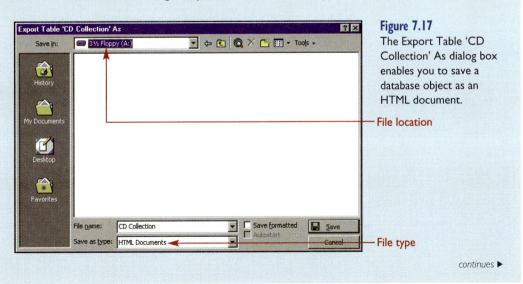

Figure 7.17
The Export Table 'CD Collection' As dialog box enables you to save a database object as an HTML document.

— File location

— File type

continues ▶

To Save a Table as an HTML Document   (continued)

5 **Click the Save button.**

The program determines a format for the data, and then writes all the data to a text file, with HTML instructions embedded in the document. This enables any browser to read the file and display it in the proper format. You will look at the results of this exercise in the next lesson.

 Many viewers and Internet server computers do not support filenames longer than eight characters or file extensions longer than three characters. Access saves the files with a four-letter extension, .html. If you view these files directly from your disk in the next lesson with an older browser, they will not link to each other properly.

When Access saves database objects as HTML documents, it adds a sequence number to the name of the file. For example, Form.html becomes Form_1.html. If the name of the table, query, form, or report is longer than six characters, the resulting filename will be longer than eight characters.

To avoid problems with older browsers and Internet servers, make a copy of any of the tables, queries, forms, or reports that will be saved as HTML documents to a name that is six characters or fewer. Export these copies as HTML documents. After the files have been created, edit the names and change the extensions to .htm rather than .html.

You use the same procedure to save a query as HTML as you used to save the table. In the following exercise, you will follow the same steps you followed above, but with one simple change that will significantly alter the look of the Web page.

To Save a Query as an HTML Document

1 **Click the Queries object button and select the Jazz/Big Band CDs query.**

This query displays a subset of the CD Collection table.

2 **Click the Open button to open the query.**

Notice that the query has a pale blue background with dark blue, italicized letters (see Figure 7.18).

Figure 7.18
The query has had several formatting changes added to it.

Jazz/Big Band CDs : Select Query	
Artist/Group	**CD Title**
Baker, Chet	Compact Jazz
Baker, Chet	Embraceable You
Baker, Chet	Pacific Jazz Years, The (4CD)
Baker, Chet	Songs for Lovers
Baker, Chet & Stan Getz	West Coast Live
Bolling, Claude and Jean-Pierre Rampal	Suite for Flute and Jazz Piano Trio
Brubeck, Dave	Time Out
Brubeck, Dave	Time Signatures: A Career Retrospective, Disc 1
Brubeck, Dave	Time Signatures: A Career Retrospective, Disc 2
Brubeck, Dave	Time Signatures: A Career Retrospective, Disc 3
Brubeck, Dave	Time Signatures: A Career Retrospective, Disc 4
Davis, Miles	Love Songs
Desmond, Paul and Gerry Mulligan	Two of a Mind
Desmond, Paul Quartet	Like Someone In Love
Dolphy, Eric	Out There
Dolphy, Eric and the Latin Jazz Quintet	Caribe
Dolphy, Eric Quintet featuring Freddie Hubbard	Outward Bound

Record: 1 of 46

3 Choose **File**, **Export** from the menu. Select a file location, choose **HTML Documents** from the Save as **type** drop-down list, and accept the default name.

4 Click the Save **formatted** check box.

The HTML file will now retain the formatting of the original document. The data is saved in table format by default. Your Export dialog box should look like Figure 7.19.

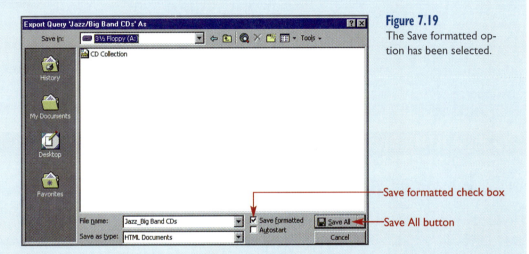

Figure 7.19
The Save formatted option has been selected.

Save formatted check box

Save All button

5 Click the **Save All** button.

The HTML Output Options dialog box is displayed (see Figure 7.20). You can use this option if you have design templates that you want to use. In this case, you will skip this step, because you are already using a formatted query.

Figure 7.20
The HTML Output Options dialog box enables you to add a design template if you so desire.

6 Click OK.

The HTML file is saved, along with your formatting.

7 Close the query and close **Access**.

You will not need Access to view or edit the HTML files in Lessons 4 or 5.

 The Select an HTML Template dialog box may not display HTML templates. To find them, you can use the **A**dvanced search to look for files with .htm extensions. If Microsoft Office is installed on your hard drive, the HTML files are usually found at C:\Program Files\MicrosoftOffice\ Templates\1033\.

Lesson 4: Viewing HTML Pages on a Local Drive Using a Browser

HTML documents are made to be viewed by a browser on the Internet. If you have a browser on your computer, you can open and view the documents created in the previous lesson, even if you are not connected to the Net. There are several brands of World Wide Web browsers, but the most popular ones share the features that are used in this lesson. The examples shown use Microsoft's Internet Explorer 5.0 browser, but you should be able to adapt the following commands to most other browsers.

It is common practice to check your HTML documents on your computer before transferring them to the computer that makes them available on the Internet.

In this lesson, you open both of the HTML files you created in Lesson 3, "Saving Database Objects as Static HTML Pages," so you can see the difference between the look of the file you saved using the default format and the file you saved with its own formatting.

To View HTML Documents Using a Web Browser

1 **Open the Windows Explorer and select drive A (or the folder in which you placed the HTML files you created in Lesson 3). Click the Details button, if necessary.**
If you are using a floppy disk, the Explorer window should look like Figure 7.21. You can identify your default browser by checking the file type.

Figure 7.21
The Explorer window identifies the Web browser you are using.

Internet Explorer icons

HTML files

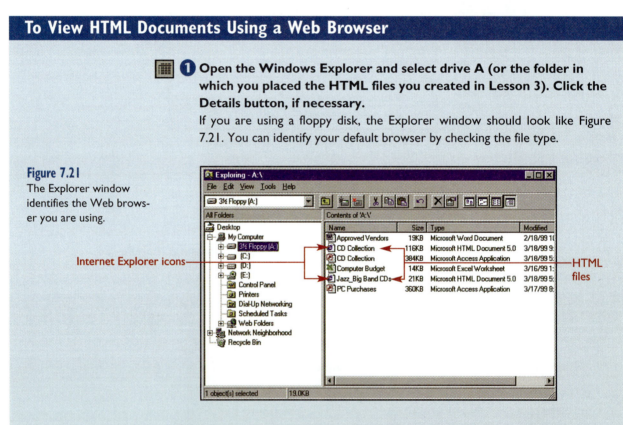

2 **Double-click the CD Collection file. Maximize the window, if necessary.**
The CD Collection table is displayed in the default HTML format (see Figure 7.22). The name of the table is automatically used as the page title. Notice that the information is wider than the screen, so a horizontal scrollbar has been added.

Access table name   Browser

Figure 7.22
The table is displayed in HTML format.

Address box

X If the file type for your HTML files says HTML File in Windows Explorer, and double-clicking the filename does not result in a table as shown in Figure 7.22, you probably do not have a Web browser in-stalled (or working properly) on your computer. Install (or re-install) a browser, or skip the rest of this lesson.

---

3 **Click the down arrow in the A̲ddress box.**

A directory of your computer is displayed (see Figure 7.23). If you were on the Web, you would see URLs instead.

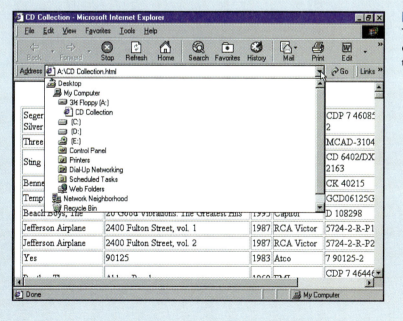

Figure 7.23
The Address box drop-down list displays a direc-tory of your computer.

continues ▶

To View HTML Documents Using a Web Browser (continued)

4 **Select 3 1/2 Floppy (A:) from the drop-down list.**
All the files on the floppy drive are displayed.

5 **Double-click the Jazz_Big Band CDs file.**
Internet Explorer opens the Jazz_Big Band CDs file created from the Jazz/Big Band CDs query (see Figure 7.24). The query name is again used as the page title, but the Access query formatting has been transferred to the Web page.

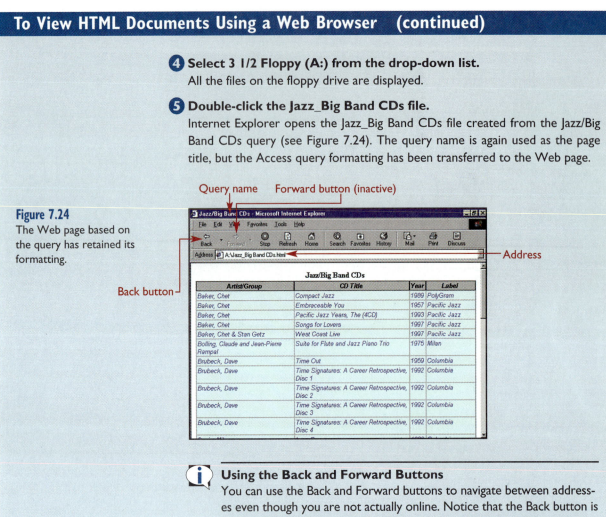

Figure 7.24
The Web page based on the query has retained its formatting.

i **Using the Back and Forward Buttons**
You can use the Back and Forward buttons to navigate between addresses even though you are not actually online. Notice that the Back button is active, indicating that you can click on it and move back to the previous document. If you click the Back button, the CD Collection page is displayed, and the Forward button becomes active.

6 **Try the Back and Forward buttons to move between pages. When you are done, close the browser.**
In the next lesson, you will edit the CD Collection HTML document.

Lesson 5: Editing HTML Pages in WordPad

The Hypertext Markup Language, HTML, is a standard method of describing the contents of a document so that the document can be displayed on a variety of computer platforms and monitor types. It is beyond the scope of this text to describe HTML in detail, but you should know how an HTML file is constructed and how to make simple changes.

In this procedure, you learn how to use WordPad to edit the HTML file you created for the CD Collection table in the CD Collection database.

To Edit the HTML Document

1 **Click the Start button in the taskbar. Select Programs, Accessories, WordPad.**
WordPad, a word processor often used to edit text files, is launched.

 Editing HTML Files
WordPad is a word processor included with Windows. It is used to edit text files. Because HTML files are saved in text format, WordPad is a popular HTML editor because it is so easy to use. It is not, however, the only program you can use to edit an HTML file. You can also use Word (or any other word processor) if you remember to save the file in text format.

You can also edit HTML files in Access. To do this, click the Pages option button, double-click the Edit Web page that already exists button, and find and open the HTML document. You will use this editor in one of the Challenge exercises at the end of this project.

2 **Choose File, Open from the menu. Select All Documents (*.*) from the Files of type drop-down list, and then choose the file location in the Look in box.**
Your two HTML documents should appear in the Open dialog box.

3 **Select the CD Collection HTML file and click Open.**
The CD Collection document is displayed in the WordPad window (see Figure 7.25). Because this data was taken directly from a table, there are no column headers; the data starts in the first row of the table.

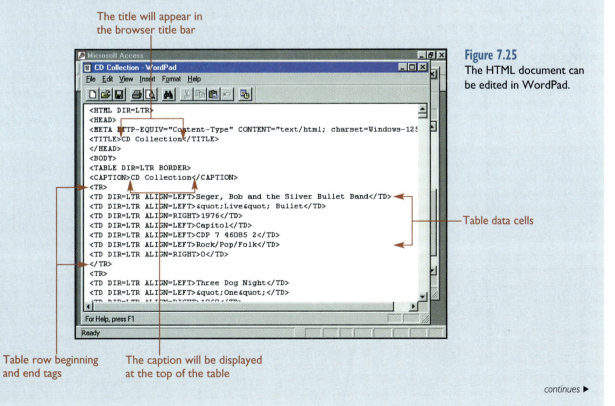

Figure 7.25
The HTML document can be edited in WordPad.

continues ▶

To Edit the HTML Document (continued)

 If the file does not open correctly, it could be that you tried to open the Access file called CD Collection. Try again, making sure that you select the HTML file.

 HTML Structure

HTML instructions are transmitted with *tags*—codes enclosed in angle brackets that begin and end an instruction. For example, in the fourth line of the example on your screen, the *title* of the document (which is the text that appears in the browser title bar) is enclosed by a <TITLE> beginning tag and a </TITLE> end tag. Notice that the second tag uses a slash to indicate the end of an instruction. The paired tags do not need to be on the same line of text (notice lines two and five). Finally, HTML tags are not case-sensitive—<TITLE> and <title> are identical instructions.

Each record in the table takes eleven lines in WordPad. Each row of the table begins with a table row (<TR>) tag and ends with an end table row (</TR>) tag. In between are the individual table data cells, which begin and end with the <TD> and </TD> tags. Notice that there are some further instructions in the beginning table data cell tags.

4 **Highlight the caption text and replace it with** The CD Collection of <your name>.

The caption is always given the default name of the database object on which it was based. Put your name in the title in place of <your name>.

5 **Add bold tags (<B> and </B>) before and after your new title.**

Your title will now be formatted as bold text. The WordPad document should look like Figure 7.26.

Figure 7.26
The caption text has been edited and bold tags have been added.

New tags have been added to the caption

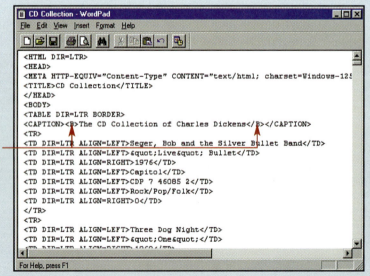

6 **Click the Save button on the toolbar.**

A dialog box informs you that saving the document in text-only format will remove all formatting (see Figure 7.27). This is exactly what you want.

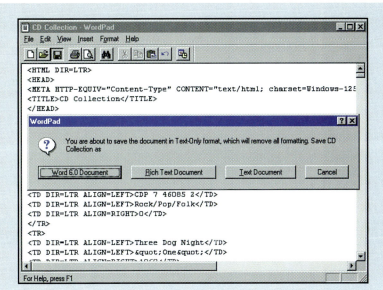

Figure 7.27
A dialog box asks if you want to save the document as text-only.

7 **Click the Text Document button, and then close WordPad.**

8 **Find the CD Collection document in the Windows Explorer and double-click it.**

The document is opened in your default Web browser. Notice that the caption is changed and the caption text is boldfaced (see Figure 7.28).

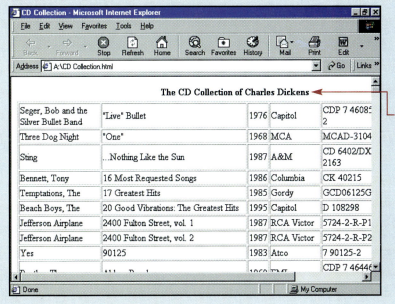

Figure 7.28
The edits you made in WordPad are reflected in the Web page when it is displayed in the default browser.

Caption reflects changes made in WordPad

9 **Close the Web browser.**

You have learned to edit the text in an HTML document. If you want to learn more about creating and editing HTML code, many books are available on the topic.

Summary

In this project, you worked with links, both from Access to other programs, and from Access to the Web. You added links from Access forms to a Word document and to an Excel worksheet. You saved a table as an unformatted static HTML page, and a query as a formatted static HTML page. You viewed both of these pages on a browser, and then you edited text in the file and added tags to make the caption bold.

You can enhance your knowledge of HTML by getting one of the many good books on the subject and then making changes and testing your changes using the Web browser without ever having to put your pages on a Web server.

Checking Concepts and Terms

True/False

For each of the following statements, check *T* or *F* to indicate whether the statement is true or false.

__T __F   **1.** Hyperlinks can only be used to jump to other HTML pages. [L1]

__T __F   **2.** You can place hyperlinks in Access forms or reports. [L1]

__T __F   **3.** Static HTML pages can be viewed but are no longer linked to the database. They cannot be used to edit data in the database table. [L3]

__T __F   **4.** It is possible to use a browser to check HTML files without connecting to the Internet. [L4]

__T __F   **5.** You can use a word processing program such as Word to edit HTML documents. [L5]

__T __F   **6.** A tag is an HTML instruction contained in parentheses. [L5]

__T __F   **7.** You can choose to save the formatting of a table or query when you create the HTML file. [L3]

__T __F   **8.** To save a query as an HTML file, the first step is to choose File, Save As from the menu. [L3]

__T __F   **9.** If you open more than one HTML document in your browser, you can move back and forth between them using the Back and Forward buttons. [L4]

__T __F   **10.** When a query is saved in HTML format, the default layout is tabular. [L3]

Multiple Choice

Circle the letter of the correct answer for each of the following questions.

1. After a hyperlink has been used to jump from an Access form to a Word document, how do you return to the Access form? [L1]

   a. Click the Page Up button on the keyboard.

   b. Use the roller button on the mouse.

   c. Click the Back button on the toolbar.

   d. Click the Forward button on the toolbar.

2. You can insert hyperlinks to other documents into which of the following database objects in Access? [L1]

   a. forms

   b. forms and reports

   c. forms, reports, and queries

   d. forms, reports, queries, and tables

3. A tag is _____. [L5]

    a. an HTML instruction, displayed in angle brackets, that is used in pairs

    b. an HTML instruction, displayed in square brackets, that is used in pairs

    c. an instruction inserted into an Access table

    d. the link between an Access form and a Word document

4. Which of the following best describes HTML? [L5]

    a. a Web server operating system such as Windows NT or UNIX

    b. an application software similar to Word or Access

    c. a type of Web browser such as Netscape or Internet Explorer

    d. a language code that enables different browsers to display the same document

5. To save a static Web page, use the File, _____ option. [L3]

    a. Save As

    b. Save as HTML

    c. Export

    d. Web Page

6. You can edit an HTML document in _____. [L5]

    a. WordPad

    b. Word

    c. Access

    d. all of the above

7. A URL is _____. [L1]

    a. another name for an HTML document

    b. an acronym for the Universal Relay Language

    c. an HTML instruction

    d. an Internet address

8. When formatting a hyperlink in a form, it is a good idea not to change _____. [L1]

    a. the font size

    b. the font type

    c. the font color

    d. none of the above

9. An advantage of using the Internet or a company intranet to disseminate information in static form is _____. [Intro]

    a. you don't have to worry about updating the information

    b. anyone who wants to can change the information

    c. you retain control of the data

    d. there's no cost involved

10. Which of the following statements about HTML is false? [L5]

    a. HTML tags are case-sensitive.

    b. A slash is used to identify the end tag of a pair of tags.

    c. The text between the TITLE tags appears in the browser title bar.

    d. The name of the table or query is used as the default caption.

Screen ID

Label each element of the Access screens shown in Figure 7.29 and Figure 7.30.

Figure 7.29

A. Text that appears in the browser title bar

B. Click here to browse the Web site to which to link

C. Hyperlink text that appears on the form

D. Tag to end bolded text

E. First data cell in first table row

F. Document to which to link

G. End of first record or row in the table

H. Text that appears at the top of the table

I. Click here to add pop-up text to the hyperlink on the form

J. Click here to browse the document to which to link

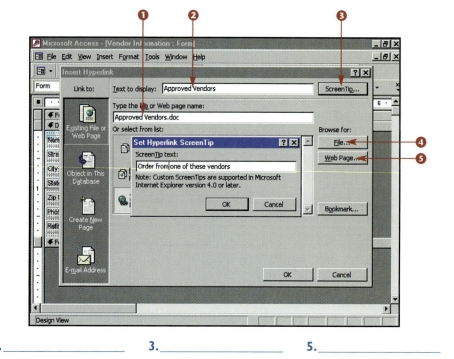

1._____   3._____   5._____

2._____   4._____

Figure 7.30

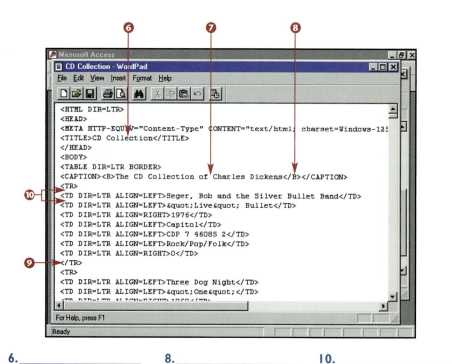

6._____   8._____   10._____

7._____   9._____

Discussion Questions

1. If you add hyperlinks from Access forms or reports to Word or Excel documents, you can connect people from one department in a company to another via the company intranet. The advantages to this type of information dissemination are obvious, but can you think of any drawbacks?

2. When would static HTML pages be preferable to interactive data access pages?

3. You used a table and a query to create static Web pages in Lesson 3. You can also make pages from Access reports. What could you do using a report that you couldn't do using a table or query?

4. This project has dealt with interactivity and interconnectedness. Do you think the ability to link programs and data is going to change the way you do business? The way you learn? The way you relate to others in your private life?

Skill Drill

Skill Drill exercises reinforce project skills. Each skill reinforced is the same, or nearly the same, as a skill presented in the project. Each exercise includes a brief narrative introduction, followed by detailed instructions in a step-by-step format.

In these exercises, you will work with database interactivity using a customer information database.

1. Linking an Access Form to a Word Document

The Accounting department has just put out an emergency document on the company intranet to notify the sales force of new credit ratings for some of the customers. The notice is in Word. Although the new ratings will be added to the database soon, you need to see the new credit ratings immediately to find out if prepayment is necessary for some of the customers whose ratings have dropped.

To link an Access form to a Word document, complete the following steps:

1. Copy the AC2-0705 file to your disk, remove the Read Only status, rename it **Customer Information Management**, and open the database.

2. Copy the AC2-0706 Word file to your disk and rename it **New Credit Ratings**.

3. Click the Open Customer Information Form button, and then click the View button to switch to Design view.

4. Click the Insert Hyperlink button.

5. Click the File button. Find and select the New Credit Ratings document, and then click OK.

6. Remove the .doc extension from the Text to display box.

7. Click the ScreenTip button and type **Make sure you check the new ratings before shipping orders!**

8. Click OK twice. Move the hyperlink to the right of the first field, and then click the View button to switch to Form view. Your form should look like Figure 7.31.

9. Click the New Credit Ratings hyperlink to switch to the Word document. Click the Back button to move back to the Access form.

10. Close the form and save your changes when prompted.

11. Use the taskbar to find and close Word. Leave the database open for the next exercise.

Figure 7.31
A hyperlink has been added to the form, linking the form to a Microsoft Word document.

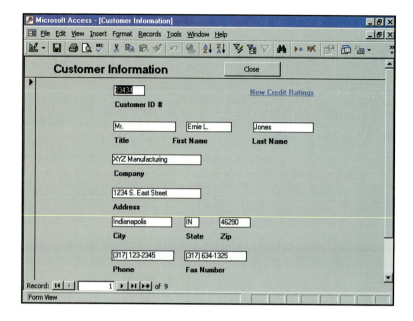

2. Saving a Table as an HTML Document

You want to make a complete list of recent orders available to everyone, but you do not want to give anyone the option of making changes to the data. You decide to create a static HTML document to place on the Net.

To save a table as an HTML document, complete the following steps:

1. Click the Close button on the switchboard to move to the database window.

2. Click the Tables object button, if necessary, and select the Orders table.

3. Choose File, Export from the menu. Select a location for the file using the Save in box, and call the File name **Recent Orders**.

4. In the Save as type box, select HTML Documents. Do not click the Save formatted check box, but click the Save button.

5. Leave the database open for the next exercise.

3. Viewing the Table Using the Default Browser

You created an HTML document from a table, and now you want to see if it works.

To view the table using the default browser, complete the following steps:

1. Go to the Windows Explorer and find the Recent Orders file you just created.

2. Double-click the Recent Orders file. Make sure the document opens in your browser.

3. Scroll down using the vertical scrollbar.

4. Leave the browser open, but use the taskbar to move back to the database. Leave the database open for the next exercise.

4. Saving a Query as an HTML Document

Because the new credit ratings are coming out, the salespeople want to know which of their customers have not paid their bills, and how far behind they are. This isn't the only factor in determining credit ratings. The Fifth District Court, for example, has not paid for four shipments, but they have never missed a payment, so their rating is high. You decide to post the unpaid bills, again in static form because you don't want anyone changing the data.

To save a query as an HTML document, complete the following steps:

1. Click the Queries object button, if necessary, and select the Unpaid Purchases query.

2. Choose File, Export from the menu. Select a location for the file using the Save in box, and call the File name **Unpaid Orders**.

3. In the Save as type box, select HTML Documents.

4. Click the Save formatted check box and click the Save All button. Ignore the HTML Template option.

5. Leave the database open for the next exercise.

5. Viewing the Query and Navigating Between Pages Using the Default Browser

You created an HTML document from a query, and now you want to see if it works. You also want to move back and forth between the new file and the Recent Orders file you created in the second exercise.

To view the query and move between pages using the default browser, complete the following steps:

1. Use the taskbar to switch to your browser.

2. Choose File, Open from the menu.

3. Click the Browse button in the Open dialog box.

4. Select the Unpaid Orders file, click Open, and then click OK.

5. Click the Back button to move to the Recent Orders page. Click the Forward button to move back to the Unpaid Orders page. Notice what a difference a little formatting makes in the look of the page!

6. Close the browser. Close Access unless you are going to proceed to the Challenge section.

6. Editing an HTML Document

Your formatted Unpaid Orders HTML file looks pretty good, but you'd like to change the title in the title bar and the caption at the top of the table. You'd also like to customize the caption.

To edit an HTML document, complete the following steps:

1. Click the Start button and select Programs. Choose WordPad from the Accessories option.

2. Click the Open button, change the Files of type option to All Documents (*.*), find and select the Unpaid Orders document, and click the Open button.

3. Select the title and change it to **Unpaid Orders Since January 1, 1999**.

4. Scroll to the right and change the caption to **Unpaid Orders Since January 1, 1999**.

5. Add italic tags (`<I>` and `</I>`) around the new caption, which already has bold tags around it.

6. Click the Save button and select the Text Document option.

7. Close WordPad, find the Unpaid Orders file, and double-click it. Notice that the title in the title bar has changed, as has the caption at the top of the table (see Figure 7.32).

8. Close your browser.

Figure 7.32
The HTML document has
been edited in WordPad.

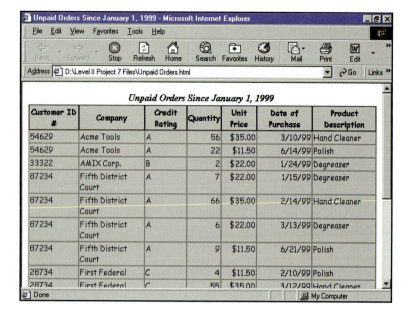

Challenge

Challenge exercises expand on or are somewhat related to skills presented in the lessons. Each exercise provides a brief narrative introduction followed by instructions in a numbered step format that are not as detailed as those in the Skill Drill section.

The database you will use for the Challenge exercises is a revised version of the CD Collection database you used earlier in this project.

1. Adding a Hyperlink to a PowerPoint Presentation

In this exercise, you add a hyperlink to a form that will open a PowerPoint presentation.

1. Copy the AC2-0707 PowerPoint Show file to your disk and rename it **CD PowerPoint Presentation**.

2. Copy the AC2-0708 file to your disk, remove the Read Only status, rename it **Updated CD Collection**, and open the database.

3. Open the CD Input form in Design view and add a hyperlink to the CD PowerPoint Presentation. Use the filename without the extension as the text to display, and add a ScreenTip that says **Click here for instructions.**

4. Move the hyperlink to the right of the Category field. Click the View button, and then click the hyperlink. Click (PgDn) to move through the slides.

5. Close the PowerPoint presentation to move back to the Access form. Leave the database open for the next exercise.

2. Adding a Hyperlink to Connect to a URL

In this exercise you add another hyperlink to the CD Input form, this time to connect the form to a site on the Internet.

1. Switch to Design view of the CD Input Form.

2. Click the Hyperlink button. Type the following URL: **http://www.microsoft.com**. Note: If you want to use a different URL, please feel free!

3. The hyperlink on the form should read `Go to Microsoft for Help`. Do not add a ScreenTip. Your form should look like Figure 7.33.

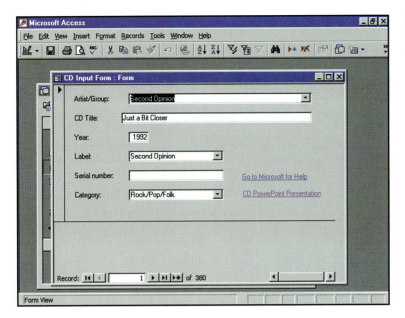

Figure 7.33
A second hyperlink has been added to the form.

4. Move the hyperlink above the other one. Click the View button and test your new hyperlink.

5. Close your browser, close the form, and save your changes. Leave the database open for the next exercise.

3. Creating a One-page HTML Document from a Report

In this exercise you create an HTML document from a one-page report.

1. Click the Reports object button and select the Country/Western CDs report.

2. Export the report to an HTML file. Skip the template dialog box.

3. View your new Web page on your Web browser. Notice that the headers and footers are displayed on the Web page.

4. Close your Web browser.

4. Editing a Hypertext Document in Access

In Lesson 5, you used the WordPad program to edit an HTML file. You can also edit these files in Access. You have more control over the edit, but look at the screen and decide which you like best!

To edit an HTML file in Access, click the Pages option button in the Updated CD Collection database. Double-click the Edit Web page that already exists icon. Find the Country_Western CDs file and click the Open button.

Use the available help to find out how to change Artist/Group to Artist or Group, and put your name before the CD Collection caption at the top of the table. Also, move to View, HTML Source and change the date to the current date. Also, change the color of the date to a bright red. Test your changes with your Web browser.

5. Adding New Lines to an HTML Report

Sometimes you will want to do more than just edit existing text. In the Country_Western CDs document, you want to make the caption more descriptive. Use the available help to add a second line just below the CD Collection line. This second line should be the same font size, face, and color, and should say `Country/Western`.

When you are finished, test your page and print it. Close the browser, and then close Access, unless you are going to move to the Discovery Zone exercises.

Discovery Zone

Discovery Zone exercises help you gain advanced knowledge of project topics and application of skills. These exercises focus on enhancing your problem-solving skills. Numbered steps are not provided, but you are given hints, reminders, screen shots, and references to help you reach your goal for each exercise.

1. Creating a Multiple-page HTML Document

So far, you have created only HTML documents that are contained in one page. In this exercise, you will create an HTML document that consists of several linked pages. You will be using a database of tornadoes in the state of Arizona.

Goal: Create a multi-page HTML document from a report.

In this exercise, you should

- Move the AC7-0709 file to your disk and rename it `Arizona Tornadoes Online`.
- Save the Arizona Tornadoes report as a multiple-page HTML document.
- Test the HTML document and test the links between the pages.

2. Uploading HTML Files onto a Web Server

After you have created the Web pages you want and you have made any editing changes you feel are necessary, you will need to get your file(s) onto a Web server to share your pages with the world. Unfortunately, there is no set way to put Web pages on a Web server.

The method you use depends on what type of server you have—**UNIX**, VMS, **Windows NT**, and so forth. It also depends on what utility programs you use to upload the files. You will need to find out what types of permissions need to be set; that is, who can read the pages and who has the rights to change the pages. Finally, you will need to use an **FTP** (File Transfer Protocol) program to transfer the files to the server.

Note: You can also use any number of Web publishing tools, including the Microsoft Web Publishing Wizard, to upload your document(s). This program should be available at C:\Program Files\Web Publish. The filename is Wpwiz. You will need all the information mentioned above to run this program successfully. If you do not have the Microsoft Web Publishing Wizard, you can download it from Microsoft. Go to http://www.microsoft.com and search from there.

Goal: Upload the Arizona Tornadoes pages onto your Web server.

In this exercise, you should

- Create a folder on your server to hold your files.
- Transfer the files to your server folder using one of the many FTP programs (WS-FTP LE is available online, and is free to students).
- Set the permissions on your server so that people can see your pages, and you can make changes to them.
- Find out the URL you will need to use to get to your pages.

Hint: Talk to your network administrator if you have never done this before!

Task Guide

A book in the *Essentials* series is designed to be kept as a handy reference beside your computer even after you have completed all the projects and exercises. Any time you have difficulty recalling the sequence of steps or a shortcut needed to achieve a result, look up the general category in the alphabetized listing below, and then quickly home in on your task at hand. For your convenience, some tasks have been duplicated under more than one category. If you have difficulty performing a task, turn to the page number listed in the third column to locate the step-by-step exercise or other detailed description. If a task does not include a page reference, it is a bonus task from the author that was not within the scope of the book. For the greatest efficiency in using this Task Guide, take a few minutes to familiarize yourself with the main categories and keywords before you begin your search.

To Do This	Use This Command	Page Number
Application and File Management		
Back up database file	Use the Windows Explorer (or My Computer) to copy the file and send it to a floppy disk, Zip disk, or network drive.	[pg. 170]
Back up table data	To save just the data in a table, select the table and choose Export from the File menu. Type a filename, and then choose the type of file from the Save as type drop-down list. Click the Save button, and then answer the Export Wizard questions.	[pg. 167]
Compact files	Launch Access, but do not open a database. If the database is on a network, make sure that no one else has the file open, and then highlight the file and select Tools, Database Utilities from the menu. Select Compact and Repair Database. Type a filename in the File name box, and then save the compacted file.	[pg. 172]
Detect and repair Access problems	Launch Access, but do not open a database. Choose Help, Detect and Repair from the menu. Click the Start button. Identify the location of the installation source and click OK. Restart your computer to complete the repair.	[pg. 173]
Save as an Access 97 database	Select Tools, Database Utilities, Convert Database, To Prior Access Database Version from the menu. Give the database a unique name, and then click the Save button.	[pg. 171]
Field		
Data entry: create lookup column	In table Design view, click the drop-down arrow in the Data Type column for the field you want to work on, and choose Lookup Wizard from the drop-down list. Choose to type your own data, and then enter the data.	[pg. 18]

continues ▶

To Do This	Use This Command	Page Number
Data entry: prevent duplicates	In table Design view, select the field on which you want to work, and click in the Indexed property box in the Field Properties area. Choose Yes (No Duplicates) from the drop-down list.	[pg. 16]
Data entry: required entry	In table Design view, select the field on which you want to work, click in the Required property box in the Field Properties area, and then select Yes from the drop-down list.	[pg. 14]
Data entry: validation criteria	In table Design view, select the field on which you want to work, click in the Validation Rule property box in the Field Properties area, and then click the Build button to activate the Expression Builder. Start the expression with the equal sign (=), and then build your expression.	[pg. 11]
Format: apply Input Mask	In table Design view, select the field you want to format, click in the Input Mask property box in the Field Properties area, and then click the Build button to start the Input Mask Wizard. Select the appropriate input mask and follow the wizard instructions.	[pg. 8]
Format: create conditional	In table Design view, select the field you want to format, click in the Format property box in the Field Properties area, and then enter the character(s) needed for each component of the series of commands. Separate the components with a semicolon (;).	[pg. 6]
Format: create consistent	In table Design view, select the field you want to format, click in the Format property box in the Field Properties area, and then enter the character(s) needed to format the data.	[pg. 4]
Format: in form	In form Design view, select the field you want to format, click the Properties button, go to the Format tab, and enter your format in the Format box. You can also select a field and use the buttons on the Formatting toolbar to alter the format.	[pg. 67]

Form

Date and time stamp: enter	In form Design view, choose Date and Time from the Insert menu. Select date or time, or both, and choose the format you want. Move the date or time fields to the desired location, and format them using the Formatting toolbar.	[pg. 80]
Date: enter automatically	In form Design view, select the date field on which you want to work, choose Properties from the shortcut menu, and then click in the Default Value property box. Click the Build button, and then choose Common Expressions, Current Date.	[pg. 78]
Field: add list box selections	In form Design view, select the field to which you want to add a list, and choose Change To and List Box from the shortcut menu. From the shortcut menu, choose Properties. In the Data tab, change the Row Source Type to Value List, and then type your list in the Row Source box, using semicolons between values.	[pg. 70]

To Do This	Use This Command	Page Number
Field: fill from query information	Click the Forms object button, click the New button, and then choose a query that contains merged data from two tables. Using the Form Wizard, select the fields that you want to include, and then select a format and a style.	[pg. 75]
Field: fill from table or query	In form Design view, select the field you want to use for look-up, and choose Change To and Combo Box from the shortcut menu. From the shortcut menu, choose Properties. In the Data tab, make Table/Query the Row Source Type. Using the drop-down menu from the Row Source, choose the Table or Query to use as a source.	[pg. 73]
Field: format	In form Design view, select the field you want to format, click the Properties button, go to the Format tab, and enter your format in the Format box. You can also select a field and use the buttons on the Formatting toolbar to alter the format.	[pg. 67]
Labels: create for mailings	Create a mailing label report using the Label Wizard. Select a standard label size, and then assemble the fields for the label. Follow the directions in the wizard to sort the labels and to select font attributes.	[pg. 105]
Print	In Form view, select Page Setup from the File menu. Change margins and other options as necessary. Choose Print Preview from the File menu to see what your printout will look like. Choose Print from the File menu, and then select which records to print.	[pg. 89]
Subform: create	Click the New button to create a new form. Select the table with the "one" relationship and select the Form Wizard option. Add all the fields from the table, and then select the "many" table and add all the fields except the related one. Answer the rest of the wizard's questions about the setup.	[pg. 84]
Tab order: change	In form Design view, select Tab Order from the View menu. Click on the Detail button. Click the Auto Order button to select a left-to-right, top-to-bottom order. Click OK.	[pg. 83]

Integration with Web

Browse HTML page on local drive	Find the file by using the Windows Explorer. Double-click the file to activate the default browser. If this doesn't work, launch the browser. Select File, Open from the menu, and open the page.	[pg. 206]
Edit HTML page with WordPad	Click the Start button, and then choose Programs, Accessories, WordPad. Click the Open button and select All Documents (*.*) from the Files of type drop-down list. Find and open the file. Make your changes, save the document, and test the document using your browser.	[pg. 209]
Hyperlink from form to Excel worksheet	Open the form in Design view. Click the Insert Hyperlink button on the toolbar. Specify the document and its folder location. Type the text to display and the text for a ScreenTip. Move the hyperlink, and then click the View button. Click the hyperlink to test it.	[pg. 200]

continues ▶

To Do This	Use This Command	Page Number
Hyperlink from form to Word document	Open the form in Design view. Click the Insert Hyperlink button on the toolbar. Specify the document and its folder location. Type the text to display and the text for a ScreenTip. Move the hyperlink, and then click the View button. Click the hyperlink to test it.	[pg. 194]
Save database object as HTML page	Choose the object, and then select File, Export from the menu. Select where you want to put the file and give it a name. Select HTML Documents from the Save as type drop-down list.	[pg. 203]
Upload files to a server	Obtain permission to publish Web pages to an Internet server. Write down the URL of the folder that will contain your pages, your username, and password. Use an FTP program or the Microsoft Web Publishing Wizard to transfer the files to your folder. Set the necessary permissions for that folder.	[pg. 220]

Macro

Create, to close a form	Select the Macros object button and click New. Select the action Close. Save and close the macro. Use a name that would work as the label on a command button—in this case, Close is best for generic use.	[pg. 145]
Create, to launch Main Switchboard	Create a macro to open the Switchboard form. Add a second action to maximize the Switchboard window. Name the macro Autoexec, and save it.	[pg. 152]
Create, to open form in Add mode	Select the Macros object button and click New. Select the OpenForm action. Select the form to be opened in the Action Arguments section. Select Add Mode to only add new records. Save and close the macro. Use a name that would work as the label on a command button.	[pg. 141]
Create, to open form in Edit mode	Select the Macros object button and click New. Select the OpenForm action. Select the form to be opened in the Action Arguments section. Select Edit Mode to edit existing records. Save and close the macro. Use a name that would work as the label on a command button.	[pg. 139]
Create, to open form in Read Only mode	Select the Macros object button and click New. Select the OpenForm action. Select the form to be opened in the Action Arguments section. Select Read Only Mode to disable add and edit capabilities. Save and close the macro. Use a name that would work as the label on a command button.	[pg. 142]
Create, to open report in Preview view	Select the Macros object button and click New. Select the OpenReport action. Select the report to be opened in the Action Arguments section. Select Preview as the View argument. Save and close the macro. Use a name that would work as the label on a command button.	[pg. 144]
Run from button on form	Open the form in Design view. Use Window and Tile Vertically to split the screen to show the opening Database window and the form design. Click the Macros object button in the Database window. Drag the name of a macro to the form design to create a command button. Save and close the form design.	[pg. 146]

To Do This	Use This Command	Page Number
Run two queries: create macro	Click the Macros object button and click <u>N</u>ew. Choose <u>W</u>indow, <u>T</u>ile Vertically from the menu. Click the Queries object button and drag the queries to the first two action rows in the new macro. Close and name the macro. Add the macro to a switchboard, if appropriate.	[pg. 180]
Switchboard: create	Create a new form that is not based on a table. Open it in Design view. Use the Labels tool in the toolbox to create a title. Choose <u>W</u>indow and <u>T</u>ile Vertically to split the screen to show the opening Database window and the form design. Drag macro names from the Database window onto the form. Save the form and close it.	[pg. 150]

Query

To Do This	Use This Command	Page Number
Archive table: append records	Copy the Delete query, click in an open area of the Queries window, and then choose Paste. Enter a new query name in the Paste As dialog box. Highlight the new query and then go to Design view. Click the Query Type button and change the type to Append Query. In the Table <u>N</u>ame box, choose a path and a table to which to send the records. Close the query.	[pg. 179]
Archive table: create	Click the Queries object button, click the <u>N</u>ew button, and then select Design View. Add the table you want, and then add all fields to the Field row. Enter your criteria, and then click the Query Type button. Choose Make-Table Query, give it a name, and then close the query. Run the query to create the archive table.	[pg. 175]
Delete records using Make-Table Query	Create an archive table (Make-Table Query), rename it, and then switch to Design view. Click the Query Type button and select Delete from the menu. Save and run the query.	[pg. 177]
Duplicate records: find	Create a new query designed for that purpose using the Find Duplicates Query Wizard. Identify the field you want to check, and then add fields that help you identify what to do with duplicate records.	[pg. 50]
Field: choose from joined table	Add both tables to the query design. Add the foreign key from one table, and the fields you want to automatically fill from the table with the corresponding primary key.	[pg. 44]
Field: choose from two tables	Add both tables to the query design. Drag fields from either table to the query, and view the results in Datasheet view.	[pg. 39]
Run two queries: create macro	Click the Macros object button and click <u>N</u>ew. Choose <u>W</u>indow, <u>T</u>ile Vertically from the menu. Click the Queries object button and drag the queries to the first two action rows in the new macro. Close and name the macro. Add the macro to a switchboard, if appropriate.	[pg. 180]
Update table by editing query data	Open the query in Datasheet view. When you enter a value for the foreign key, the other fields from the corresponding table will be automatically filled in. Do not try to enter a new value in the foreign key field.	[pg. 47]

continues ▶

To Do This	Use This Command	Page Number
Report		
Field: add calculated, to Group headers and footers	Open the report in Design view. Click the Sorting and Grouping button. Go to the Group Properties section of the dialog box and select Yes for the Header and Footer options. In Design view, drag a text box into the footer or header. Add an expression such as =SUM, =AVERAGE, or =COUNT to the text box. Make sure you enclose field names in square brackets.	[pg. 123]
Field: create calculated	Open the toolbox and click the Text Box button. Drag a box into the Detail section. Enter an expression in the box that starts with an equal sign and encloses each field name in square brackets.	[pg. 110]
Group data	Open the report in Design view. Click the Sorting and Grouping button. Select the field on which to group.	[pg. 117]
Group data: keep together	Open the report in Design view. Click the Sorting and Grouping button. Go to the Group Properties section of the dialog box and select Whole Group from the Keep Together box.	[pg. 121]
Sort data	Open the report in Design view. Click the Sorting and Grouping button. Select the field on which to sort and choose how you want the records sorted.	[pg. 117]
Table		
Back up data	To save just the data in a table, select the table and choose Export from the File menu. Type a filename, and then choose the type of file from the Save as type drop-down list. Click the Save button, and then answer the Export Wizard questions.	[pg. 167]
Duplicate records: find	Create a new query designed for that purpose using the Find Duplicates Query Wizard. Identify the field you want to check, and then add fields that help you identify what to do with duplicate records.	[pg. 50]
Query: choose data from joined table	Add both tables to the query design. Add the foreign key from one table, and the fields you want to automatically fill from the table with the corresponding primary key.	[pg. 44]
Query: choose data from two tables	Add both tables to the query design. Drag fields from either table to the query, and view the results in Datasheet view.	[pg. 39]
Related: design for repetitive data	Create separate tables to hold data that would otherwise have to be entered repeatedly. Make sure related tables contain fields of similar data types that can be joined.	[pg. 33]
Relationship: create join	Click the Relationships button and use the Show Table dialog box to select the tables to be joined. Drag a connection between the two related fields. Identify the type of join, and then decide whether to enforce referential integrity and whether to cascade deletes and updates.	[pg. 35]
Update by editing query data	Open the query in Datasheet view. When you enter a value for the foreign key, the other fields from the corresponding table will be automatically filled in. Do not try to enter a new value in the foreign key field.	[pg. 47]

All key terms appearing in this book (in bold italic) are listed alphabetically in this Glossary for easy reference. If you want to learn more about a feature or concept, turn to the page reference shown after its definition. You can also use the Index to find the term's other significant occurrences.

action   An Access-defined function that performs some process within the database, table, form, or query. [pg. 138]

archive table   A table designed to hold inactive or completed records to remove them from an actively used table. [pg. 174]

argument   A value needed for a macro to perform its function. [pg. 138]

cascade   A table-relationships option that enables you to change one field, which then automatically changes related fields in other tables. [pg. 37]

combo box   A data entry drop-down list that looks up valid entries from a table, query, or source list. [pg. 34]

compact   To reduce the size of a database file. [pg. 171]

delimiter   An ASCII character, such as a tab, comma, semicolon, or space, that separates fields in a text file. [pg. 168]

Detect and Repair   A feature in most Office 2000 applications that detects problems with a program and fixes them. [pg. 173]

dynaset   A temporary table of data that is assembled from other tables by running a query or filter. It is not stored as a separate table. [pg. 43]

encrypt   To protect a database from being broken into by word processors or to prevent other utility programs from extracting the text data. [pg. 189]

expand indicator   A plus or minus symbol to the left of a field to indicate that related information from another table is attached to that record. [pg. 38]

Expression Builder   A program that helps the user create formulas for many Access uses. [pg. 11]

Find Duplicates Query Wizard   Creates a query that finds records with duplicate field values in a single table or query. [pg. 49]

Find Unmatched Query Wizard   Creates a query that finds records in one table that have no related records in another table. [pg. 49]

foreign key   The corresponding field in another table that is linked to the primary key. [pg. 35]

format   The way that data is displayed. [pg. 2]

FTP   File Transfer Protocol; a method for transferring files between computers over a network or the Internet. [pg. 220]

HTML   Hypertext Markup Language; the standard programming language used for writing documents that can be viewed on the Internet by many different browsers. [pg. 203]

hyperlink   A connection between one document and another document stored on the user's personal computer, local area network (**LAN**), or the World Wide Web. [pg. 193]

indexed field   A field for which Access builds a location guide; an index speeds up sorting or searching on a field. [pg. 15]

Input mask   A data entry structure that forces data entry into a selected format. [pg. 7]

Internet   The worldwide computer communication network that is based on open standards for operating systems and communication. [pg. 192]

intranet   A communication network within a company that uses the same software and standards as the Internet. [pg. 192]

LAN Local area network; a group of personal computers connected through a computer that coordinates their communication with each other and the outside world. [pg. 193]

list box A data entry list that looks up valid entries from a table, query, or source list, and does not allow the user to type new data. [pg. 69]

macro A group of instructions that provide additional commands or functionality to a program. [pg. 138]

MDE file A file saved in a protected format so that the user has access to the database but cannot change forms, reports, or Visual Basic code. [pg. 190]

null value A field with no data entered into it. It is not the same as an entry of zero. [pg. 5]

one-to-many A relationship that links one record in a table to many records in a different table. [pg. 35]

placeholder A character used to reserve a place for another character in an Input Mask. [pg. 9]

primary key field A field that contains a unique value for each record in the table. [pg. 15]

sans serif A typeface without serifs. [pg. 107]

serif A horizontal line finishing off the main strokes of a letter, as at the top and the bottom of the letter M. [pg. 107]

static HTML pages Web pages that are not interactive. [pg. 203]

subdatasheet A secondary datasheet in a table that shows related information from another (related) table. [pg. 38]

subform A form within a form; a subform shows the "many" records related to the selected record in the main form. [pg. 64]

switchboard The term Access uses for a menu of choices represented by buttons on a form. Clicking a button on a switchboard runs an associated macro to perform functions such as opening forms or printing reports. [pg. 138]

tab order The sequence of fields in a form that the insertion point follows as you press (Tab) or (↵Enter). [pg. 64]

tag An HTML instruction enclosed in angle brackets, such as <TITLE>My Page</TITLE>. The second tag instruction is preceded by a slash. [pg. 210]

text qualifier Single or double quotation marks that surround text entries in a delimited text file. [pg. 169]

title In HTML, the text between the title tags that is displayed in the browser title bar. [pg. 210]

unbound object An object in a form or report that is not connected to an underlying table. [pg. 112]

UNIX A non-proprietary operating system language for computers. It is commonly used to run servers for Internet communication. [pg. 220]

URL Uniform Resource Locator; an Internet address. [pg. 195]

validation rule An expression that Access uses to check the data entered into a field. [pg. 11]

validation text The text that is displayed when data that doesn't match a validation rule is entered into a field. [pg. 11]

Web browser A software application used to view and interact with sites on the World Wide Web. Two popular examples are Netscape Communicator and Microsoft Internet Explorer. [pg. 192]

Windows NT An operating system used for stand-alone machines and for running local area networks. [pg. 220]

World Wide Web A graphical interface that links sites on the Internet and enables the user to easily jump from one site to another. [pg. 193]

Index

Q

queries

appending records to archive tables, 178-180

exercises, 187

creating archive tables, 174-177

exercises, 186

deleting archived records from tables, 177-178

exercises, 186

forms, automatic data entry, 75-78

macros

running delete and append queries, 180-182

exercises, 161

saving as HTML (Hypertext Markup Language) pages, viewing with browsers (exercises), 217

saving as static HTML (Hypertext Markup Language) pages, 204-205

exercises, 217

tables

duplicate records, 49-52

filling in fields automatically, 44-46

multiple, 39-44, 57-59

unmatched records (exercises), 56

updating tables, 47-49

text files, from table data (exercises), 188

R

Read Only mode, forms, opening

with macros, 142-143

exercises, 158

records

adding to main forms/subforms, 87-88

fields, calculated (exercises), 131

finding duplicates, 49-52

sorting/grouping

reports, 116-123

reports (exercises), 129-130, 133

sorting/grouping on multiple fields, reports (exercises), 135-136

referential integrity, 37, 49

exercises, 56-61

relationships, tables, 34-39

repetitive data, 32-34

Repair and Compact feature, databases, 171-173

exercises, 185

Repair and Detect feature, databases, 173-174

Report Wizard, grouping records (exercises), 133

reports

adding page breaks (exercises), 130-131

calculated fields, 110-116

adding to group headers/footers, 123-125

adding to group headers/footers (exercises), 131-133

creating HTML (Hypertext Markup Language) documents

exercises, 219

multiple-page documents (exercises), 220

file folder labels (exercises), 132

mailing labels, 105-110

exercises, 129

multiple fields, sorting/grouping (exercises), 135-136

opening

with macros in Preview view, 144

with macros in Preview view (exercises), 158

records, sorting/grouping, 116-123

exercises, 129-130, 133

subtotals/grand totals (exercises), 136

summary, formatting (exercises), 134

S

saving Access 2000 databases as Access 97, 171

exercises, 186

security, databases, MDE format (exercises), 190